POLITICAL ANTHROPOLOGY

POLITICAL ANTHROPOLOGY

Power and Paradigms

Donald V. Kurtz

A Member of the Perseus Books Group

Copyright © 2001 by Westview Press, A Member of the Perseus Books Group

Westview Press books are available at special discounts for bulk purchases in the United States by corporations, institutions, and other organizations. For more information, please contact the Special Markets Department at The Perseus Books Group, 11 Cambridge Center, Cambridge MA 02142, or call (617) 252-5298.

Published in 2001 in the United States of America by Westview Press, 5500 Central Avenue, Boulder, Colorado 80301–2877, and in the United Kingdom by Westview Press, 12 Hid's Copse Road, Cumnor Hill, Oxford OX2 9JJ

Find us on the World Wide Web at www.westviewpress.com

A CIP catalog record for this book is available from the Library of Congress.
ISBN 0-8133-3804-2 (pbk.); 0-8133-3803-4 (hc.)

The paper used in this publication meets the requirements of the American National Standard for Permanence of Paper for Printed Library Materials Z39.48–1984.

10   9   8   7   6   5   4   3   2   1

To Liz,
WITHOUT WHOSE LAUGHTER AT MY TITLES
MY LIFE WOULD BE INCOMPLETE.
YOU MAKE IT ALL WORTHWHILE.

CONTENTS

vii

FIGURES

INTRODUCTION

A while back I talked to a colleague about this project. He was a generation younger than I and specialized as an economic anthropologist. He
was surprised when I mentioned the different theoretical orientations
that have directed research into political anthropology historically. And I
was surprised when he commented that political anthropology had always appeared to him to be a dispersed field without a theoretical center.
That has not been the case since the field was formally established in 1940
with the publication of *African Political Systems* (Fortes and Evans-
Pritchard 1940). But to a younger scholar who came to the practice of anthropology after the 1970s, the field might appear to be dispersed because
since the mid-1970s the methodologies by which anthropologists study
political phenomena have emanated from different theoretical centers.

Many political anthropologists of my generation recall with some nos-
talgia the advent of the actor-oriented processual approach to political
phenomena in the mid-1960s. They consider the decade until the mid-
1970s to be the heyday of political anthropology and think that it subsequently lost its vigor. But the decade from approximately 1965 to 1975
was a heady period for cultural anthropology at large. Anthropologists
heatedly debated the importance of theoretical orientations, such as
ethnoscience, structuralism, cultural evolution, and the primacy of substantive and formal economics, as well as the social significance of hot-
ticket interests, often faddish, such as the culture of poverty, the causes
and morality of war, and whether human aggression is biologically or
culturally motivated. None of these concerns, including political anthropology, has survived with the same level of urgency that practitioners as-
signed to them during that time. But the field of political anthropology as
a whole remains alive and well, and political anthropologists continue to
expand into new directions, as they have since the inception of the field.

In the 1940s and 1950s, political anthropology served as a handmaiden
to the structural-functional orientation of British social anthropology.
That unfortunate relationship was gradually superseded in the mid-1960s

by a processual approach concerned with the role of the political agent. By the 1970s, that orientation was complemented by anthropological approaches to political economy in social anthropology and to political evolution in cultural anthropology and archaeology, each of which was influenced by Marxist theory. Today the role of the agent in political processes is being recuperated in a practice-theory approach to political phenomena. And, although this shift has not yet been acknowledged by many, postmodern anthropologists are taking political anthropology in still other directions, despite naive threats by radical postmodern anthropologists to deconstruct anthropology as a social science. Each of these orientations in one way or another is implicated in the concern anthropologists have with the "state." Instead of lacking a theoretical center, political anthropology, if anything, suffers from too many theoretical sources. But they are not mutually exclusive, and together they comply with the breadth and depth that the anthropological perspective brings to the study of the human condition, which is its best conceit.

As is the case in most other anthropology subfields, political anthropologists study and analyze political phenomena in all the kinds of human societies of which we have any record and from the earliest prehistoric formation of these societies to the present. This scope may sound audacious, but that is what the anthropological enterprise is all about, and what makes it at once exciting and frustrating. One can never know all there is to know, even within the narrow specialties, such as political anthropology, by which we in our guise as scholars identify ourselves. The earned conceit that anthropologists bring to the study of political phenomena is obvious if we compare the anthropological approach to political phenomena to that of other social sciences. These approaches can be identified as *minimalist* and *maximalist* (Balandier 1970).

Political scientists and sociologists, for example, have a minimalist view of political phenomena. To most of them, especially political scientists, government and political phenomena transpire and exist within formal political institutions, almost all of which are associated with modern state formations. That the government of a political community might exist in other nonpolitical institutions is largely alien to their thinking. Yet that is exactly what political anthropologists confronted and had to sort out.

Anthropologists developed a maximalist approach to study political phenomena because they discovered that in the preindustrial, precapitalist, non-Western societies that provided their research subjects, practices and structures of government and other political practices often transpired in unlikely contexts, such as witchcraft and sorcery, and in curious institutional settings, such as kinship associations, age sets, secret societies, and among shamans. Simply put, not all the kinds of societies for which anthropologists have written ethnographies, such as nomadic hunters and gatherers and some horticultural and pastoral peoples, have formal political institutions. But every human society, regardless how institutionally simple, has some form of political organization and leadership, despite early, romanticized ideas to the contrary (Radcliffe-Brown 1922; MacLeod 1931; Redfield 1956; Murdock 1957; Sharp 1958). The different approaches that anthropologists use to understand political phenomena are responses to the variety and complexity of the human political condition that is either largely unknown or of little interest to political scientists and political sociologists.

Just as I have written above, in day-to-day discourse political anthropologists (and others) commonly refer to the "orientations" or "approaches" by which they study political phenomena. Each of the approaches by which anthropologists try to understand and explain political phenomena is characterized by a compatible body of theory, concepts, and strategies that direct their research. Yet it is more accurate to think of each of these research constellations as a *paradigm* that provides its dedicated practitioners with the scientific tools to investigate and explain political phenomena through normal scientific practices (Kuhn 1970). The paradigms through which political anthropologists have pursued their research agendas are the focus of this work.

The theoretical subject matter of political anthropology is represented by five paradigms: structural-functionalism, process, political economy, political evolution, and postmodernism. Historically, different paradigms have dominated the anthropological study of politics at different times. Today, many of the hallmark ideas of earlier paradigms, such as structural-functionalism and process, are included without acknowledgment in more recent paradigms, such as the postmodern, because they have been absorbed into anthropological thought and discourse, but without the specific emphasis given to them previously. In this way, the major and important contributions of each paradigm remain alive and well and provide a holistic view to political phenomena unlike that in any other social science.

This book differs from others that claim to introduce political anthropology and runs against the traditional mode of anthropological presentation. In the traditional practice of writing about anthropology, theoretical statements, often brief, are buttressed by copious amounts of ethnographic data. I emphasize theory over data because I am of the conviction that political anthropology is fundamentally about the ideas, theories, and concepts that direct research on political phenomena. Ethnographic data are the means by which anthropologists present and

display politics and political organization, and these data are rich and exciting. They are also the means to test theory deductively and to construct
theory inductively. But it is the theory embedded in the paradigms of political anthropology that provides the catalyst for the anthropological
study and analysis of political phenomena. That theory is the major concern of this work.

This does not mean that I reject the idea of relating theory to data. That
relationship is the essence of scientific methodology. But this book is not
an introduction to political anthropology per se. Rather, it is an introduction to the theory of political anthropology. Ethnographic data that relate
to these paradigms are readily available, and most of the major ethnographic writings on political anthropology are referenced in this book.

I try to present this theory, including my own contributions, in a coherent, readable, and interesting manner through a discussion of each paradigm and its major exemplars who have contributed to the theoretical
foundation of political anthropology. I believe the presentation is complete, but not exhaustive. For those anthropologists who might choose to
assign this work in classes, it leaves ample room for interpretation and argument from other viewpoints.

The major purpose of this work is to introduce and critically analyze
each of the paradigms within which reside the theory, concepts, and research strategies that imbue the field of political anthropology. The paradigms considered here do not include all the concerns of political anthropologists. Some of these concerns are simply nonparadigmatic; that is,
they can be and often are explored and addressed differently in different
paradigms. Various interpretations of the idea of political power, for example, recur in all the paradigms. Likewise, particular aspects of the
structure, organization, idea, and evolution of the "state"—recurrent interests of political anthropologists—also are embedded in each paradigm.
Neither the study of political power nor of the state constitutes a paradigm. To cover these interests, the book is divided into three parts.

The first part, Chapter 1, introduces the idea of a paradigm and the
paradigms of political anthropology. The second part goes against the
current trend in anthropology that denies that any idea or phenomenon is
"essential" to the study of the human condition. The idea of political
power, discussed in Chapter 2, is utterly essential to any consideration of
political phenomena and, as noted, pervades all the paradigms. Perhaps
less essential, but critical nonetheless, are ideas related to political leadership (Chapter 3) and succession to political status and office and the legitimation of authority (Chapter 4).

I devote the third part to a critical analysis of each paradigm and the
concerns they have spawned, such as the politics of kinship (Chapter 6)
and the state (Chapter 11), the ideas that its exemplars have contributed

to the study of political phenomena, and its historical background. The paradigm of structural-functionalism is the topic of Chapter 5. Practitioners of this paradigm discovered, among other things, the political importance of kinship relations and practices in societies without identifiable political institutions. Chapter 6 explores the results of the twenty-plus years of debate that this discovery triggered as anthropologists worked to understand the intricacies of the political organizations embedded in kinship relations and the algebra of the practices and politics they involved. The processual paradigm and the paradigm of political economy are the topics of Chapters 7 and 8, respectively. Chapters 9 and 10 consider the paradigm of political evolution. Chapter 9 is devoted to an analysis of the traditional evolutionary approaches to political phenomena. In Chapter 10 I take the novel approach of trying to account for political evolution as a result of the practices of political agents—the evolution of politics, as I think of it—that are represented by the different kinds of political leadership that anthropologists have identified.

In Chapter 11 I provide a critical analysis of the anthropological study and interpretation of the state and explore the idea of the vertical entrenchment of state governments. Postmodernism introduced a new and experimental genre of ethnographic writing to anthropology. In Chapter 12, which concludes this work, I identify a body of writing in this genre that appears to be congealing into a postmodern paradigm of political anthropology, despite disclaimers of identity with any subfield of anthropology by radical, postmodern anthropologists.

ACKNOWLEDGMENTS

Several colleagues contributed comments and helped to make this a better book. Jim McDonald, Jerry Hanson, Jon McGee, F. G. Bailey, Grace Keyes, Richard Warms, and two anonymous reviewers for Westview Press read various parts of the book and provided comments, insights, and criticisms, some of which, at my peril I'm sure, I ignored. But their substantive and sage contributions enhanced the quality of the work above what it would have been otherwise. I extend my deepest thanks to each of them. Of course, with the usual disclaimer, I alone am responsible for the final product.

I appreciated Bobbie Buczyna's patience in helping me to sort out my bibliographic problems. Kathryn Sauceda made sense out of my crude drawing to do the kinship diagrams that grace Chapter 6. Jane Moss did all she could to enhance the photograph that abuses the cover.

The staff at Westview Press were a delight to work with. I extend a special thanks to Karl Yambert, Senior Editor at Westview. His faith in this project, his patience and understanding, and his assistance throughout were invaluable in bringing the work to conclusion. I also want to thank John Thomas, a sensitive and perspicacious copy editor who knows his anthropology, Katharine Chandler, a diligent and gracious project editor, Michelle Mallin, marketing manager, Paula Waldrop, marketing coordinator, Jennifer Chen, associate editor, and Jennifer Thompson, editorial assistant. Each in their own way helped to make the experience with Westview Press rewarding and memorable.

PART ONE

Paradigms and Science

1

THE PARADIGMS OF
POLITICAL ANTHROPOLOGY

The implications of the noun *politics* and the adjective *political* represent related yet separate domains in the subject matter of political anthropology. Dictionary definitions of these two words elicit complicated and overlapping relationships. Drawing a distinction between the idea of "politics" and those ideas that "political" qualifies, such as organization, structure, process, and the like, involves more than merely splitting lexical hairs. The implications reflect different orientations that are important to the analysis of the subject matter of political anthropology.

Anthropologists who analyze problems associated with the idea of the political focus on social-political structures, such as lineages and age-grades, or political systems, such as chiefdoms or the state. These analyses often are synchronic, static, and functional. They emphasize the integration and maintenance of these systems. Anthropologists concerned with the political are apt to establish typologies of political structures and systems and worry about the constituent parts by which they identify them. Even when anthropologists cast their analyses in diachronic and evolutionary frameworks, they generalize political process and attribute it to nonhuman agencies and interventions, such as technology, systems of economic distribution, environmental forces, and the like. Human political agents are usually passive elements in these analyses, subject to forces either beyond their control or that the anthropologists involved generalize theoretically to the exclusion of the practices of human political agents.

The idea of politics, on the other hand, refers to the practices of agents who either operate within political structures and systems or are somehow related to them. In this context anthropologists explore how political agents, usually leaders, use skill, power, cunning, wisdom, and numerous strategies to pursue goals and attain ends. Political agents and leaders, such as big men, shamans, Sicilian bandits, chiefs, Pathan saints, and the like, are the sources and means of political process. A study of Western leaders might include Winston Churchill, Adolph Hitler, Joseph Stalin, Martin Luther King, and Bill Clinton. Leaders engage in strategies to acquire power to increase their authority, enhance their legitimacy, defeat a competitor, retain the right to govern, and bend others to their will. In politics, these goals are usually identified as public and are prosecuted in the service of political constituencies and the public good. But politics also is self-serving and aimed at ensuring the political survival and social and economic well-being of the agents involved. In either case, analyses concerned with the idea of politics focus on dynamic, processual, and goal-oriented practices of specific human agents as they develop and use power to gain ends and win prizes. Regardless of the commitment that anthropologists make to study either political structures and organizations or the politics that engage human agents, their research is almost always conducted within the context of a particular paradigm.

PARADIGMS

Kuhn (1970) promoted the idea of a scientific research paradigm in response to his interest in the history and philosophy of science. He bequeathed to those who are involved in scientific research a framework to analyze why and how a research community at any particular historical moment is committed to a particular research agenda and strategy and why these commitments change. The idea of paradigmatic research penetrated anthropology in the 1970s and sharply clarified the various theoretical approaches that anthropologists used to analyze their subject matter. The idea that anthropological research is paradigmatic is now well established, and the paradigms within which anthropologists conduct research are agreed upon, with minor variations (Lett 1987; McGee and Warms 2000). Vincent (1990) has commented that research in political anthropology is structured paradigmatically. But the idea of a paradigm has not been developed sufficiently to identify and delineate the subject matter of political anthropology. Even so, all scientific anthropological research is paradigmatic, including that related to political anthropology. The idea of a paradigm as delineated by Kuhn helps in understanding the historical trajectory of the subject matter and research interests of political anthropologists since the subfield developed over the last half of the twentieth century.

According to Kuhn, the history of science shows that paradigms have historical roots and that any field of scientific research will rely on more than one paradigm to try to solve the puzzles and problems that pervade the field. To qualify for this task, a paradigm must meet certain criteria. Kuhn suggests two major characteristics that define a paradigm.

The first requires the subject matter of the paradigm to be sufficiently unprecedented that it attracts practitioners from other paradigms in that field of study. The second requires that the subject matter is sufficiently open-ended to leave all sorts of problems for the practitioners to resolve. When these characteristics are met, the paradigm gains status because in the early stages of its development its practitioners are especially creative and more successful than those in other, older paradigms in solving acute problems. In its established form, the methodologies of a paradigm represent a body of concepts, propositions, models, and epistemology that distinguishes it from other paradigms. The paradigm's methodologies are consummated when through "normal" scientific activity the corpora of scientific factors provides research strategies to resolve the problems and puzzles in the subject matter with which its practitioners are concerned.

However, after the initial creative phase of a paradigm's development, its practitioners become less creative. Increasingly they merely tinker with the paradigm's subject matter and mop up the research detritus that the paradigm does not incorporate well. Paradigms eventually cease to respond creatively to the problems that birthed them, either because the nature of the problems and/or the environment of the paradigm's subject matter has changed. When this occurs, an existing paradigm is replaced by one that responds better to these changes. Still, ideas related to the previous paradigm do not necessarily phase out of existence. Often they are recuperated in various ways in the new paradigm.

POLITICAL ANTHROPOLOGY AND PARADIGMS

The subject matter of political anthropology has been explored in five paradigms. These include the *structural-functional* paradigm (or simply *functionalism*), the *processual* paradigm, the venerable paradigms of *political economy* and *political evolution*, which precede historically the previous paradigms and continue to thrive, and the arguable paradigm of *postmodernism*. Postmodernism may also be conceived as a literary genre, although the attributes that distinguish genres are very similar to those of scientific paradigms (Kurtz n.d.).

Of these paradigms, only the processual is exclusive to political anthropology. Yet its conceptual field owes more to ideas established in political science than in anthropology. Its practitioners, however, applied these ideas to subject matter that was uniquely anthropological. Each of the other political paradigms is an analogue of a larger anthropological paradigm. Only after each paradigm was established did some of its practitioners generate sufficiently unique subject matter related to political problems to sanction a paradigm that was exclusive to the subfield of political anthropology.

Each paradigm is a product of a history that largely determined whether its practitioners focused on politics, the political, or some combination of the two. Each has its exemplars, anthropologist practitioners who provided the repertoire of theory and political data that constitutes the paradigm. No paradigm has been totally superseded by any other paradigm, but some are more vital today than others in the work of political anthropologists.

THE STRUCTURAL-FUNCTIONAL PARADIGM (FUNCTIONALISM)

In the first half of the twentieth century, structural-functionalism, derived largely from the work of Malinowski and Radcliffe-Brown, engaged the energies of most British social anthropologists. The exemplars of the functionalist paradigm focused on synchronic analyses of social structures and systems and investigated the proposition that social structures function to maintain social stability and integration. In essence, functional explanations are those in which the consequences of a structure enter into the explanation of its persistence (Donham 1999). Except for the specific focus of its exemplars on political subject matter, the emerging field of political anthropology reflected the research methodology and strategies of the structural-functional paradigm (Fortes and Evans-Pritchard 1940; Radcliffe-Brown 1940, 1965 [1952]). Research in the paradigm by practitioners who would establish the field of political anthropology ascertained how elements of political structures functioned to maintain social order and to enforce conformity within larger social systems. They were not concerned with an agent-driven politics.

Today the functional paradigm is largely defunct and much maligned, in part because of the service of its practitioners to the colonial enterprise. But as F. G. Bailey (1960) noted, functionalism was essential to the development of the field of political anthropology. It identified political structures, such as the lineage, and attributes that had not been considered before, such as the significance of the ritual functions and mystical values of political offices. Functionalism opened vistas for future research that might otherwise have remained obscure.

THE PROCESSUAL PARADIGM

Other political anthropology paradigms are more dynamic and agent oriented. For example, the processual paradigm, as noted earlier, emerged quite apart from any paradigmatic analogue in anthropology. It grew out of the gradual rejection of the functional approach in political anthropology (and anthropology at large) and crystallized around the work of American cultural anthropologists in the mid–1960s (Swartz, Turner, and Tuden 1966; Swartz 1968; Bailey 1969).

The analytic power of the processual paradigm came from its major proposition: the rejection of structures of government as a primary focus for political analysis. Instead, its practitioners emphasized conflict, an idea that was sufficiently tainted by Marxist ideas to be eschewed by functionalists for ideological reasons. Processual exemplars argued that politics was a process in which political agents used power and a variety of strategies to attain public goals. Their research focused on the politics of political communities at the local level. Politics at higher levels of government, such as the state, were considered only when they related to problems at the local level.

The paradigm's practitioners introduced a rich array of concepts, many of which were adopted from political science, to analyze these processes. Ideas of conflict, power, agents, support, and a plethora of novel concepts, such as the authority code and political field and arena, provided the early stages of the paradigm with considerable energy. But true to Kuhn's evaluation of a paradigm, after this initial burst of novel ideas the analyses of many its practitioners lost their vigor, largely because they remained functional in practice. In part this was because many of the ideas they introduced as alternatives to the functional concepts, such as the political field and arena, proved difficult to work with.

In the late 1960s, Bailey (1969) resuscitated the paradigm with new ideas in a neo-processual context. Bailey introduced another set of concepts for analyzing political processes, and his redefinition of structure, this time as the rules that regulated competition for political prizes instead of an array of functional statuses, became central to the paradigm. Analyses now focused on political agents, leaders, and teams, and on the qualities and dynamic tensions that led to changes in these relationships as a result of competition over public and private goals. Process became truly dynamic. It was marked by changes over time in political structures that regulated the practices and competition of organizations of agents.

POLITICAL ECONOMY AND POLITICAL EVOLUTION

In political anthropology, the paradigms of political economy and political evolution overlap methodologically (Kurtz 1979). Political anthropologists who used evolutionary models to explain political phenomena, such as Fried (1967), often relied on ideas from political economy for their dynamics. Those who engaged in political economy analyses, such as Sahlins (1960, 1963), often relied on evolutionary models to demonstrate political economic processes. Practitioners in each paradigm also utilized research strategies that involved both the processual dynamics of an agent-oriented politics and concerns with the functional integrity of political structures. Though these paradigms have not always been mutually discrete, in political anthropology the distinctions between them have sharpened as the subject matter of political anthropology has changed. I will consider these more sharply defined paradigms here.

Political Economy

The paradigm of political economy has a venerable tradition that dates back at least to the Enlightenment. During the nineteenth century, it became embedded in both non-Marxist and Marxist philosophies. In either context it addressed the relationship between economics and political policies of the governments of state societies. These policies were the products of institutions and structures of governments, not the politics of particular agents, and they had impacts on broad categories of social systems, such as nations, classes, and colonial subjects. Political economists in this tradition examined the proposition that governments of state formations are implicated in the production, acquisition, and distribution of economic resources for social and political purposes. Marxists elevated production to a preeminent place in these analyses.

Excursions by political anthropologists into political economy retain the proposition that mutually implicates economics and politics in social processes. But anthropologists do not restrict political economic relations to governments of state societies. Their analyses also include the political structures and practices of political agents whose study are peculiar to political anthropology, such as chiefs and big men. Political anthropologists retained much of the paradigm's Marxist bias. They grounded their work in materialist explanations and analyses of inequality in different kinds of societies. Until recently (Wolf 1982, 1999; Donham 1999), however, they largely ignored the Marxist emphasis on production and ideology. Instead they focused on systems of distribution, a decidedly non-Marxist orientation that precluded ideology. In its anthropological context, no single exemplar stands out in this paradigm. But Karl Polanyi (1944, 1947, 1957, 1966), Marshall Sahlins (1958, 1960, 1963, 1972), Morton Fried (1967), Donald Donham (1999), and Eric Wolf (1982, 1999) have made major contributions to understanding puzzles in the paradigm.

In the early phases of the paradigm, anthropologists analyzed the political economy related to redistributive practices suggested by Polanyi (1957) of big men and chiefs (Sahlins 1960, 1963, 1968), the development of inequality in precapitalist societies (Sahlins 1958; Fried 1967), and political economic processes in precapitalist state formations (Polanyi, Arensberg, and Pearson 1957; Polanyi 1966). Later studies explored the development of specific alternative political formations, such as the Sicilian Mafia (Schneider and Schneider 1976), and the global consequences of the expansion of Western-style capitalism (Wolf 1982). Many of these efforts drew inspiration from Wallerstein's (1974) concern with the impact of dominant political economic centers on subordinate societies on their geographical peripheries. Others began to emphasize the importance of ideology in political economic practices and related it to ideas of resistance and hegemony (Donham 1999). Ideology may also provide resistance to domination (Taussig 1980) as well as dilute that resistance (Nash 1979).

Gramsci's (1971) idea of hegemony as an ideology-generating process looms large in some of this research. Woost (1993), Linger (1993), the Comaroffs (1985, 1991), Carstens (1991), and others explore how culture mediates the relationship between resistance and domination. Kurtz (1996a) and Kurtz and Nunley (1993) used the idea of hegemony to account for how an ideology of work is inculcated in a population to promote economic production for the benefit of a society's rulers and elites. The paradigm of political economy remains a vital paradigm for exploring the agent-driven politics of dominant and subordinate social categories in different kinds of political systems.

Political Evolution

Similar to the political economy paradigm, the paradigm of political evolution sprung from roots established in the Enlightenment. Some of its concerns and strategies are an extension of research into problems related to political economy. The major proposition of political evolution argues that qualitative changes reflected in the differentiation and specialization of a political system's roles and institutions are a consequence of the material relations of a political community to its environment.

Exemplars of political evolution have devoted most attention to the qualitative changes in sociopolitical systems. In this paradigm, different exemplars suggest that political evolution is demonstrated through different typologies. Bands, tribes, chiefdoms, and states represent sociopolitical categories (Service 1962). Nomadic hunters and gatherers, horticulture, pastoralism, and agriculture represent technological systems (Y. A. Cohen 1968). Egalitarian, ranked, and stratified political communities account for political economic differences (Fried 1967). Changes in these systems are thought to emerge largely because of the dynamic relationship of sociopolitical institutions, their environments, and the technolo-

gies by which they exploit them (Fried 1967; Y. A. Cohen 1968). Others
have explored the evolution of political roles, such as the transition from
big men to chiefs (Sahlins 1963), sometimes as a result of their relationship to qualitative changes in political systems (Fried 1967).

It is difficult if not misleading to isolate the evolution of political agents
from their anchor in political systems. So far the paradigm's practitioners
have focused on the evolution of political systems instead of political
agents. But if politics is to be theorized as a causal force in the evolution
of political systems, the practices of political agents and their historical
transformations require more attention (Lewis and Greenfield 1983; P. B.
Roscoe 1993; Donham 1999). This is an underdeveloped component of the
paradigm of political evolution that I will try to rectify in Chapter 10.

STATE FORMATIONS

Except for the processual paradigm, the state is the only political structure that practitioners in each paradigm address in abundance. Still, the
study of the state does not represent a paradigm. Instead, in political anthropology it is conceived of as a political structure, organization, or system, and as a context for the analysis of politics. The state is better
thought of as a topic of special interest to political anthropologists.

In part this is because the invention of the state was a critical watershed
in the development of world politics owing to the impact of its govern-
mental structures on other societies. As a result of this impact, it is likely
that no topic has received more attention than the state by anthropologists who study politics and political structures and organization. Yet the
idea of the state defies clear definition and is badly muddled methodologically (Kurtz 1993). Regardless, the state was introduced as a major research consideration of political anthropology in the functionalist paradigm (Fortes and Evans-Pritchard 1940). Analyses of the state dominate
anthropological thinking and practice in the paradigms of political economy and political evolution, and their exemplars were important in establishing its preeminence. However, for many postmodern anthropologists, the state is primarily a "deconstructed" entity.

POSTMODERNISM

Postmodernism may not qualify as a paradigm in the Kuhnian sense.
Kuhn's idea of a paradigm explicitly denotes scientific research strategies.
Postmodernists eschew positivist science in favor of an epistemology and
research practices that often are embedded more comfortably in the humanities and the analytic framework of genres (Kurtz n.d.). There also is
no agreement among postmodernists regarding what exactly postmodern

studies represent and what the proper focus of research and concern should be. Indeed, the denial of such a focus is one hallmark of postmodernist thinking.

Nonetheless, within the farrago of subject matter related to postmodernism, a significant portion in anthropology deals with both agent-driven politics and political systems and structures, but in unorthodox ways. Postmodern practitioners address a variety of ideas and topics, such as hegemony, gender, domination, and resistance, that political anthropologists have explored in other paradigmatic contexts. They also explore ideas that anthropologists in other paradigms have ignored or de-emphasized, such as citizenship, nationality, and identity in a "deconstructed" world political order, and a plethora of other "decentered" concerns garbed in a fluid and changing vocabulary. This eclecticism may appear to deny that postmodern anthropologists bring a focus to their political ideas. Yet some postmodern exemplars appear to be defining state terror and violence as the nexus of a postmodern paradigm of political anthropology (Feldman 1991; Mahmood 1996; Nordstrom 1997; Slyomovics 1998; Linke 1999; Sluka 2000). Nonetheless, the eclecticism of postmodern concerns and the various methodologies, even of those who share an interest in state terror and violence, represents the "strategically agnostic" paradigm that some anthropologists deplore (Harris 1979:289; 1998; Gellner 1992). But it also embodies the most remote ideas of politics and the political that are not clear, embedded, accountable, or fashionable in any of the other paradigms related to political anthropology.

PART TWO

Political Essentials

2

POLITICAL POWER

THE DOMAIN OF POLITICAL POWER

In anthropology political power is only one dimension in a range of ideas of power that imbue human practices as diverse as economic distribution, religious worship, and healing rituals (Fogelson and Adams 1977). In these contexts, power represents a catchall to describe protean practices and processes that were not always appreciated by scholars to be powerful. These insights into the various dimensions of power were a major contribution to the concept of power in general, and recently anthropologists have rushed to examine the role of power in almost every human activity. Many of these activities are neither political nor involve politics, except in the sense that when some human practice defies easy explanation the outcome is often attributed to politics, usually by those whose goals or desires have been thwarted.

Political power is much more specific. Politics is all about power: about how political agents create, compete for, and use power to attain public goals that, at least on the surface, are presumed to be for the common good of a political community. Yet just as often and more covertly, political power is used to attain private goals for the good of the agents involved. Without power, political agents, especially political leaders, are ineffective and probably ephemeral.

Despite its significance to politics, the idea of power remains elusive and defies definition. "Power" is used widely inside and outside academic circles in both metaphorical and concrete senses to apply to many different situations and conditions. Many of these contexts do not refer to political power. Yet ideas of political power derive from these contexts and are so generalized that they include much more than they should.

This contributes to the tiresome intellectual exercises by which philosophers and social scientists unnecessarily mystify the idea of power.

The most common sense of political power derives from Weber's widely used and popular notion of power. Weber suggests that power is "the probability that one actor within a social relationship will be in a position to carry out his own will despite resistance" (1964 [1947]:152). In other words, power is the ability of A to bend B to his or her will. This idea of power is very much taken for granted and usually not open to question. But it does not identify specifically what property or attribute provides some with the capacity to force others to do things. It is in this context especially that the idea of power as the control of resources becomes important. Unfortunately, the resources that political scholars suggest as a basic formula for political power are not very satisfactory.

Political scientists and sociologists noted the importance of resources to power long ago. Lasswell and Kaplan (1950:87) suggested eight resources, largely ideational, that are the basis of political power: power itself (an ambiguous redundancy), respect, rectitude, affection, well-being, wealth, skill, and enlightenment. Dahl (1961:229ff.) distinguishes resources that are more material. These include social standing, distributions of cash, wealth, and credit, access to legal means, popularity, control over jobs, and information. These ideas of power fail to illuminate the idea of resources as power because they are too Eurocentric, modern, and situationally particular.

Indeed, it is because the consequences of political power are so obvious and ubiquitous in the societies with which political scientists and sociologists are involved that finer distinctions of power itself may not be perceived to be necessary. Power conceived as a laundry list of resources in these examples does not do much to demystify the relationship between power and politics that has been created by social scientists and philosophers. Instead, they contribute to the breadth of ideas concerned with power and so dilute its significance for understanding politics. This makes power more abstract than it needs to be when it is considered in the context of an agent-driven politics.

In politics, as opposed to other contexts in which ideas of power may have relevance, the power of any political agent does indeed derive fundamentally from the control of resources. But from an ethnographic perspective, the itemization of discrete features of political power is self-defeating. There are simply too many variations of political formations, agents, and potential resources of power identified in the ethnographic record. Instead, from a cross-cultural perspective, the resources that constitute the power of an agent-driven politics can be subsumed succinctly, without being reductionist, under material (tangible, human) and ideational (ideological, symbolic, informational) resources. Acquisition and maintenance of these resources endow political agents with power, and political power from this perspective may be fruitfully defined as the control of resources. In general, political agents who control more resources tend to win out against those who control less. However, agents who control less power but use it wisely and skillfully often win out against other agents with more power, but who squander it.

Some think the sharp distinctions that anthropologists draw between material and ideational domains are self-indulgent, and that even in political practice these domains of political power represent false oppositions (Wolf 1999). Still, the idea that power is grounded in distinct categories of resources permits a wider, cross-cultural consideration of the relationship among power, political leadership, and their environmental contexts. It also provides insight into the evolution of political power. The belief that there is a critical relationship between resources and power is neither new nor unique, but I will demonstrate below a novel approach to this relationship.

POLITICS AND POWER

Economists have identified an "economic man" whose purpose in life is to maximize profits. The ethnographic record suggests the existence of a "political person" whose goal in life is to maximize political power. The gender-sensitive idea of a "political person" complies with the fact that political power is not the exclusive property of men. There are numerous examples of leadership, political practice, and uses of political power by women, and their sources of power are no different from those available to men. For example, women had power to select the sachems of Iroquois society (Morgan 1901 [1851]), and the women's council of the Barabaig, cattle herders in Tanzania, had power to punish males for transgressing rules regarding traditional rights of women in the society (Klima 1970). In each instance, women controlled material resources, land and cattle, respectively, and drew upon an ideology and symbols of women's power to support their actions.

In the sixteenth century, Queen Elizabeth I used the power available to her to manipulate successfully English policy against the military might of Spain and conspiracies at home. This power included the material and ideational powers of her office, the material booty captured from the Spanish by her corsairs, and the constructed myth of her exalted virgin status. Three hundred years later, Margaret Thatcher's conservative agenda relied on the power vested in her office of prime minister to reshape British domestic and foreign policy. In the patriarchal tradition of Indian politics, Indira Gandhi's power included support from India's impoverished masses and her symbolic status as an heir to the Nehru name.

These and powers derived from her office as prime minister enabled her politics of opportunism, redefinition, and accommodation to redefine India's domestic and international policies during the 1970s and early 1980s. In these instances, women could draw upon considerable material and ideational power available to them as heads of state to pursue their political agendas.

Although power infuses politics no matter which gender uses it, politics has been and largely remains a male prerogative. Men have been more successful than women in creating, accessing, and controlling power. More important, they have been very successful in keeping it out of the hands of women. The message is clear: If more women want to compete more successfully with men in political arenas, they must either figure out ways to take power away from men or develop their own.

The ethnographic description of political power appears to vary widely in the political communities and polities that anthropologists have explored. This variety derives from cultural relativism, currently very fashionable in anthropology, which considers the culture of human societies to be infinitely variable and individually distinctive. An alternative, ethnological perspective exposes cross-cultural regularities that reveal that political power is not infinitely various. Its constituent material and ideational components often cohere to the types of societies with which that power is associated, such as chiefdoms, state formations, or big man polities.

Political scientists and political sociologists have a more exclusive view of political power than do most anthropologists. In part this is because they explore political power primarily in contemporary state formations. In these formations, political power is more highly centralized in specialized institutions of governments than is the case among stateless formations. In the latter, political institutions consist of less centralized arrangements of political statuses and roles, and power is more diffuse and uncertain. The totality of resources that provide power that is available to leaders in state polities is quantitatively and, to some extent, qualitatively different from that which is available to leaders in stateless formations.

Despite the amalgamation of the material and ideational factors that anthropologists use to demonstrate political power ethnographically, this power also is simpler, more specific, less mysterious, more substantial, and less abstract than philosophers make it. This is because the political power that drives politics is empirically grounded in human agencies. In philosophical contexts, power often is rendered mysterious or relegated to abstractions such as discourse, sovereignty, knowledge, or nationalism. Nonetheless, power is materialized in the practices of the human agencies that develop, acquire, and use it in politics. If power relates to politics that are agent driven it is not very mysterious, although much of what constitutes power politics may be hidden from public view.

PARADIGMS AND POWER

The paradigms that direct political research by anthropologists are not equally concerned with political power. Anthropologists involved in functional analysis gave little attention to the dynamics of political power. In the development of functionalism, Radcliffe-Brown asserted that the study of political organization was concerned with "the maintenance of established social order, within a territorial framework, by the organized use, or the possibility of use, of physical force" (1940:xiv). After this depiction, power was largely used as a synonym for coercion and force.

The functional idea of power as force used to maintain order implies that political power is concerned with the Weberian capacity of someone or some group to force others to do things. The capacity of power to bend another to one's will suggests a process of action and reaction of the parties involved and the potential for dynamic alterations in the social system. But anthropologists invested in the functional paradigm did not explore these relations much. Instead, the capacity of power to change sociopolitical systems was relegated to a process dedicated to maintaining order and enforcing conformity in the service of social cohesion and integration. They assumed that sociopolitical systems changed as whole entities to retain their structural integrity. This perspective of power begs many questions. Still, anthropologists did not establish alternatives to this view of political power for over a decade.

Following World War II, American anthropologists expressed renewed interest in the paradigm of political evolution. They gradually resurrected the role of power in the materialist domain and began to explore the cross-cultural regularities related to power. These explorations did not specifically address political power, but they had an impact on the concept of political power.

The paradigm of political evolution focused on materialist dimensions of power and was grounded largely, if not covertly, in Marxist thinking. Some practitioners broadly conceived of power as an energetic process (R. N. Adams 1975). The impact of Marxist ideas on this formulation was vague. Others took a vulgar Marxist position and explored power in economic contexts related to systems of distribution (Sahlins 1958, 1960, 1963; Service 1962). Still others handled Marxist ideas more expertly and explored power in terms of relations of production (Wolf 1982) and ideology (Wolf 1999).

ADAMS AND POWER

Richard Adams (1975) diluted the impact of the energetics of power with an unfortunate juxtaposition of ideas. Instead of rethinking the issue, Adams accepted the Weberian concept of power as the ability of one to force others to do things. His subsequent analyses of power had little to do with politics. Rather, they were concerned more with varieties and relations of power in different contexts. This is a recurrent theme in the literature on power: The consequences of power are considered without exploring the dynamics of power outside the Weberian framework.

For example, Adams attached relations of power to types of power that he identified broadly as independent and dependent power. Independent power refers to the abilities and capabilities related to knowledge, skills, and fortuitous and systematic attributes of individuals or social units to direct or control relations of dominance in society. Dependent power exists when one agent gives another the right to make decisions on his or her behalf. These relations may exist in some conditions where power is used, such as a healing ritual. But in politics, power is never independent of the resources that constitute it; all political power is dependent on them.

Adams did make a useful contribution to understanding politics by distinguishing between power that is granted, allocated, and delegated. Granted power is that which is given by a leader to another. In politics this is not very common, unless a leader wants to relinquish power over some domain or retire from the political field. Power that is given away may be very hard to reclaim.

It is more likely that leaders will delegate power to another for a specific purpose, such as collecting taxes or implementing policy. Leaders may reclaim delegated power or delegate it to another. Delegated power suggests a strong leadership because the leader has a reservoir of power to draw upon. But this is not always the case. Weak leaders may be required to delegate power to retain their political status, which may be more titular or symbolic than real.

Allocated power is given by a political community to a leader. Here the political community may reclaim the power and allocate it to another. In contemporary democracies this is accomplished through voting. In a hunting and gathering society or where a big man prevails as leader, as in Melanesia, the political community may simply refuse to obey or pay attention to the leader. And they may or not reallocate the power. Power allocated in this manner is indicative of a weak leader.

Adams does not identify the constituent ingredients of granted, allocated, or delegated power. Instead, through a turgid academic exercise, he developed an idea of power as "a relational quality that exists contingent on controls that can be exercised over elements of the external world [and exists] differentially and independently for all men and may be extended to many things" (R. N. Adams 1975:395). In trying to provide a universal model of power that includes politics, Adams obscures the idea of power and the relationship between power and politics.

WOLF AND POWER

The concept of a mode of production became acceptable in anthropological thinking in the 1960s and 1970s. It was related to the emergence of political economy as a research concern in anthropology. Anthropologists involved in the paradigm of political evolution had long held to a form of vulgar Marxism that related leaders to supporters through rules of reciprocity and redistribution (Polanyi 1957; Sahlins 1958, 1960, 1963; Service 1962). But leader–supporter relations were not the major concern of anthropologists in either the political economy or evolutionary paradigms. They focused on political systems and emphasized the political economic integration of the political community. Little was said about the creation and use of power.

This oversight was redressed in the paradigm of political economy, in which power became a derivative of either influence over or control of the means of production, and this control provided both a source of political power and a means of extending it. Wolf (1982) configured these practices in three modes of production: the kinship, the tributary, and the capitalist. Each mode identified means by which political agents and structures became increasingly centralized and powerful as a result of controlling how tangible materials are produced, who motivates the production, and why. This led Wolf to think recursively about how forms of leadership and government related to the acquisition and use of material forms of political power. To accomplish this, he identified four *modes of power* (Wolf 1990). They are neither mutually exclusive nor exclusive to material forms of power. He returned to them later to explore relationships between ideology and power (Wolf 1999).

One mode refers to power as an attribute of a person's potency or capability in power relations. A second mode refers to the ability of an ego to impose his or her will on another. The third refers to tactical power, that is, the instrument by which a political agent or unit circumscribes the actions of another within a political field and arena. The fourth mode refers to structural power. Wolf adopted this latter mode from Michel Foucault's notion of power as "the ability to structure the field of possible action of others" (1984:428). Wolf singles out this last mode for special consideration. It provides the framework within which the three other modes of power are combined as a unified strategy of power practices in both material and ideational power domains (Wolf 1990, 1999).

Structural power refers to power that configures a society's political economy by deploying and allocating social labor. In this context, structural power exists at a level of abstraction above the individual political agent. But Wolf (1990) uses the idea of structural power, in conjunction with tactical power, to consider the organization of a capitalist political economy. He examines how tactical and structural powers are extensions of modes of personal and psychological power. These latter modes relate individuals to the field of political action by which events and behaviors are organized and orchestrated in a setting to influence the distribution and direction of power. The tactics of individual political agents allow certain kinds of behavior while rendering other less likely or impossible. Structural power emphasizes how social labor is deployed and allocated in the material domain. In the ideational domain, structural power emphasizes how power is imbued with ideological potency and meaning through communication and discourse. Structural power transpires within a structured social field of action to the advantage of power holders (Wolf 1990, 1999).

From the cross-cultural perspective provided by the paradigm of political evolution, Wolf's ideas of power account for the development and peculiar organization of contemporary political systems. However, the four modes of power that Wolf addresses also can be used to account for material and ideological concerns with power in the precapitalist, less institutionally complex political communities to which anthropologists traditionally gravitate. The deployment of social labor by political agents to produce tangible goods to use for political purposes is not as exclusive to modern political economies as Wolf's analysis suggests.

Wolf's work on power is less abstract than its representation in the paradigms of political evolution. Still, he suggests that the tactical uses of power are a product of the personal and psychological attributes of individuals. These attributes connote qualities of leadership; they are not reserves of power. Many people, such as aspirants to the political field, can demonstrate personal and psychological attributes that suggest their ability to compete in political arenas. But unless they have political power to do so, those qualities mean little. The aspects of Wolf's ideas that relate to personal and psychological qualities are close to Adams' notion of personal power. They are insufficient. Nonetheless, Wolf did inject a powerful dimension of Marxist thinking into the study of power. On the one hand, he displaced the attention given to systems of distribution as the basis for political economic thinking in political anthropology. Instead, he identified modes of production as vital sources of political power. On the other hand, he demonstrated how ideas are involved in relations of power. As ideologies they comprise united schemes that underwrite the power of leaders and become intertwined in the relations of rulers and ruled.

FOUCAULT AND POWER

Few individuals have influenced how anthropologists think about power more than Michel Foucault (1972, 1979, 1980, 1984, 1991) (recall it was Foucault from whom Wolf extrapolated the idea of structural power). Foucault infused a philosophical perspective into discourses about power in dramatic and epigrammatic pronouncements. Taken as a whole, these pronouncements can easily overwhelm the reader and obfuscate even more the complexity of Foucault's thoughts on power. Such complexity is responsible for the tendency to reduce his ideas to misleading clichés, such as the popularized notions that "knowledge is power" (1979) and "power is everywhere" (1980).

Foucault's major concern was to develop an "analytics" of power (1980). But his analytics is not concerned with the essence or substance of power. Instead his purpose is to account for what power does, the effects it produces for and to individuals and social categories, such as prisoners, homosexuals, and the insane. To accomplish this, Foucault parses power as a noun that he disguises in a variety of contexts. Power is a force, a sphere, a moving strata, an instrument, a multiplicity of forces all of which function as "force relations" that affect individuals as mechanisms of control. Power is not a force controlled by agents in Foucault's scheme. Indeed, agents are not important to him for power is not something held by someone. In effect, his "Power" is an anthropomorphized agent that exists in many shapes and forms and comes from many directions as a vector, an instrument, a technology, a technique, or a discourse that produces effects, such as knowledge, reality, and regimes of truth. As biopower, Power influences matters of life and death. As a microphysics of power, perhaps his most original and best idea (Garland 1990), Power inserts itself into the actions, attitudes, discourses, knowledge, learning, and practices of people in everyday life. Foucault dazzles with his relentless kaleidoscopic reconstitutions of ideas of Power's myriad causes and effects. Ultimately, for Foucault, Power is "the overall effect that emerges from all these mobilities" (1980:93).

Regardless of the complexity of Foucault's visions of Power, his Power also is Weberian in essence. It relies on Weber's notion that power provides A the ability to force B to do things. This is Foucault's "productive" aspect of Power. Knowledge is not power per se. Power produces knowledge that may then become Power, but which remains nonetheless a production of Power that then has wider effects in those situations where it is implicated.

Clearly this is an important aspect of the universal relationship between power and the production and control of information. But Foucault diluted the importance of the relationship between knowledge and power and the generalized productive capacity of power when he suggested that "Power is everywhere ... because it comes from everywhere" (1980:93). To think of power as a universal agent that is embedded in everything everywhere is novel. But its magnitude reduces the idea of *political power* to insignificance. But then, Foucault is not really interested in politics. Nor does he like power. Instead he is hostile to it in any form because of the pernicious effects it produces on individuals and social categories of people.

The creation of power as an agent limits the value of Foucault's ideas of power as a necessary aspect of politics. From Foucault's analytics there is no way to discern, distinguish, or compare qualities and degrees of power. Power to Foucault is ultimately an abstract, quasi-structuralist force that emanates from what it produces—knowledge, discourses, social relations, reality, truth, and so forth—with a crushing social effect.

POWER, POLITICS, AND PROCESS

Each of these paradigmatic and philosophical constructions of power suffers from a single flaw that mitigates their value for understanding the politics related to political power. They overlook the fundamental resources of power that enable its capacity for powerful human action. The idea that political power provides the capacity that enables someone to act against another, to bend them to their will, to inhibit their actions, to shape a field of action, to delegate power, or to produce knowledge begs a fundamental question: What precisely is the source of power that provides an agent or structure or Foucault's anthropomorphized Power with the capacity to force others to act in ways that may be and often are inimical to the other's interests?

A response to this question must first acknowledge that political power is not an abstraction or an anthropomorphized force. It does not exist apart from those who use it. Radcliffe-Brown recognized this when he said, "There is no such thing as the power of the State [an abstraction]. There are only, in reality, powers of individuals—kings, prime ministers, magistrates, policemen, party bosses, and voters" (Radcliffe-Brown 1940:xxiii). The relation between political power and the actions of political actors was recognized most emphatically by anthropologists involved in the processual paradigm.

Research strategies developed by anthropologists in the processual paradigm revealed the specifics of political power as they explored the dynamic relationship between power and people in discrete ethnographic contexts. Nicholas said it most succinctly, although incompletely: "'Power' is control over resources, whether human or material. . . . Participants in political activity attempt to expand their control over resources; or, if they do not, they are not engaged in political action" (1966:4; also 1968). Without acknowledging it, exemplars of the processual paradigm recovered Radcliffe-Brown's ignored and forgotten legacy that situated political authority and power in the practices of human agents. The processual anthropologists incorporated the idea of political power as the control of resources.

POWER RESOURCES

The ethnographic record suggests that the identification of political power with the control of resources can be accommodated in five common resources. Besides human and material resources identified by Nicholas, ideology, symbols, and information provide three other critical resources of political power. The five resources that constitute political power may be divided into two domains—the material and the ideational—to help distinguish relationships among them.

The material domain includes human and what I think of as tangible resources. Human resources refer to the allies and supporters—people— that any political agent requires to be a leader. Tangible resources provide the culturally defined goods, such as money in the United States, pigs in highland New Guinea, cacao beans among the Aztecs, and the like. Politics is obvious when agents compete for human and tangible resources and use them to attain their goals.

The ideational domain of power includes ideology, symbols, and information. The power they provide is more subtle. Ideational resources, especially symbols, are used largely to impose meaning on political actions. Ideologies and information are used to manipulate that meaning. In concert, ideational resources help leaders to convince others of the legitimacy of their authority and to enhance the leaders' abilities to acquire additional material resources.

Political power does not exist apart from agents who forge it creatively out of the resources available in their environments. From the perspective of cultural relativism this is obvious in the politics of particular societies. Some agents always have more power than others, and agents with less power tend to lose out to those with more.

It is less obvious that these power resources exist and are available in different degrees in different types of societies. The officeholders and political aspirants in state governments and chiefly polities have access to more resources than do leaders in nomadic hunting and gathering societies or big man polities. Between the extremes—nomadic hunting and gathering societies and state formations—political power resources vary greatly in abundance, accessibility, and distribution. The variations depend largely on the institutional and environmental complexity of the society in which politics transpires. These differences demonstrate the evolution of political power.

But whether explored from a relativist or cross-cultural bias, the resources of power are inextricably intertwined in complex equations and can be separated practically only for analysis. It is difficult to say without fear of contradiction which resource of power is most fundamental. But a case can be made that human resources are the most basic. In the following sections, the resources of power are separated only for discussion. Their crucial relationships are considered here only where necessary. These relationships and the evolution of political power will be considered in context later.

THE MATERIAL RESOURCE DOMAIN

Supporters

It is axiomatic that a leader cannot exist without someone to lead. Most often those who support a leader are identified as followers (H. S. Lewis 1974). But, as I think of it, followers are merely one category of political supporters, albeit the largest and arguably the most important, upon which a leader relies. This is because the single biggest problem that any leader confronts is how to attract and retain supporters.

Without supporters a leader could not generate the tangible resources that are necessary to compete successfully in political arenas. An aspiring leader may attract supporters based on his or her ideational qualities—ideas, rhetoric, symbols. But if he or she cannot produce what is promised, their tangible support will be withdrawn and the leader will not last for long. The recursive nature of power suggests that while a leader may attract supporters, the paucity of tangible resources ultimately will affect the relationship and destroy it. A serious lack of any material resource, tangible or human, is an indication of the bankruptcy of a leader's politics.

The supporters upon whom a leader relies may be thought of as *followers, benefactors,* and *loyalists.* They are not mutually exclusive, and the relationship of any of these supporters to a leader is likely to be fickle and subject to change.

Followers are the fundamental human resource that a leader must develop. They are the foundation of a leader's status. They also are the most fickle. Followers tag along in a leader's wake and provide support if the leader does not disappoint them. A leader's reciprocal relations with followers are often distant, abstract, and generalized. These relations often depend on ambiguities, such as the leader's promise to protect them from enemies or to provide them a better way of life. Policies and practices that respond immediately to followers' expectations are most likely to ensure support, such as sponsoring a feast, reducing taxes, or overseeing a period of economic growth. But specific policies always risk alienating some followers. Without a body of followers a leader will lose, or at least have difficulty retaining, benefactors and, possibly, loyalists.

Benefactors provide a leader access to tangible resources, however they are defined culturally: money, pigs, automobiles, shells, yams, furs, and the like. Benefactors have a stronger commitment and closer relationship to a leader than do followers, and this relationship is based on different reciprocal principles. Reciprocity between leaders and benefactors is more immediate and quickly balanced. Benefactors provide a leader with tangibles if there is an acceptable return for their commitment in a culturally determined reasonable time. That could mean government contracts, access to trade routes, rights to property, favoritism in the resolution of a dispute, or simply the right to bask in the heated glow of the leader's shadow, under which tangible returns may be incubated.

Loyalists provide the most enduring support, for they are morally committed to a leader. But even they may fade away if a leader falls on protracted hard times. Still, loyalists are more likely to hang on when all other supporters have deserted. Loyalists may not reap any tangible gain from their commitment to a leader. Often they are alter-symbols of the leader, and devote much energy to developing the leader's image, meaning, and policies to followers. For loyalists, the fact that they and the leader share fundamental ideas, beliefs, and ideology is sufficient reward.

Leaders must be mindful of the cost they pay for supporters. The closer supporters get to leaders in their reciprocal expectations, the more the exchanges are likely to cost leaders and drain away his or her power. Power is never static. It can be acquired and lost. The cost to leaders for nurturing supporters, especially benefactors, can put them so deeply in debt that they lose power as their supporters gain it. If leaders' debts become too unbalanced, supporters can dictate the policies they want to have implemented. Leaders who become too indebted to supporters may be unable to implement their own policies and be forced to respond only to those of their supporters. If a leader's actions become inimical to the moral and material interests of her supporters, they may transfer the power they represent to other leaders.

Tangible Resources

Tangible resources of power are culturally specific. In Western societies, money is the primary tangible that leaders translate into political power.

New Guinea big men rely heavily on pigs, some African chiefs on cattle. Feathers of the quetzal bird and cocoa beans were two among many tangibles upon which Aztec kings of pre-Columbian Mexico relied.

As a rule, popular leaders to whom followers allocate authority also will derive tangible resources from benefactors. Often supporters are encouraged rhetorically, sometimes by force, to create tangibles from which leaders derive power. However they are obtained, tangibles enable leaders to gain access to other tangible sources of power. Leaders may develop access to credit (Oliver 1955; Read 1965; Bailey 1969) or trading partners (Oliver 1955; Pospisil 1963), or they may gain control of trade routes (Helms 1979). They may have access to land holdings (Berdan 1982), rights to productive fishing grounds or slaves (Codere 1950; Ruyle 1973), or control of the distribution of scarce resources whose flow through the society they regulate, such as breadfruit, coconuts, taro, and yams (Firth 1957 [1936]). Some leaders may be able to exact tribute from conquered people, control the flow of precious goods, tax their subjects, and require corvée labor on their estates from their subjects (Claessen and Skalník 1978). However obtained, tangible resources enable leaders to gain access to other tangible sources of power.

Still, the acquisition of tangible resources is a major problem for leaders. One may deduce from the ethnographic record that acquiring tangibles is a universal political problem. But even more fundamental in the quest for tangibles is the difficulty of creating them in the first place. That is why leaders actively promote the production of gross surpluses above the minimal per capita levels of biological necessity in their political communities (R. M. Adams 1966; Fried 1967; Kurtz 1984, 1996a; Kurtz and Nunley 1993). This may be accomplished by coercion, rhetoric, or a combination of both.

It is to the advantage of every leader to rule a productive society. Unless tangibles are available over minimal survival levels, there will be little for a leader to expropriate. Without tangible resources, leaders flounder in the face of the demands from their supporters. Leaders may try to coerce their subjects to produce gross surpluses of tangibles, which is well reported in the literature. But if they do, sooner or later they will generate a threat to their legitimacy. Coercion is costly in terms of both human and tangible resources.

Wise leaders seek an alternative route. They try to instill the idea that the production of tangible resources above minimal levels of survival necessity is for the common good. There is considerable truth to this (Kurtz 1996a). But when gross surpluses of goods are produced, those surpluses always fall under the control of political and economic institutions of authority and power. In effect, no society produces a gross surplus of tangible resources. Most tangibles that exceed minimal per capita levels neither trickle down to the people nor float free for people in the society to garner. Rather, surpluses are mobilized in institutions that constitute a society's political economy and are used by a society's leaders for political ends.

THE IDEATIONAL RESOURCE DOMAIN

Ideological Resources

A political ideology is a system of hypotheses, principles, and postulates that justify the exercise of authority and power, assert social values and moral and ethical principles, set forth causal connections between leaders and the people they govern, and furnish guides for action (Kurtz 1996a). The primary functional relevance of an ideology is that it enables leaders to mobilize people for action around a set of beliefs and ideas (Carlsnaes 1981; Wolf 1999). This may include mobilizing people for warfare or social causes and convincing them that it is proper for them to labor for the common good of the society. Political ideologies are likely to be more diverse and interwoven in more institutionally complex societies.

Some ideas are more important to a polity than others. Those that are critical to the survival of a government are likely to receive special attention. These might promote the perceptions that the government is just, is concerned with the well-being of its citizens, and protects them from their enemies.

Political ideologies are likely to be specific to types of polities and their political communities. Ideas related to social justice are likely to be concerns of the governments of state formations. Political ideologies that emphasize the generosity of leaders are likely to be promoted in polities where leaders are not especially powerful. Ideologies related to the value of productive work seem to be universal (Kurtz and Nunley 1993; Kurtz 1996a; Wolf 1999).

Symbolic Resources

A symbol is a material object, mental projection, action, idea, or word that human beings infuse with ambiguous, multiple, and disparate meanings. Political symbols may be anything in the social and physical environments that helps to convince people to follow and support a leader or leadership structure: money, pigs and cattle, flags and fasces, gods and utopian worlds, genders and kinship structures, rituals and ceremonies, notions of democracy and freedom, brotherhoods and sisterhoods, abortions and family values, words, and rhetoric. Symbols are fluid and changeable as they respond to shifting social, cultural, and political conditions (A. Cohen 1969, 1974, 1979).

Symbols are polysemic, that is, they have different meanings. A symbol that has positive value in one polity can have negative value in another context. The meaning of the swastika in Hinduism and some American Indian cultures—well-being or good luck—is qualitatively different from its meaning on the flags and banners of Nazi Germany.

Symbols may establish and maintain a leader's identity and intentions. They may also hide and disguise them. Ronald Reagan was the Teflon president; Bill Clinton the Velcro president. A symbol can evoke strong feelings and emotions, and therein lies a symbol's potential for political power.

Leaders manipulate symbols. They appropriate them from the past and refashion them to fit current needs. They create new symbols, such as the imagery of sisterhood or Black and Brown and Red power. Leaders may oppose their symbols to those of their opponents. Shrewd political leaders use symbols to impel people to act in ways that are desirable to the leader (A. Cohen 1974; Dolgin, Kemnitzer, and Schneider 1977; Wolf 1999).

Symbols may help a leader dominate others. They also may provide resistance to domination. Leaders themselves can become powerful symbols and embody the values and ideals of a political community. As a symbol, a leader can unify followers for action. A leader's failure may also reproduce the leader as symbolically negative.

Politics and the competition for power are replete with symbols that may mystify people thoroughly and effectively. In his film *The Cow of Dolo Ken Paye*, James Gibb pointed out how Dolo Ken Paye, a paramount chief of the Kpelle of Liberia, could infuse his spirit into his cattle; they symbolized him. Therefore, anyone who attacked Dolo Ken Paye's cattle attacked Dolo Ken Paye himself, and could expect to be punished. Followers know their leaders through the meanings the leaders impose upon them (A. Cohen 1969). Meanings are conveyed orally and in print media through words and rhetoric. In their oral and written contexts, symbols become a component of the informational bases of power.

Informational Resources

Information both includes and produces knowledge. To the extent that leaders can harness the flow of information, it can become and produce knowledge as power. Information also provides access to other resources. It is a means to support or subvert existing ideologies, or to develop alternative ones. When information is used by a skilled orator, it can dramatically increase the reservoirs of supporters. Similarly, if a political community is linguistically homogeneous, people may be more easily politically socialized by their leaders. This is because leaders are likely to talk more directly and with less obfuscation about matters of concern to the community (Mueller 1973).

In an ethnographic sense, the most common source of information as political power is the rhetoric of the spoken word. Political rhetoric is the deliberate exploitation of eloquence in public speaking (or in writing) by leaders to persuade others. However and by whomever political talk is presented, the basic purpose of the talk is rhetorical. The extent to which rhetoric persuades is one gauge of a leader's power. In most societies, leaders are expected to be good talkers. Those who are not may find that this limits the height to which their political star may rise. But just as importantly, a leader must know when not to talk and be silent.

The qualities that people accept in a leader are always specific to a time and place. The paladin of one set of supporters may be another's scoundrel. Leaders who are exceptional orators and able to sway people with their rhetoric run the gamut from demagogues, such as Adolf Hitler, to humanitarians, such as Martin Luther King. The oratorical abilities and viewpoints of most leaders lie between these extremes. It is rare that any leader, no matter how eloquent, will be acceptable to everyone in their respective political communities.

In some societies the ability of leaders to exercise power and authority is contingent on their anonymity. For example, in some big men societies or in divine monarchies, where leaders are less visible and not easily approached by common people, the style by which leaders talk and present information is likely to be illocutionary. Their talk is guarded, formal, and stylized. At the extreme it is frozen and impoverished semantically (Bloch 1975). The formalization of illocutionary talk enables leaders to coerce more easily the responses of ordinary people because their talk directs and predicts others' responses. The style of their talk conveys power over others beyond the information at their disposal.

In societies where leaders are more visible, even if their physical proximity to their political communities is distant, as among many contemporary democracies, the elocutionary style of leaders is free, informal, less stylized, and semantically rich and expansive (Paine 1981; Bailey 1983). The skill with which the spoken work is presented can be a route to political success and power. Social distance between leaders and followers is mitigated somewhat by modern media, which brings the image of the leader into the homes of subjects. Where cultural complexity is the result of linguistic heterogeneity, leaders may find it to their advantage to be able to speak the high and low dialects of their community. They also are likely to talk more in generalities, be more ambiguous, and be prone to political doublespeak (Mueller 1973; Paine 1981).

In technologically advanced polities, where information is processed cybernetically, so much information is available that it causes a sharp dialectic of power as the pronouncements and opinions of different leaders clash. Information can be detrimental to leaders' power, or they can turn it to their advantage. Information, in either written or spoken form, always exists, and current and aspiring leaders can use it to contradict each other, often to the detriment of their followers. Misuse or misunderstanding of information can also cost leaders and aspirants credibility and power. Shredding machines, speech writers, and thoughtful elocution are several responses to haunting informational concerns, such as what the definition of is, is.

In the industrialized and Western world, notions of rationality prevail. There also is some expectation that rhetoric should be based on facts and that good leaders will present rational arguments and act rationally. However, the reality of politics in practice suggests a simple alternative proposition: Political leaders rarely win support by rhetorical tactics and strategies that employ reason and rationality. Reason is dull and rarely moves people to action. Instead it is passion that sways people. In politics, passionate and hortatory talk is a more effective rhetorical tactic than reason. Leaders are more likely to be successful and powerful if their rhetoric is passionate (Bailey 1983).

This does not mean that reason has no place in politics. It is most effective when a leader must respond to abominations, things better left unsaid, or problems of image and credibility. In these contexts, reason will probably prevail, or at least help. But in the daily political contests of winning the hearts and minds of people, acquiring supporters, conveying ideologies, manipulating symbols, and, probably, enhancing a leader's total power base, passionate talk is a good tactic (Bailey 1983).

3

POLITICAL LEADERS AND
AUTHORITIES

POLITICAL LEADERSHIP AND
POLITICAL PARADIGMS

embedded

Practitioners in each political paradigm study political leaders and authority figures in some context or other, and there is often overlap in how they approach and treat these issues. Most, for example, use anthropologically familiar terms, such as big men, chiefs, or states, to refer to ethnographically depicted leaders, authority figures, and structures. But agents involved in political processes are not necessarily practicing politicians. They may include shamans, priests, influential individuals, and the like. Nonetheless, some distinctions can be made between paradigmatic usages and the applications of these ideas.

Exemplars of the structural-functional paradigm were concerned more with the idea of authority than of leadership. They generally disregarded leadership and the dynamics of leadership practices. Instead they considered the nature and characteristics of the authority vested in or associated with different political structures, such as the mystical offices held by chiefs and kings in African societies (Fortes and Evans-Pritchard 1940).

Exemplars of the paradigms of political economy and political evolution focus primarily on the consequences of economic practices of specific types of leaders, such as big men, chiefs, or *mafioso*. Their analyses generalize about the sociopolitical dynamics and consequences of economic practices, such as economic production and distribution (Sahlins 1963; Fried 1967; Schneider and Schneider 1976), or modes of production (Wolf 1982) and the resulting effects on types of leaders and authority structures.

Anthropologists who work in the processual paradigm also use the traditional terminology of leadership types, such as big men and chiefs. But they are concerned with the practices, tactics, and strategies that leaders use to gain ends and their significance for an agent-driven politics (Barth 1959; Swartz, Turner, and Tuden 1966; Swartz 1968; Bailey 1969, 1988, 1991; Ottenberg 1971; H. S. Lewis 1974; Kracke 1978).

As mentioned earlier, the distinctions between "politics" as an agent-driven process and the "political" as a functional structure are useful primarily for analysis. In practice, the relationship is more complex. For example, political structures, such as big men and governments, exist and change largely because of the politics by which agents respond to internal and external pressures on the political community. While leaders are undeniably critical to any consideration of politics, the value of any single leader to a political community may be highly exaggerated.

It is not possible to develop an economic equation for the price of leadership based on leaders' importance to politics and political processes. But it is easy to conclude paradoxically that political leaders represent an incredibly cheap commodity in the political marketplace. There are so many qualified existing and potential leaders in every political community that they are literally a dime a dozen. Consider for a moment the political process in the United States or other contemporary democracies. In each election season it is likely that several individuals will contest for an office in government. The one who prevails is the one with the most support and largest following. Taking scale into account, this holds true for most political communities, even nomadic hunters and gatherers. Positions of leadership in the world's political communities do not lack qualified and capable individuals who aspire to be leaders. Qualified aspirants are deeply stacked at any given position.

But if leaders are cheap commodities in the political marketplace, supporters, who by their sheer numbers should represent even more of a glut on the market than leaders, are nonetheless a very expensive commodity. This is because the major challenge that any leader confronts is how to acquire supporters and/or how to hold onto those that she or he has. As we saw in the previous chapter, that is why supporters are important as a primary resource of power.

POLITICAL LEADERSHIP AND AUTHORITY

Practitioners of the paradigms of political anthropology use the ideas of leaders and authorities interchangeably. But leadership and authority are not necessarily the same. They can be separated practically and for analytic purposes.

Authority connotes the condition of an incumbent, agent, or structure of statuses recognized by a political community to make decisions on its behalf. A person with strong authority may be able to make decisions that are binding on the community and also delegate authority to others. A weak authority may be only a symbol or may represent a static condition with no practical political consequence. This is the condition of current European monarchies. Authority figures or structures may be more or less legitimate. Some may produce good leaders, and others may produce bad ones.

Leadership exists in a dynamic and ongoing time frame in which individuals seek goals and try to channel the actions of others to their advantage and the advantage of those for whom they act as political agents. Leaders try to make things happen for a body of supporters. Most leaders also expend considerable physical and rhetorical energy convincing their political communities that whatever they do is for the good of the community. Those who convey this message successfully may have considerable authority. Others who are less successful may have very little authority and are required to renew constantly through practices and rhetoric their claim to leadership and whatever authority they hold by virtue of that leadership.

There is no obvious correlation between power and competent leadership. An abundance of power, such as that which may be inherited by a king, may help bad leaders lead badly. Leaders who use power wisely on behalf of their political community usually represent a legitimate authority, that is, they have the support of their political community. The political environment of any political community sets ambiguous limits to the practices of leaders, and leaders test the environment constantly to see what they can get away with. Politics is very much about what leaders can get away with. Skillful leaders often get away with a lot and redefine the normative rules of political process. Leaders who are not successful in politics do not receive much attention in political analyses. Depending on how well they are known, they may be forgotten, remain as historical footnotes, or be doomed to postmortem analyses of why they failed.

By definition a leader must have supporters. How leaders acquire them raises the question of what constitutes the qualities, styles, dispositions, attributes, behaviors, and practices of individuals that enable them to attract supporters and become leaders? This requires consideration of the social and psychological characteristics of leaders.

SOCIAL AND PSYCHOLOGICAL ATTRIBUTES OF LEADERS

With rare exceptions (Kracke 1978), anthropologists have not considered in much detail the social and psychological characteristics that authorize the cultural construction of leaders across societies. But these characteristics have been explored by sociologists, political scientists, business administrators, psychologists, philosophers, leadership trainers, and others (Gouldner 1950; Gibb 1969; W. Roberts 1989). These studies focus largely on Western societies. The qualities of leadership they identify are variations of a universal theme, whether the leaders practice in the boardrooms of multinational corporations, the state-houses of great nations, or the mens' houses of highland New Guinea villages.

Social attributes are those qualities of a leader's public persona and performance that comply with the community's *authority code*, that is, the normative expectations to which a political community holds its leadership responsible. *Personality attributes* are those qualities that derive from the leader's presentation of self and its interpretation by a political community. It is misleading to separate personality and social qualities of leaders. In practice they operate in concert and are mutually reenforcing. Which attributes are more important is difficult to determine. Nice guys and gals may finish last. Less personable and more corrupt individuals may prevail. The political context and the environment in which politics transpires may determine these outcomes.

Leaders operate within a social and cultural environment. When a political community allocates and agrees to the authority of a leader, it also allocates and agrees to the codes of performance and values expected in leaders. These values influence the rules by which politics is conducted and are materialized in a leader's comportment. Leaders respond to these constraints in a variety of ways, but the constraints impose social expectations on the behavior of leaders that they ignore at their peril.

Some political communities may expect a leader to be bombastic and aggressive. Others may require the leader to be unassuming and deferential. But a leader who is totally mute is not leading at all and will last no longer than one who is all talk and no action. Knowing when to talk and what to say and when to be quiet and deferential are important skills. A leader with considerable skill but little power at his or her disposal may prevail over one with lots of power but little skill. Skillful leaders respond to these expectations by mobilizing their social and personality attributes. There is no formula by which a leader may be acceptable to everyone in a political community, but there are qualities related to leadership that indicate why a political community prefers a particular leader. These seem to recur among different polities.

A leader must make things happen, at least when it is expected. A leader must be a *doer* at crucial moments. A leader who does nothing loses support quickly.

A leader need not always be visible. But when he or she causes positive things to happen, *visibility* is important to claim credit, establish authority, and build power. Negative outcomes can be costly.

A leader's *charisma* can be a hedge against negative outcomes. Not all leaders can be charismatic. Of course, one person's charismatic inspiration is another's demon. Charisma relies on more than just personality, performance, and appearance. It usually relies heavily on a leader's *rhetoric.*

Leaders must be *talkers.* Even in situations, as among big men, where leaders often are retiring, their rhetorical skills are important to their status when events require it.

A leader's *political skills* are never honed in a vacuum. A leader must make wise decisions. He or she need not always be effective. But neither can a leader fail consistently.

Leaders are *androcentric,* that is, they enjoy the company of other "political men" from whom they learn much. Women, such as Margaret Thatcher and Indira Gandhi, are no exception. Such learning transpires in smoke-filled backrooms, men's houses, and tepees, wherever males convene to conspire and collude, prior to displaying publicly their authority in assemblies, at pig feasts, or around council fires. Most politics exclude women. To operate in this world of men, women must hold positions that are solidly legitimate, that is, strongly supported by the political community, and must possess special qualities, many of which would appear to be quite androcentric.

Margaret Thatcher, Indira Gandhi, and the women's council of the Barabaig in Tanzania (Klima 1970) were aggressive and dominant figures. Thatcher and Gandhi used the support that their charisma provided to challenge openly the authority and abilities of their male counterparts. Barabaig women used their numbers and control of ideology, symbols, and cattle wealth to punish males for transgressions. To show their utter disdain for these transgressors, the women often beat to death the cows that males paid them in fines. Despite the androcentric tendencies that skillful male or female leaders display, they still ought to balance the application of a big stick with compassion and generosity.

No leader, no matter how charismatic, is universally loved. A strong ego may blunt criticism, and paradoxically so can a reasonable dose of *narcissism.* This enables leaders to finely hone their *self-focus,* sense of self, and preservation reflexes. Practical narcissism allows leaders to know themselves and to believe in their abilities.

Confidence is good for leaders' power building. Confident leaders are more likely to accomplish what their rhetoric says is good for the political community and what their *political savvy and intuition* tell them the community thinks is good.

A leader is expected to be *wise, insightful, perspicacious,* and aware of the total sociopolitical field and environment within which she or he operates. Ambiguity in action disturbs followers.

On the other hand, a certain amount of *ambiguity* in a leader's actions can enhance the mystique of leadership and keep opponents off balance. Ambiguity is also an antidote to the constraints imposed by the rules that regulate all political practices. No leader wants to be so hemmed in by rules that they impede novel strategies. Most leaders cherish a certain amount of ambiguity in their political environment because it may facilitate action.

Politics is governed by rules, but most are unwritten and sufficiently ambiguous to be manipulated by practical leaders. Even codified rules are often tested by leaders as they try to see how far they can go without sanction. Recall the earlier maxim: *Politics is very much about what a leader can get away with.*

Still, *decisiveness*, knowing when to be tough and when to be compassionate, when to follow a rule and when to break it, suggests a leader's wisdom regarding followers' expectations, their political community's authority code, and the environment. A skillful leader is aware of the total social field in which she or he operates and upon which their decisions and actions have an effect.

Nonetheless, leaders must by necessity be *paranoid*. To be otherwise is to be totally insane. To paraphrase both Karl Marx and F. G. Bailey, there is one thing of which any leader can be absolutely certain: Lurking in the wings of every political structure are other structures itching to show that they can do the job better. Recall that no society suffers a shortage of potential leaders. Any extant leader is always fair game for others on the prowl for authority and power. To persist and prevail in this environment requires the ultimate aphrodisiac for political performance—power. Political power is a major gauge of a leader's strength or weakness and the ability to attain goals and ends.

STRONG AND WEAK LEADERS

Leaders range across a continuum from weak to strong regarding the authority and power they exercise over their political communities. The implication is that leaders who adhere to the normative rules of political practice expected by their political communities will be more acceptable than leaders who do not. A fundamental difference between strong and weak leaders is the extent to which they embody the appropriate combination of social and psychological attributes to enable them to develop the power to attain their goals. Most leaders operate somewhere between these polar positions.

Success and failure and whether the leader is strong or weak are conditioned by the situations that the leader confronts. Some leaders simply are more skillful in coping with problems than other leaders. Some have talents in some contexts and not in others. These qualities are reflected in their strategies, tactics, and outcomes and are identified most powerfully by Bailey (1969, 1988, 1991).

According to Bailey, strong leaders command. They have others at their disposal, much as mechanics have tool kits and spare parts. They have high credit with those who provide resources. Skillful and wise use of resources translates into more resources. The possession of such a constellation of features is likely to correlate with leaders who conduct affairs from the high ground of a public persona wrapped in moral principles. Where these prevail, politics will be conducted by adhering to the normative rules and expectations of the community.

Weak leaders, as Bailey argues, can only ask that their wishes be followed. They may have to seek consent before they act. Weak leaders have allies whose commitments to them are transactional, that is, based on what they can get for their support, which therefore is tenuous. As a result, the political credit of weak leaders is low and their access to additional resources is limited. This impedes their ability to sustain sufficient resources to attain their ends. Because they are flexible by necessity, the actions of weak leaders are directed by pragmatic, often unethical, considerations as a means to attain their ends. However, a weak leader who becomes successful may become stronger. If he or she becomes legitimate, that is, acquires the support of a political community, their behaviors and the rules that regulate them will change and become more normative (Bailey 1969, 1988; Kracke 1978).

But many factors influence and affect these scenarios. Even the strongest leader will not always be successful, and weak leaders may survive for different reasons. In a particular political environment a weak leader may be the best that is available to a political community. Weak leaders also may exist where central authorities are strong and brook no challenges to their authority. A powerful and existing political structure may even maintain a loyal opposition composed of weak leaders whose presence enhances the legitimacy of the existing structure. This is not uncommon among governments in modern state formations, such as that represented by the PRI (Revolutionary Institutional Party) in Mexico for much of the twentieth century. A weak leader also may be retained in a position of authority by a more covert leadership to provide the symbol of unity and to obfuscate and mystify the intentions of the covert leadership. Medieval kings in Europe and the Japanese emperor during the Tokugawa period were such symbolic figureheads.

The code by which political communities allocate authority suggests that the rules that communities deem to be acceptable will be normative, that is, they will operate in the public sector of politics. Public politics are visible to the entire community and enable it to evaluate and assess the quality of its leadership. But leaders know that politics is more a matter of manipulating pragmatic rules behind the scenes in ways that may not even be legal.

Rules, as Bailey (1969) makes clear, are critical to winning the fundamental political prize: power. Power is the wellspring from which all other political prizes are rendered possible. Leaders constantly challenge the normative rules of the game in an effort to establish new rules and new means to attain power. The competition for power, which is what politics is all about, is largely a matter of changing rules and thereby the political environment in which politics transpires. Issues and ideas related to political leadership, such as the authority codes and the normative and pragmatic rules by which the leaders actually play the game, have been well developed in the processual paradigm. They will be explored in more detail in that context.

For now it is sufficient to introduce the types of leaders that anthropologists have identified ethnographically: episodic leaders, big men, and chiefs. I will address the nature of leadership in state formations separately, in Chapter 11. The dynamics by which the attributes of leadership are materialized in their actions will be dealt with later in context. Of these leaders, only those in state formations and perhaps chiefs have been a concern of social scientists other than anthropologists. Ethnographic depiction of these leaders' practices provides the empirical foundation of politics and the political in the preindustrial, precapitalist, and now largely postcolonial non-Western societies in which anthropologists have honed their research skills.

EPISODIC LEADERS

The politics of episodic leaders may be a misnomer. Episodic leaders have minimal authority, almost no power, and little possibility of building any. They are significant because they represent the most rudimentary form of political leadership that exists at a suprafamilial level in a political community. They are ignored by scholars largely because their status has been superseded by more centralized authority structures. Ethnographically they are associated with nomadic hunting and gathering societies. Yet they exist in all polities, even the most complex, at the most local level of power and authority relations.

Episodic leaders are allocated temporary authority over a sphere of activity by their political community. In hunting and gathering societies they may be allocated authority to direct a hunt or ritual, because of special skills, paraphernalia, or instruments they possess that will assure a successful completion of the task. In contemporary state formations their authority may be recognized to organize events such as a class reunion, a picnic for their workmates, a community cleanup project, or a block party, and perhaps to mediate a dispute among peers.

The authority code under which episodic leaders operate is a product of these relations and dictates practices commensurate with their lack of authority and power. Episodic leaders are the classic prototypes of weak leaders: They must lead by example. They cannot command or order. They can only request, suggest, plead, and sometimes do themselves what needs to be done in the hope that by their example others will respond. Should episodic leaders become overbearing, people may ignore or reject them and transfer authority to another. Or the people may do without and use other interpersonal means to manage their affairs. When people do comply with the authority of an episodic leader it is of their own volition because the episodic leader is respected and persuasive. Authority that can be exercised only for a specified time or event imbues an authority status with no special rights, privileges, or longevity.

BIG MEN

In general, the model of the big man depicts an individual who has some authority and some power, and is trying to develop more. His primary political function is to resolve disputes that emerge in a community of sedentary peoples. These groups do not have the luxury of moving away from their problems as hunters and gatherers are prone to do. The big man is the central actor in the political economic practices and community rituals that entail redistribution of goods and foodstuffs at culturally prescribed intervals.

The model of the big man is based on authority figures who were identified first in Melanesia, on New Guinea and on nearby islands. The literature on big men is restricted largely to this geographic area and is as voluminous as that on episodic leaders is small.[1] But the political characteristics of a big man appear in many cultures. Political agents who act like big men have been identified among the Nuer (Worsley 1955), Tallensi (Fortes 1945), Swat Pathans (Barth 1959), South American Indians (Clastres 1977; Kracke 1978), in Gondo parish in Uganda (Vincent 1968), and in the United States Congress (Weatherford 1985.) Big men probably also had counterparts among some North American Indian polities.

Big men polities extend across a range of variation from less too more complex. In the least complex polities, big men are not easily distinguished from episodic authority figures. At the other extreme, big men approximate the power and authority of chiefs. The ideal model of a big man falls between and corresponds to the image of the big man as a *primus inter pares*, a first among equals.

The idea that a politician is a servant of the people is accorded some validity by the status and practice of a big man. A big man is a leader to
whom a community allocates some authority over a particular sphere of
activity, such as warfare, trade, ceremonies, or work activities. Despite
this, big men do not have much power to enforce their authority. Like an
episodic leader, a big man is required to lead by example. He can recom-
mend, persuade, and request, but he can rarely command.

Big men are not always visible. Much of the time they appear to reside
in the wings of a social structure. Big men live, act, and look like other
members of their communities. They have no emoluments of prestige to
mark their status. They are allocated authority by the political communities because of their personal attributes.

The authority code to which a big man must conform contains several
values. In the role of *primus inter pares*, a big man is expected to be generous and to comply with requests for material items, such as a replacement
for a broken tool. This is fundamental to the reciprocity that bonds him
and his political community. Their support is necessary to any aspirations
he might harbor for higher status.

A big man is expected to manage activities internal to his community,
such as organizing work, rituals, ceremonies, and raids. Big men also may
be expected to represent the community in external relations with other
societies, which may include establishing alliances or conducing hostili-
ties and fighting. Sometimes these activities may become specialized in
different big men.

Perhaps the foremost political function of big men is to maintain order.
They are expected to respond to the needs of the community, such as me-
diating quotidian altercations and resolving disputes with the minimal
power at their disposal. This requires a big man to mobilize his skills and
wisdom, traits that are commensurate with the authority code by which
communities select big men and allocate authority to them. The ability of
a big man to comply with these expectations depends largely on the
credit he has established and the goods—and goodwill—he has amassed
in dealings with others. How a big man manages these relations depends
on how well he manages the political economy of his career.

The most reported primary political economic function of big men is
to redistribute material goods. Less well reported, but probably more
important, is the role the big man plays in persuading followers to produce material goods in the first place. By definition redistribution requires that a political community surrender part of the result of their labor to a centralized authority. The authority then is required to
redistribute all or part of the accumulated capital to its political community. It is in their capacity as political leaders that big men begin to influence the production and distribution of economic resources. This pro-

vides them a means to fulfill and exceed the expectations of their communities' authority codes.

The ability of big men to redistribute goods is a major index of their power. Some big men control very little power. Others may have considerable power. Most fall between these poles. Big men strive to build a personal base of political power through redistributive practices and whatever other means that will help them build power. They are notoriously unscrupulous wheelers and dealers, and pressure their communities to produce more.

Big men do not occupy an office vested with authority and power. Their political practice is vested in their personal qualities as leader over a particular activity. Because big men do not acquire power vested in an office, they must continually earn the support of their followers. If they fail, they are easily replaced. Followers need only to transfer their support to another aspiring big man. One always seems to be waiting in the wings.

As a generalized status, the big man usually represents a permanent position. But big men who approximate episodic leaders in practice are dispensable. The spheres of activity over which a political community allocates them authority can continue without a leader, at least for a while. Problems can be resolved through other means, such as convening a council, negotiations among elders of households, or through self-help.

Powerful big men are at the opposite end of the pole. Their competence may result in sufficient power to bend the rules of a community's authority code to their advantage. Leaders who can either alter the expectations of an authority code to their advantage or respond to changes in expectations of their political communities usually end up with increased power and authority.

CHIEFS

Chiefs are leaders of polities identified as chiefdoms by Oberg (1955; also see Steward and Faron 1959; Service 1962; Carneiro 1981; Earle 1991). A major distinguishing criterion of a chiefly polity relates to the office that a chief occupies. Chiefs can transfer the power and authority of the office to an heir or otherwise designated successor.

Chiefly polities may be constituted along a continuum from weak to strong chiefs. At one extreme, chiefs may possess less power than strong big men. The only distinction will be the heritability of the office of chief. A chief in this situation may be one among several peers, each of whom represents a particular political community composed of a lineage and/or clan that is relatively equal in status. However, the relative equality between the peer chiefs and the communities they represent does not disguise the increase in social distance between the chiefs and their political communities. Because of the status a chief holds, the social distance between even a weak chief and his political community is a measure of social inequality. Under different conditions the social distance can also be one of an economic inequality.

A weak chiefly polity is likely to prevail over a political community that is egalitarian in its values and sentiments. Weaker chiefs are more likely to lead societies whose constituent kinship components, lineage and clan associations, stand in a relatively equal relationship. Accordingly, their office will probably be more precarious and subject to challenge. Their emoluments, symbols of authority and power, attendants and retainers, bureaucracy, and ability to transfer that power to heirs also will be less secure than in the case of stronger chiefs. Considerable authority and power will remain within the descent associations—lineages and clans—that constitute the political community. The affairs of these communities probably will be directed by a polity comprising a council of the elders of those associations. They may challenge the legitimacy of the chief by asserting their right to name the holder of the office that constitutes the basis of the chiefly polity.

Stronger chiefs may be associated with different kinds of political communities. Some may consist of ranked lineages, or ramage. The right of succession to the chiefly offices of these polities is challenged less. These polities approximate and may be preadaptive to the stratified social structures that constitute the governments of state polities. The highest-ranked lineage will provide the highest-ranked chief. Chiefs of lower-ranked lineages will be subordinate in some affairs to those that are higher. But in affairs that affect the chiefdom, the most comprehensive political community, each chief will have some say. Rarely does the highest-ranked chief control the power to force his decision on others. When this happens, the distinction between a chiefdom and an inchoate state polity is difficult to discern.

Chiefly polities of considerable power need not always be ranked. Some chiefly polities may reflect the power and authority vested in the office that a paramount chief occupies. In such a polity, a chief presides over a bureaucracy of lesser chiefs and headmen. Here the chief may delegate authority to them over some affairs of local political communities and their kinship and voluntary associations. This polity is sufficiently centralized in authority and power, legitimate in its methods of succession to office, and involved in political problems to make their distinction from an inchoate state polity a matter of debate.

Because chiefs control power, they also can build more power outside the context of the office: Power begets power. For example, as well as having access to taxes and tributes, they often acquire other sources of tangible power, such as lands and herds. A good portion of the resources acquired from emoluments related to the office may have to be redistributed among their subjects to maintain their support. Resources from private reserves of power are more at the chief's discretion. They may be used to extend alliance through marriage, support a retinue or military force, or employ witches, magicians, and sorcerers to counter supernatural attacks on their person. Private resources provide additional means by which chiefs and most other leaders acquire additional power.

The office also brings with it ideologies and symbols of power and prestige that sharply distinguish the chief (the ruler) from his subject (the ruled). Chiefs generally are wealthier and live more opulently than their subjects. The right of the chief to these privileges and emoluments commonly is supported by ideas based on mythic beliefs accepted by the political community. As symbols of the status they hold, they may live apart from their subjects, either spatially or in designated compounds with restricted access, which also symbolize the chiefs' high status. Symbolic and ideological social distance distinguishes the rulers from the ruled and adds another dimension to the economic criteria that distinguishes the class hierarchy that emerges in chiefdoms.

NOTES

1. Among other writings on the big man, see Berndt and Lawrence (1973), Brown (1972, 1978), Godelier (1986), Godelier and Strathern (1991), Heider (1970, 1979), Herdt (1981, 1984), Koch (1974), Meggitt (1977), Newman (1965), Oliver (1955), Pospisil (1958, 1963), Rappaport (1968), Read (1959, 1965), and Rogers (1970).

4

SUCCESSION TO POLITICAL STATUS AND OFFICE AND THE LEGITIMATION OF POLITICAL AUTHORITY

Leaders must be concerned with how they succeed to positions of authority and establish a legitimate claim to their statuses as leaders. Succession and legitimation are mutually implicated processes. Succession refers to the means by which leaders attain positions of authority. Legitimation refers to the strategies by which leaders acquire and maintain the support of their political communities. This includes the people at large (supporters) and those that are close to them, such as benefactors, loyalists, and kin who often are most likely to try to usurp their authority. Every polity is subject to rules and strategies that influence these processes.

As we shall see, the legitimacy of leaders' authority is an outcome of their strategic use of power. But power may have little to do with the succession of leaders to positions of authority. For example, the succession of a prince to the hereditary office of king usually is independent of the considerable power at a king's disposal. And princes have little political power until they succeed to the office of king and acquire access to the power and authority vested in the office the king occupies. On the other hand, although big men control far less power than kings, an aspiring big man must invest deeply in the power at his disposal to attain the acknowledgment of a political community of his status as a potential big man. Leaders whose authority relies on their political statuses—*status leaders*—and leaders whose authority is the result of the political offices they occupy—*officeholders*—signify important differences in succession and legitimation and mark important distinctions between institutionally more and less complex polities and political communities.

Leaders whose authority and power are products of the status they occupy are common among institutionally less complex political communities. These include episodic leaders and big men. Status leaders must constantly renew their right to leadership through their actions. They are not endowed with this right or any authority and power by the incumbency of an office. Their authority is allocated to them personally by their political communities based on their psychosocial qualities and attributes. Political communities that allocate authority to leaders who are not incumbents of offices may easily withdraw it and divest leaders of their authority. In some of these polities, stronger status leaders attempt to formalize succession, usually in the favor of a kinsperson, through some pattern of inheritance.

Political offices constitute an abstract structure of positions that are vested with political power and authority and provide incumbents (of the offices) access to other sources of power. A political office is established when leaders can transfer authority and power without objections from the political community to heirs, most commonly eldest sons (primogeniture). A political office enables authority and power to be transferred to the next incumbent without requiring the individual to build a base of authority and power anew, as status leaders must. Political offices are associated with more institutionally complex polities, such as chiefdoms and state formations.

The existence of a political office has nothing to do with the quality of leadership. In fact it may dilute it. Some officeholders, for example, may be totally incompetent and unfit to lead. But incumbents of offices are not so easily divested of their authority and power as status leaders. This is because of the peculiarly sacred or mystical status that a political office often acquires apart from the officeholder.

A violent challenge to the legitimacy of the incumbent of a political office does not necessarily include a challenge to the existence and legitimacy of the office. Such challenges, or rituals of rebellion (Gluckman 1963), are directed only at the officeholder. Once the office exists, it is rarely challenged, and persists long after any particular incumbent is disencumbered. Rituals of rebellion also provide a means by which aspiring leaders may demonstrate their competence to govern and thereby enhance their claim to legitimacy.

The transition from polities dominated by status leaders to those governed by officeholders is a product of political evolution. The paradigm of political evolution is the topic of Chapters 9 and 10. Succession to established statuses and offices is not necessarily evolutionary. But as a process, succession provides insight into the intricacies of the rules of succession and changes in those rules.

Competition over succession to authority and power often involves conflict. Leaders usually want more power and authority. They are prizes worth fighting over. Despite the drama attached to conflict over succession, the transition of authority most often is orderly because the rules and factors that influence modes of succession function to reduce conflict. Yet conflict over succession seems central to changes in the rules that regulate succession, for the means by which leaders attain an authority status depends on the rules of succession to which they are subject.

SUCCESSION TO POLITICAL STATUS AND OFFICE

Goody (1966), following Weber (1964 [1947]), suggests that the rules concerned with *inheritance, appointment,* and *election* account for succession to political office. Goody also suggests that the rules of succession are conditioned by factors related to the *uniqueness* of the office held by a leader, the *time* of succession, the *selection* of the successor, and the *relationship* between officeholders.

Goody's (1966) model is thorough, yet it is not complete because it does not account well for the succession of status leaders. Goody implies, as Weber asserts, that the succession of status leaders is accomplished by inheritance. This is not so. Succession to political status is better accounted for by the *allocation* of authority by a political community to a status leader. Status leaders also may usurp the authority of another, although *usurpation*, primarily as a *coup d'état* (or *golpe de estado* in the Latin American version), plays a larger role in succession to office.

Succession to authority and perhaps power along the continuum of leadership from episodic leaders, such as the Washoe antelope shaman, to the governments of state formations, such as the Aztecs or the United States, is subject to these rules and factors, and they are related in complicated ways. They do not guarantee a peaceful transition. Nor do they establish parameters for practices that may mitigate conflict over succession. Still, conflict, in the form of either rituals of rebellion or coups d'état, is common, especially when succession pertains to attaining a political office. I will begin by considering the rules of succession.

RULES OF SUCCESSION

Allocation

Richard Adams's (1975) idea of the allocation of authority, the upward flow of authority from a political community to a leader or political structure, applies primarily to status leaders, although the idea of government by the people has ideological vigor in contemporary democracies. Nonetheless, allocation represents the most fundamental means of attaining authority and is common where weak leaders prevail. For example, allocation of authority to an individual by a political community accounts largely for the succession to leadership of episodic leaders and the less powerful big men of Melanesia.

Allocation of authority by a political community is a gradual process. Aspiring leaders must earn their authority based on their performance and psychosocial qualities. No formal legal or ritual mechanism establishes their authority over a political community. Nor do formal mechanisms, legal or otherwise, exist by which to divest them of their authority. If their performance falters, the political community simply withdraws support, ignores them, and allocates authority to others. Recall that leaders as commodities are cheap and that no one can lead without followers.

Succession by allocation of authority from a political community to a status leader tends to be informal and the support provisional. The durability of a status leader is contingent on two factors. The first is the degree to which the performance of the status leader is acceptable to the political community. The second is the extent to which the status leader is willing and able to risk his or her status in the quest for more authority and power and get away with it.

Usurpation

Usurpation refers to a rule of succession that breaks existing rules of succession. Usurpation represents the mode of succession most likely to invoke conflict because, depending on circumstances, it may be either improper or clearly illegal. Where rules of succession are not codified, as is common in societies where status leaders prevail, usurpation by one of another's status as leader may be merely an improper and annoying way of replacing an existing authority. Where succession is governed by laws, either traditional or codified, usurpation of the power and authority vested in an office is generally an illicit means of appropriating the authority and power of an office. Each condition of usurpation may involve violence, although violent usurpation is most common when the incumbency of a political office is at stake.

In either instance the potential for a big political payback often is worth the risk. This is obvious. But perhaps more important and less obvious is the fact that those who risk usurping the power and authority of another and get away with it may establish a new rule of succession. When usurpation involves status leaders, such as an aspirant to the status of big

man, it may represent the transition from a community's reliance on allocated authority to the establishment of a more permanent status vested in
an office to which one succeeds by inheritance. Where usurpation involves an office, as in state formations, it may involve transition from
some form of democracy to despotism, or vice versa. In either case the
threat of violence is real.

The attempt to appropriate the status of an existing leader represents
perhaps the most fundamental form of risk that an aspiring leader can
take. Usurpation without a connotation of legally binding precepts relates
largely to the displacement of a status leader, such as a big man. This is
executed when an aspirant to the status displaces an existing big man and
is not challenged by either the political community or the big man subject
to the challenge. Such a case occurred among the Dani of highland New
Guinea (Heider 1970) when an existing big man who aspired to higher
status appropriated the symbols of the status of the dominant big man at
a ceremony and was not challenged. He took a political risk and got away
with it.

Violent usurpation is more likely when the prize is a political office,
such as chief or king. Succession to office by usurpation implies a coup
d'état, although usurpation may also take the form of Gluckman's (1963)
ritual of rebellion. The *coup d'état* is most common in state formations
and is a high-risk option. The ritual of rebellion may be encoded in the
community's values as an acceptable practice for succession and be fully
legitimate from the point of view of the political community. Therefore it
does not represent the same degree of risk as the *coup d'état*, which is
rarely encoded as a legitimate practice in a political community. Rather, it
is an illegal usurpation of power and authority and represents a big risk.
But, as noted, it has the potential for a big payback.

Inheritance

Inheritance of an office is well established ethnographically in chiefdoms
and state formations. Inheritance formalizes succession by passing the
authority and power of a political office to an incumbent's heir through
some cultural rule, such as primogeniture or ultimogeniture, inheritance
by the eldest or youngest son, respectively. Inheritance of an office is
likely to involve considerations of kinship that smack of nepotism. This is
common in preindustrial state formations (Claessen 1978). Nepotism in
these formations also has practical applications. It permits leaders in high
offices to retain the right to rule within a descent line and to keep an eye
on those who are most likely to threaten their right to the office, namely
their close kin. Nepotism of this sort often is eschewed and may be illegal
in contemporary state formations.

Appointment

Leaders who either inherit an office or are elected to it are also likely to appoint others to political offices. Appointment to an office is different from allocation. Appointment implies a leadership that is sufficiently powerful, perhaps legitimate, to *delegate* and perhaps even *grant* (R. N. Adams 1975) some authority, and perhaps some power, to others. It is characteristic primarily of polities based on the political office, such as chiefdoms and state formations. Appointment may involve some form of nepotism, but more commonly leaders appoint loyal followers who are less likely to challenge their status. Close kin, such as brothers, often aspire to the office and are not safe candidates for appointments, unless, as noted, the appointment is designed to mitigate the threat they pose to the incumbent.

Election

Succession, appointment, and election to office may be coterminous in the politics of some polities, such as most contemporary state formations. But succession to office by election exclusively is not common in the ethnographic record. Election to office, a characteristic of contemporary state formations, is a recent phenomenon that correlates to the emergence of democracies and industrial capitalism. The ethnographic record of state formations pertains largely to preindustrial, precapitalist monarchical polities in which inheritance to office prevails, with its attendant problems, of course, such as the *coup d'état*.

CONDITIONING FACTORS

Uniqueness

The principle that infuses the uniqueness of the office or status with significance for succession can be stated simply. The more unique the office or status, the greater is the potential for conflict over succession. Conversely, the less unique the office or status, the less likely is the potential for conflict over succession. It follows, therefore, that the principle of uniqueness bears more upon officeholders than status leaders. Violence over competition for political status among big men or episodic leaders is not very common. The rewards and prizes in terms of political power are not that great. Political power is a prize to be gained by the incumbency of an office, and violence over succession to the office is more likely.

Time

The significance of the time of succession depends on whether succession involves a status or an office. The time of succession to a political status is less important. In the least complex polities, the status may go unfilled for long periods. And when it is filled, neither the authority nor the power it accords is very great. The affairs of the community often can be managed by heads of the households or lineages, severally or perhaps in council, that constitute the society.

In institutionally complex polities where succession pertains to the incumbent officeholder, the tendency is to fill a vacated office as quickly as possible. On the one hand, incumbency assures continuity of political and administrative functions of government. On the other, the interregnum is often perceived by a political community to be fraught with mundane and supernatural danger. This is especially important when the office is at the apex of a hierarchy of offices.

The offices of the highest-ranking leaders commonly are imbued with mystical if not sacred qualities. Even where these qualities are not thought to be especially important, as with the presidency of the United States, an unexpected vacancy due to assassination of the incumbent may be construed nonetheless as a supernatural as well as an occult secular threat to the well-being of the political community. "The king is dead. God save the king," implies more than continuity. It suggests both divine and secular intervention against occult threats to assure the well-being of the political community.

Recruitment

The recruitment of the successor is never totally automatic. It is more automatic where the successor becomes the incumbent of an office and the succession is accomplished by any means other than allocation, such as inheritance, appointment, or election. But even where succession is associated with a legitimate polity supported by the political community, tradition, and law there is always the chance of some problem upsetting the recruitment process. The competence or health of claimants may become an issue. Death might occur. Officeholders might be involved in criminal acts. Challenges might develop and escalate into the violence of usurpation, or conflicting claimants to the office may fight behind the scenes.

Where succession relates to status leaders, individuals have to prove their qualities in practice for the community to allocate authority to them. If their demonstrated abilities to lead are suspect, political communities wait for someone else to demonstrate acceptable qualities. The ability of status leaders to exercise much power to help them attain political status is difficult. Status leaders, such as episodic leaders, big men, and even weak chiefs, do not control much power. Power is a prize to which at least some of them aspire, and status leaders must devote considerable energy and time holding on to what power they have acquired. The extent to which succession is free of conflict depends largely on the legitimacy of the authority structure involved.

THE LEGITIMATION OF POLITICAL AUTHORITY

Legitimacy accrues to leaders and authority structures. It does not accrue to political power, as some suggest (Swartz, Turner, and Tuden 1966; R. N. Adams 1975). The legitimacy of any leadership or authority structure rests on the support of a leader's political community, and leaders must strive constantly to acquire and retain support (Swartz, Turner, and Tuden 1966; Kurtz 1978, 1981, 1984; Claessen 1988). Power is legitimate only to the extent that it is attached to authorities who develop and use it. Recall that without some agent to mobilize and apply it, power is merely a philosophical idea.

Support comes from two social categories in a political community. On the one hand, leaders must have the support of their loyalists and bene-factors. These individuals are those most likely to challenge the legitimacy of an existing polity and attempt to replace its leaders (Claessen 1988). They have a vested interest in the authority structure and some among them may aspire to the status of leader. They will tend to support the structure if not the person who occupies it.

On the other hand, the general population of a political community also must provide support (Kurtz 1978, 1981, 1984). Political communities think of leaders in functional and reciprocal terms. If leaders respond to and resolve problems that are important to the community, the community is likely to support them. But leaders usually try to expand their influence over the community, and by doing so they risk creating problems that are not acceptable to the community. Any political community represents an inchoate body of support. Some will always approve of a leader and some will always disapprove. The ethnographic record suggests that political communities would just as soon walk away from authority and get along without strong and permanent leaders who insist on involving themselves in the community's affairs. Political communities must be persuaded to follow and support leaders.

Legitimacy does not accrue automatically to leaders. Nor does legitimacy rely on an ideology shared by the leaders and their followers to the extent that political scientists are prone to argue. Legitimacy is the result of the dialectical process, *legitimation,* by which leaders try to resolve contradictions between more diffuse sources of authority at the local level and the more centralized and independent authority to which leaders aspire (Giddens 1979). Legitimation is a dialectic that engages leaders in actions aimed at acquiring and retaining support either directly or indirectly.

Direct support is provided most often by leaders' benefactors and loyalists. Leaders prefer this kind of support. It is obvious, tangible, and satisfying. But it is rarely sufficient. Therefore, leaders also seek support from their political communities. Most often this provides a form of indirect support, which also is an intangible form of support.

Indirect support may be mediated through intervening structures or offices. It also may come through acquiescence of the political community to the leader's authority. In any event, leaders who seek support attempt to shift the allegiance of their political communities from alternative and local-level sources of authority, such as lineages, secret societies, shamans, a class of nobles, and the like, to the supra-associational and more central status or office that leaders occupy.

Legitimacy is the outcome of five overlapping strategies that move by fits and starts depending on the orchestration of events, circumstances, and power by which leaders attempt to acquire and retain support. Leaders attempt to mobilize their communities' economy to their advantage, increase social distance between themselves and their followers, validate their right to authority, consolidate their power and authority, and socialize their political communities to the rewards and punishments they can expect for granting or withholding support from the leaders (Kurtz 1978, 1981, 1984). There are similarities and differences in the way status leaders and officeholders engage in legitimating strategies.

STRATEGIES OF LEGITIMATION

Economic Production and Distribution

Whether legitimacy is the concern of a status leader or an officeholder, the keystone to a leader's legitimacy is a robust economy that meets at least minimally the culturally perceived needs of their political community. Wise leaders strive hard to ensure such an economy. Obviously not all leaders are wise, especially those who hold high office. Where the authority of leaders is allocated to status leaders, political communities are less likely to suffer long the machinations of fools.

Any status leader and officeholder who lays claim to legitimacy will be involved deeply in the production and redistribution of material resources they have at their disposal. The extreme alternative is for the leader to govern through coercion. This is costly in terms of leaders' tan-

gible resources and also their prestige and legitimacy, because they risk
the loss of support. A better strategy is for leaders to promote the productive potential of the community and appropriate surpluses of that production in culturally acceptable ways to enhance their claim to legitimate
authority and power.

Status leaders have little control over the production of material resources by their communities. They cannot coerce people to produce
more. They can only lead by example and propound a rhetoric that extols
the value of production for the common good. Status leaders seem to ap-
preciate the importance of productive labor more than their communities
because of the difficulty they have in promoting production above minimal levels of per capita biological necessity (Orans 1966; Fried 1967;
Kurtz 1996a). Only when leaders persuade their communities to work
more can the people produce material resources that, on the one hand,
meet the community's minimal per capita biological requirements and,
on the other, provide the surpluses that leaders appropriate to bankroll
their power.

In an analysis of legitimacy among Melanesian big men, Orenstein
(1980) suggests that weak big men have little power and often are debtors
to their political communities, that is, they must continually be generous
to the community to retain the status of big man that the community allocates to them. If the big man complies with the community's expectations
and serves it well, his legitimate right to the status is not questioned.
Serving the community refers largely to resolving disputes and complying with the generosity the community expects, such as providing goods,
gifts, and feasts to individuals and community alike. The legitimacy of
the authority allocated to weak big men is sustained largely by their
benevolence and manipulation of the economy in terms favorable to the
community. Such manipulation leaves few resources upon which a big
man may build a personal fund of power. When a weak big man of this
sort dies, he may be able to pass what resources he possesses to his heirs.
But it is unlikely that he can transfer his status, and the resources are
likely to be divided among the heirs.

Officeholders generally do have some control over the productive labor
of their communities. They usually lead communities whose members
are conditioned to work more and produce surpluses above the communities' minimal survival requirements. Their problem is always one of
getting still more production out of their communities.

Some officeholders try to coerce their communities into higher production. But wise leaders establish a reciprocal relationship with their communities. They challenge the community to produce surpluses above
minimal needs for the common good. Then, supported by considerable
rhetoric that extols the common good, they appropriate a portion of those

surplus goods. Wise leaders may be no less greedy than dumb ones. Bailey correctly perceives all leaders to be masters of the "hegemonic lie" (1991:82).

One gauge of the legitimacy of a leader is the ratio of surpluses redistributed to those maintained by the leader without any objection from the community. People will not willingly follow leaders who do not satisfy their expectations. But political communities may be less aware that their expectations are usually defined by leaders. One consequence of these political economic practices is the myth of a surplus that is deployed to benefit a political community. Leaders always find some use for the bulk of surplus resources above those necessary for the minimal biological survival levels of a political community, not the least of which is to support their sybaritic lifestyles and those of their benefactors and loyalists.

Social Distance

The establishment of authority by leaders also promotes a marked increase in the real and cognitive distance between leaders and their political communities. The separation between status leaders and their communities is largely cognitive. The community acknowledges the psychosocial qualities that distinguish leader from nonleader by allocating leaders some authority. But the physical distance may not be great. Status leaders do not symbolize their distinctiveness through displays of material wealth. They can be approached, touched, confronted, rejected, and ignored by their communities.

Cognitive and material factors distinguish and establish a distance between officeholders and their communities. A community may believe that the highest officeholder has access to special supernatural or other mystical powers that are exclusive to the office. This perception may be reenforced by ritual and ceremony that connotes the symbolic and moral exclusiveness of the leader. Material or real distance is usually symbolized by the different, often more sybaritic, lifestyle that leaders enjoy. Leaders may live in larger or better houses, possess fasces of their status, maintain more than one wife, and retain a retinue and a personal military. One might recall here King Lear's lament when the size of his retinue was challenged by his daughters: "O, reason not the need!"

Social distance affirms and demarcates distinctions between leaders and their communities, enhances leaders' aura of authority, commands respect and obedience, and reduces the familiarity between peoples of different status that might breed contempt (Lenski 1966). Too much distance might impede the ability of leaders to govern if they are unable to meet the expectation of their community. This risk is ameliorated by other legitimating strategies.

Validation

Status leaders must validate their leadership through their practices. Leaders whose actions do not comply with expectations are, as noted earlier, easily deserted. Officeholders validate their status in mystical and supernatural ways that are frequently grounded in the community's religious institutions. The office itself may acquire a mystical value that is transmitted to incumbents. Some chiefs, for example, are believed to be able to make good things happen, such as rain for the crops, and to keep bad things at bay, such as drought or pestilence.

Heads of state are often involved in the development of a religion with priests that extol the virtues of the office and those who hold it. Priests who are closely aligned with the ruler or part of his government may promote the apotheosis of the office that ensures the incumbent divinity. The political community will be subjected to displays of symbols, rituals, ceremonies, and proclamations emanating from mythical charters sanctified by the state priesthood to validate the authority of these officeholders.

Consolidation

Consolidation refers to the means by which leaders entrench their authority and values in the institutions and practices of their political communities. Status leaders have limited means at their disposal to consolidate their authority and power. They hold their status contingent on the value of their practices and decisions to their political communities. Officeholders mobilize resources related to legal, political, and religious institutions to convey and bolster the authoritarian values to which they expect the community to acquiesce. Officeholders rely on traditional precedents and often, in some state formations, codified legal codes to define mutual obligations between leaders and their political communities.

Officeholders usually delegate some powers of their office to loyalists, such as tax collectors, judges, headmen, peacekeepers, priests, and the like. These individuals are charged with extending the officeholder's authority and power over the political community and entrenching it within its local-level institutions, such as the family, schools, and courts. Delegated authorities are expected to convince and demonstrate to others the leader's right to govern and to thwart local-level resistance to it. Religious sanctification of secular offices, especially at the executive level, by priests who hold high positions in state government often imbue the office with a divine quality and provide divine legitimacy to the right of the officeholder to rule. Any transgression against the leader then becomes a transgression against the mystical or divine forces that imbue the office. In some societies the threat of supernatural retribution for transgressing divine authority can be daunting.

Socialization

Leaders try to socialize their political communities into complying with their expectations. Leaders and their agents try to inculcate in the members of the community the values, beliefs, and ideologies that extol the selflessness of the leaders, as well and their authority and power. The fact that political communities do not easily accept these principles is suggested by the complementary and contradictory practices by which leaders attempt to socialize them into acceptance. Leaders attempt to develop and ensure support through strategies that dramatize what they can do for the community (benevolence), what the community is expected to do for the leadership (information), and consequences for the community if it does not conform to the leaders' expectations (terror).

Status leaders rely heavily on their rhetoric and redistribution practices to ensure support and convince their communities to follow them. They are unable to force community compliance to their expectations because they lack the power to do so. Redistribution represents a form of benevolence at a personalized level to individuals and a political community by which status leaders often retain support.

Officeholders have at their disposal more effective institutional means to manipulate these strategies. They can rely on those to whom they delegate authority and on their control of media of communication to disseminate information that extols their virtues and benefit to the community. They control resources that enable them to be benevolent in symbolically dramatic ways, such as sponsoring lavish, potlatchlike feasts or ceremonies, or to redistribute goods from their private larders in times of crisis to large numbers of people; each of these actions is a mode of communication. Officeholders also control the means to force compliance, for powers vested in their office enable them to mobilize forces and enact laws, such as the death penalty for trivial offenses, to terrorize the political opposition.

The legitimation that leaders pursue cannot be mapped out as a linear process. Leaders do not accomplish one strategy before engaging another. Rather, they apply each strategy when and where they can. The success of leaders in acquiring legitimacy depends on the kind and quality of the challenges they face. No leadership or authority structure is ever fully legitimate. Some are more successful than others. Legitimation is an ongoing sociopolitical dynamic in any polity.

PART THREE

Paradigms and Topics of Political Anthropology

5

THE STRUCTURAL-
FUNCTIONAL PARADIGM

The structural-functional paradigm (hereafter called functionalism) represents a union of the ideas of Bronislaw Malinowski and A. R. Radcliffe-Brown. Exemplars of the paradigm adopted Malinowski's concern with the functional relations of cause and effect in cultural and social systems. From Radcliffe-Brown they borrowed his interest in the intricacies of relationships in social structures, especially those of kinship. From these two premises, functional research strategies became dedicated to determining how social structures and related human practices functioned in one way or another to contribute to the cohesion and integration of social systems (Radcliffe-Brown 1965 [1952]). The functional paradigm dominated British social anthropology early in this century into the decade of the 1960s. The inclusion of politics in the functional paradigm occurred in 1940.

The publication of *African Political Systems* (Fortes and Evans-Pritchard 1940), an anthology of ethnographic research on the political structures of African societies, heralded the emergence of the field of political anthropology. The contributors to the volume provided a uniquely anthropological representation of political structures and systems. They were not concerned with an agent-driven politics, and their ethnographic depictions were largely devoid of political science ideas. Instead the authors identified social structures such as kinship associations and age sets as political structures, and that had not been done before. They explored how ideas of government in African societies related to ritual, magic, mystical values, sorcery, and other unlikely political topics. They also considered how order was maintained in societies that numbered in the hundreds of thousands of individuals and yet had no observable permanent leadership.

The topics were so uncommon to political scientists that twenty years later David Easton (1959) stated categorically that a subfield of political anthropology did not yet exist because the field lacked political theory. Some anthropologists agreed (Fried 1964; R. Cohen 1965; M. G. Smith 1968).

Although analyses within the paradigm continued into the 1960s, functional exemplars exhausted its theoretical energy within a decade. But the work spawned by *African Political Systems* provided a baseline from which other analyses of the political could develop and expand (Bailey 1960). The starting point for much current research by contemporary anthropologists still remains the identification of static social structures, political and otherwise, from which social processes emanate.

The generalized paradigm of structural-functionalism, of which its political dimensions are only one aspect, relies on a biological analogy. Its basic hypothesis contends that the structural components of an organism's system function to maintain the integration and equilibrium of the entire organism. Anthropologists, sociologists, and some philosophers expanded this to the proposition that social structures function to maintain the social integration and equilibrium of a social system. The research strategies of political anthropologists were devoted to analyzing how political structures functioned to maintain order (a political concern) and enforce conformity (a legal concern) to maintain a social system's integration and equilibrium.

BACKGROUND TO THE PARADIGM

There is a historical justification for the theoretical assumptions peculiar to the functional paradigm. Structural-functional analysis is rooted in Auguste Comte's positivist philosophy (an elaboration of Saint-Simon's "social physiology" of the early nineteenth century), which emerged in the decades following the Napoleonic era. Positivism asserted that the study of human societies should include both change, or social dynamics, and existing relationships between social forms, or social statics. In the social sciences, positivist studies largely excluded analyses of social dynamics. Instead they focused on the synchronic analysis of static social structures and the functional integration of their parts into the whole. Several factors account for this.

Positivism emerged while memories of the turmoil of the Napoleonic era still resonated in the halls of political and ecclesiastical power in Europe. European monarchies and churches were not anxious to entertain any more challenges to the reestablished social, monarchical, and religious order of European society. Agitations from the political left in reaction to the expansion of monopoly capitalism already were threatening the hegemony of religious and political authorities. By the 1840s, Karl Marx invigorated this movement and exposed aspects of capitalism that threatened the stability of the capitalist world for the next one hundred and fifty years. The goal of monarchical and church politics was to keep a tight lid on a potentially explosive situation.

European governments were also busy building their overseas empires. Imperial rule, colonial domination, and exploitation of the world's non-European peoples were the political economic order of the day. They were essential to the smooth operation and development of capitalism. None of the colonizing governments was anxious to have native leaders agitate more vigorously for alternatives to European domination and capitalist exploitation. Any social science that might upset the status quo was politically unacceptable. Functionalism complied with scholarly and political expectations of the time.

As a scholarly enterprise, functionalism was largely a British product and provided the fountainhead for British social anthropology. British anthropologists perceived functionalism to be an antidote to the strong American bias that imbued the paradigm of nineteenth-century cultural evolution and the Marxist taint it acquired in the last quarter of the nineteenth century. Once Marx and Friedrich Engels wedded Lewis Henry Morgan's ideas to their own, evolutionary thinking became unacceptable. British social anthropology and American cultural anthropology emerged to fill the intellectual vacuum.

In the early twentieth century, anthropology in Great Britain was restricted to structural-functional research strategies. The forerunners of political anthropology were both products and victims of this thinking. Functionalism was not a neutral, scientifically unbiased project. Much of the ethnographic research that provided the data base for its theory was done in support of Britain's colonial and imperial interests.

The political aspects of the functional paradigm emerged as the scientific handmaiden to the conservative ideas and discourses of the time. Its practitioners dedicated their analyses to the functional contribution that social structures made to the equilibrium and integration of existing social systems. The analysis of social dynamics was a goal honored by lip service only. Structural-functional studies made social science ideas safe and kept the colonial world tidy for those in power.

British anthropologists received considerable financial support from the British colonial administration. In return they provided knowledge of the political structures of colonized people, especially in Africa, to help the colonial administration establish policies by which they might govern "the natives" more efficiently. The analyses provided by the authors of *African Political Systems* complied with this concern of the British Colonial Administration. A major motivation for the examination of politics in the paradigm was the problem of how colonial administrators were supposed to govern people such as the Nuer. The Nuer numbered around 300,000, feuded constantly, had no chiefs, moved around a lot, and still retained a coherent society (Evans-Pritchard 1940).

Some contemporary anthropologists continue to hold the paradigm and its practitioners in contempt for their complicity in the colonial enterprises. Some, such as Harris (1968), say that the history and pressures of time and place do not excuse some lamentable oversights of these analyses. For example, Fortes and Evans-Pritchard (1940) presented as a theoretical curiosity the observation that many African state societies had a lower population density than many stateless societies. They never questioned the well-recorded and terrible devastation of African state societies because their armies often stood and fought the technologically superior European armies. The result was that African state organizations lost appalling numbers of men and suffered dislocations from which they had not recovered. These oversights were not questioned seriously or publicly for a quarter century (Skinner 1964; Stevenson 1965; Harris 1968).

It is easy today to criticize the ethics and morality of these practices. But at that time and place, supporting the empire seemed to be a good thing to do. Current fashion condemns anthropologists of the time for not protesting these policies. But in their crusading zeal some anthropologists forget that the paradigms that anthropologists engage to direct their research, today as in the past, are creations of people whose humanity and morality are nurtured in the ideas, values, and material realities of the time in which they live and work. Anthropologists are people first and thinkers second, at best. We ought not unjustly attribute to anthropologists a perspicacity and genius that deny that they are fundamentally creatures of their historical time and sociopolitical place.

FUNCTIONAL POLITICAL ANTHROPOLOGY

Comments by Radcliffe-Brown in the Preface to *African Political Systems* placed the emerging field of political anthropology squarely within the functional paradigm. He argued that, "In studying political organization, we have to deal with the maintenance or establishment of social order, within a territorial framework. . . . In dealing with political systems, therefore, we are dealing with law on the one hand, and with war, on the other" (1940:xiv). War remained in the political domain of the functional paradigm, although it was seriously understudied. Investigations into "primitive law" became the mainstay of functional concerns with how quasi-legal processes related to dispute resolution in stateless formations (Hoebel 1954; S. Roberts 1979). Anthropologists who explored explicitly political concerns in the paradigm spawned two major research strategies.

The first concern established types of political systems. One type included the political system known as the state. But the most important contribution was the identification of political dimensions of previously unrecognized political structures and systems. These included kinship structures, especially lineages, and voluntary associations, such as age-sets and age-grades, that comprised the taxon of stateless societies. The penchant for anthropologists to establish types of political systems to explore their functions became known as the *typological approach* to political analysis. This dominated political anthropology for over a decade.

The second methodological strategy engendered by the functional paradigm evaluated how various social and political structures functioned to maintain social order and enforce conformity. The maintenance of social order became identified with political relations that were external and internal to society. Political structures that maintained order were easily identified in state formations where legal and other institutions of coercion were well developed. Of more interest were the means by which order and conformity were maintained in stateless societies, many of which had no identifiable political and legal institutions. The field of *legal anthropology* developed in response to concerns regarding how native people enforced conformity to social norms and resolved disputes and trouble cases (S. Roberts 1979).

STRUCTURAL-FUNCTIONAL
TYPOLOGICAL ANALYSES

The editors of *African Political Systems* suggested a less than imaginative typology to approximate the different political structures in African societies. They distinguished type A, or states, from type B, or stateless, political systems. The elaboration of typologies aimed at refining the initial typology proliferated as a major strategy for more than a decade after World War II. It continues in some quarters in recent analyses of the state (Y. A. Cohen 1969; Claessen 1978).

Type A political systems were depicted as territorial units characterized by governments based on centralized authority, administrative machinery, and judicial institutions. The central authority and judiciary of type A systems were characterized by cleavages in wealth, privilege, and status, that is, they were socially and economically stratified. Along with their administrative machinery and bureaucratic organization, they managed the social and political affairs of these societies. But their central governments relied on sorcery, mystical practices, rituals, and other customs that were considered strange in comparison to the politics and jurisprudence of European nations. Fortes and Evans-Pritchard called these systems *primi-*

tive states. The identification of the primitive, non-Western state as a type of political system led to the proliferation of other types of states.

Vansina (1962), for example, responded to Southall's (1956) argument that the category "state" that Fortes and Evans-Pritchard established was more complex than they suggest. Vansina sought commonalities among African kingdoms based on degrees of centralization of authority. From this he deduced five types of kingdoms that he identified as despotic, royal, incorporative, aristocratic, and federated. Vansina provided some insights into the structures that characterize kingdoms, or state formations, in Africa and elsewhere. But his typology was little more than what Leach (1961) referred to as butterfly collecting. It told us little about the dynamics of government, the politics, or the history of these formations.

State formations are a matter of perduring interest among political anthropologists. Claessen (1978) established a typology of inchoate, typical, and transitional state formations. His work is noteworthy for the magnitude of structural variables he drew upon to establish the typology. Compared to previous typologies, his relied on data extrapolated from the ethnographic descriptions of twenty state societies. State formations are the topic of Chapter 11.

Type B political systems were also depicted as territorial units. But Fortes and Evans-Pritchard argued that they lacked centralized authority, administrative machinery, and judicial institutions. In short, they lacked government. They comprised egalitarian statuses related largely to systems of kinship and were identified by Fortes and Evans-Pritchard as *stateless societies.* They then identified two variants of the stateless model: nomadic hunters and gatherers and segmentary lineages, the latter of which also involved age-set and age-grade structures.

NOMADIC HUNTING AND GATHERING BANDS

Fortes and Evans-Pritchard distinguished nomadic hunters and gatherers from other types of stateless systems. Then they dismissed them because, they argued, their political and kinship structures were completely fused. This omission of band societies as political formations led to confusion. Other researchers built on the model provided by Fortes and Evans-Pritchard to argue that nomadic hunting and gathering societies contained neither structures nor practices that could be characterized as politics. Sharp (1958), for example, identified nomadic hunters and gatherers as "People Without Politics." Hoebel, on the other hand, muddled ideas by asserting that "where there is political organization there is a state. If political organization is universal, so then is the state" (1949b:376). From this logic, if hunters and gatherers had any political organization, they also were state formations!

Others saw the political structure of hunters and gatherers differently and more accurately. Schapera (1956) showed that every South African hunting and gathering society has a minimal authority structure in the form of one or more persons who are recognized and duty bound to attend to the conduct of public affairs, that is, who engage in government and politics. Schapera concluded that all societies, even the least complex, have some form of government.

Service (1962) addressed the issue later in the paradigm of political evolution, which, as we shall see in Chapter 9, depended largely on functional models. Service identified two kinds of hunting and gathering societies. He suggested that the *patrilocal band* probably represented the aboriginal condition of nomadic hunters and gathers because it maintained an organization of related males who were used to working and hunting together. The *composite band*, according to Service, had no central kinship organization. He concluded that the composite band was a recent phenomenon. He characterized it as an "expedient agglomeration" of fragments of preexisting societies ruptured beyond repair because of disruption caused by expanding Western colonial and capitalist societies. In either instance, Service concluded that government in hunting and gathering societies resided in the informal authority of family heads and ephemeral leaders (1962).

THE SEGMENTARY LINEAGE

The lineage, in particular the segmentary lineage, is a unilineal descent association common to societies in sub-Saharan Africa. It provided the other political system in the category of stateless societies. Fortes and Evans-Pritchard recognized that politics and the lineage represented distinct and autonomous spheres of social activity. But they also argued that politics and the lineage were coordinated and consistent with each other and that political relations between lineage segments were regulated by kinship relationships.

Segmentary lineages received considerable attention over the ensuing years. They were important in the political organization of societies in which centralized forms of political authority were either weak or absent. Kinship relations in lineage segments established relations based on patterns of complementary or balanced opposition. This principle identified the means by which people related by kinship reacted to unresolved internal problems and responded to an outside threat. They simply submerged their local and immediate differences and merged into ever-larger associations.

The dynamic of this principle was not fully appreciated by Evans-Pritchard (1940) in his study of the Nuer, one of the type cases for a segmentary lineage society. Evans-Pritchard's analysis emphasized how the principle of complementary opposition functioned to maintain the corporate structure of communities based on segmentary lineages. Other anthropologists demonstrated how the principle of complementary opposition enabled people with segmentary systems to retain the corporate integrity and to unify and expand against perceived or real outside threats despite internal divisive conflicts (Fortes 1945; Bohannon and Bohannon 1953; Sahlins 1968).

Some anthropologists pointed out that the lineage was only one feature of the broader category of stateless formations. Middleton and Tate (1958), for example, expanded the criteria for lineage-based stateless formations. They placed three groups of stateless formations in this category: independent lineage segments, interdependent segments, and independent segments with chiefs. A variety of factors related to each of these provided insight into other features of stateless political structures, such as the role of ancestral veneration in validating the sociopolitical integrity of the lineage and the existence of cognatic, or ranked, descent associations (ramages). True to the research strategies of the functional paradigm, political structures within each type were presumed to function to maintain order. Each type also was presented as an integrated whole in a condition of static equilibrium. Age-set/age-grade systems were identified as another politically integrating structure.

AGE-SET AND AGE-GRADE STRUCTURES

Beattie (1964) and Mair (1962) provided reasonable syntheses of African age-set formations and their political functions. Age sets and their hierarchy of internal grades provided social structures based on shared age that cut horizontally across the vertical structures based on shared descent. The political functions of age-set/age-grade structures came under scrutiny because they complemented those attributed to lineage structures.

Instead of allocating statuses, rights, and duties to individuals based on descent exclusively, age sets and their internal grades installed the males of lineage-based societies into hierarchical categories of statuses based on their age. A typical age set might allocate males to junior, warrior, and elder statuses, each of which also might be graded into finer age increments, or grades. Each set provides a means for males to learn the responsibilities of the next set and to their society.

Boys from all the lineages of the society enter the lowest grade of the junior set together. There they begin training in the cultural values and expectations related to male adulthood. Warriors defend their community and cattle herds against raids, and attack and raid enemies. Elders provide a leadership that complements that of lineage elders. Age sets and age grades provide the mechanism through which males move from junior to elder status as a category during their lifetimes.

Age sets are associated primarily, but not exclusively, with pastoral societies in Africa, but they are also found among other pastoral peoples, such as the Plains Indians of North America. Where transhumance is important, as among African cattle pastoralists, age sets provide a mechanism to cope with the risk of managing large herds of cattle. Pastoralists replenish their herds by raiding rather than through animal husbandry. Age sets distribute males across a territory in ways that disperse age and lineage mates and ensure that some of each will be available to protect the herds of member lineages and also to raid neighbors for their animals (Bernaldi 1952; Schneider 1957).

Functional analyses stressed the integrating function of age sets and age grades. They were believed to be one more structural mechanism by which order was maintained and political authority allocated on the basis of age. In the functional paradigm, age sets had two political dimensions. One was related to the warrior sets. Warriors were involved in intersocietal relations, such as protecting the property (e.g., cattle) of their political community and raiding other communities. The other dimension was more specifically political and related to the elder sets. Those who held the status of elder constituted a council that Mair (1962) referred to as a form of diffuse government. Councils of elders responded to inter- and intrasocietal problems. They resolved disputes and organized people for needed activities when descent associations were dispersed, such as defending their cattle herds or raiding the herds of others (Wilson 1951; Lambert 1956; M. G. Smith 1956; Southall 1956; Middleton and Tate 1958; Beattie 1964). Some elders had power by virtue of the size of their herds. But their decisions were sanctioned largely as a result of their relationship to symbolic resources, such as supernatural forces vested in ancestral spirits, upon whom they could call for help. Still, as with most councils, the power at their disposal to enforce their decisions was limited.

Functional research strategies provided the basis for analysis of political processes in structures that previously were not thought to be political. They also provided points of departure for exploring political dimensions of practices and behaviors that seemed far removed from politics. These contributions were made within the context of a definition of politics that emphasized the ways in which social order was maintained and conformity to existing integrating social norms was enforced. These concerns also resulted in the establishment of the field of legal anthropology.

LEGAL ANTHROPOLOGY

The field of legal anthropology grew out of concerns in the nineteenth-century study of cultural evolution that preceded functionalism (Maine 1963 [1861]). But the field's modern counterpart developed from the functional practices that Radcliffe-Brown (1940) identified as law. This muddled political–legal relations in political anthropology because it made law and politics appear to be similar features of the same structures. This is only partially so. But political and legal institutions are always intertwined (Nader 1969; Pospisil 1971). Even in state formations where political and legal institutions, such as governments and courts, are clearly differentiated and specialized structures, they overlap in functions related to maintaining social order and enforcing individual and group conformity to existing social and political norms. Distinctions between politics and law in stateless formations are murkier.

In most stateless formations the identification of mechanisms by which order and conformity are maintained presented special problems and was especially perplexing to anthropologists. Because institutions of government were underdeveloped and legal institutions all but nonexistent, exemplars of the functional paradigm conducted research to show how conformity can be enforced and order maintained in the absence of a permanent or, at best, weak authority structure. These explorations uncovered practices aimed at enforcing conformity, resolving disputes, and maintaining order that either were not part of the Western tradition or were not immediately evident in their social contexts. Ethnographic research into these concerns in state and stateless societies where political structures were not well developed laid the foundation for the subfield of legal anthropology (Hoebel 1949a, 1954; S. Roberts 1979). Curiously, while some anthropologists disputed the existence of political institutions and practices in nomadic hunting and gathering societies, no one challenged the idea that law, albeit in its customary form, was a component of hunting and gathering social structure.

In stateless societies, such as nomadic hunters and gatherers and lineage-based systems, disputes were resolved and conformity enforced by a variety of extralegal and political practices. Variation in these practices depended largely on the extent to which people were either sedentary or nomadic. For example, among sedentary farmers an accusation of witchcraft provided a warning to the accused that he or she was not complying with expected social norms. Transgressors knew that they might be killed if they persisted in their antisocial ways. In some instances, witchcraft was simply the final accusation before disposing of a socially undesirable person. The idea of the witch hunt in contemporary state formations, such as Senator Joseph McCarthy's search for communists in the United States in the 1950s, remains a way of blaming individuals for troubling social and political ills. [See Bailey (1994) for a case study of a witch hunt.]

Contests between antagonists in hunting and gathering societies often were held in formal settings where the entire political community, the band, congregated to help decide problems and resolve differences. These included practices such as spear-throwing duels, head-butting contests, and chanting rituals during which antagonists pleaded their cases before those gathered. Temporary flight, the departure of one or both litigants from the community until the problem blew over, also seemed to work in nomadic hunting and gathering societies. Saving face is not a highly regarded virtue of masculine identity in these societies. Withholding reciprocity from recalcitrant individuals or ostracizing them might be used either to force them to conform to social norms or to hasten their departure from the society. Incorrigibles and recidivists might be banished from the community. A person banished from one community was not usually welcome in others.

Underpinning most of these practices was some form of community consensus regarding the winner and loser in the case in question. Of course, if one litigant did not agree with the decision and decided to seek redress through some form of self-help, such as ambush, there was little the community could do. But self-help, essentially taking the law into one's hands, also could result in feuds. Feuds have a history in contexts other than hunting and gathering societies (Otterbein and Otterbein 1965; Otterbein 2000), and they share at least three traits: they are started easily enough; they are resolved only with great difficulty; and they could and often did lead to an expanded conflict. The extent to which litigants are aware of this possibility often seemed sufficient to impede violent forms of self-help and promote resolution. Among hunters and gatherers, community consensus was a surer way to guarantee peace and justice in the absence of a powerful authority structure.

In most ethnographically depicted stateless societies the execution of a perpetrator was an absolute last resort. The death penalty is largely a product of more advanced and "civilized" polities. In many stateless societies, every attempt would be made to reform troublemakers and recalcitrants and to reintegrate them into the social fabric. If it was decided that the death penalty was the only option for an incorrigible, the assistance of relatives of the condemned might be sought. Execution by a very close relative was one way to avoid the possibility of a feud among kin groups (Hoebel 1949a, 1954; S. Roberts 1979).

Political anthropology was only one focus of functional analysis. As we saw, functional thinking also helped to develop the closely related field of legal anthropology. Kinship organization, or social structure, was another strong interest of functional anthropologists, and the advent of *African Political Systems* merged the relationship between political and kinship structures. The politics of kinship is the topic of the next chapter. In addition to the functional approach to the politics of kinship, I also explore the nature of political alliances as they are derived from Levi-Strauss's insight into exchange theory.

6

THE POLITICS OF KINSHIP

Robin Fox tells us rightly so that "Kinship is to anthropology what logic is to philosophy or the nude is to art; It is the basic discipline of the subject." He further states that during the century between 1865 and 1967, "the anthropological literature on kinship accounts for more than half of the discipline's total literature" (1967:10). Whether the interest in kinship today remains as dominant as Fox suggests is moot. But no consideration of the paradigms and topics of political anthropology would be complete without addressing the relationship between kinship and politics.

As a result of Morgan's (1870) important work "Systems of Consanguinity and Affinity of the Human Family" and others of lesser merit, such as McLennan's (1865) *Primitive Marriage* and Bachofen's (1967 [1861]) "Das Mutterecht" ("Myth, Religion, and the Mother Right"), by the last third of the nineteenth century anthropologists were agreed that kinship relations provided the fundamental organizing principle of the societies that engaged their interests. But it was more than a fascination with the algebra of kinship relations that generated this literature. Anthropologists found that it was essential to understand the intricate workings of kinship structures and organizations before they could assess the social and cultural dynamics of the societies with which they worked, and that eventually included the dynamics of political organizations.

Problems, practices, and ideas that are specific to the relationship of kinship to politics are scattered throughout the paradigms and topics of political anthropology. However, in the field of political anthropology, problems associated with political and kinship structures first emerged as a major concern in the functional paradigm and subsequently in the paradigm of political evolution. Functional exemplars identified the main problem of the politics of kinship as the political dimensions of unilineal descent associations, especially the segmentary lineage. Later, Levi-

Strauss (1963, 1969 [1949]) identified features of marriage alliances in the paradigm of structural anthropology that also had implications for political anthropology.

By the end of the 1960s, anthropologists had resolved most of the problems related to the politics of kinship (Murdock 1949, 1960; Fox 1967; Fortes 1969). But important discoveries continue to be made. For example, Allen (1984) provided insight into the relationship between matrilineal descent and the evolution of strong leaders, such as chiefs, and nonkinship voluntary political associations, such as age-graded and secret societies. Anthropological studies of kinship relations and practices remain as important for understanding political formations and practices as they are for a general knowledge of social structures and organizations.

THE LINEAGE AND POLITICAL SYSTEMS

By the beginning of the twentieth century, the evolutionary bias that dominated kinship analyses in the nineteenth century was largely defunct. Through the early decades of the twentieth-century, British social anthropologists in particular empirically determined the variety of kinship systems—or social structures as they referred to them—that were incorporated into the British Empire, especially in Africa. Recall that much of the research by British social anthropologists was supported by the British Colonial Administration, which was concerned with how to "govern the natives." At the center of this concern was the problem of how to administer African societies whose social structures were based on lineages, especially unilineal descent associations. Occasionally a society may be characterized by double descent association. In these instances, individuals belong to a pair of descent associations that are organized on the principles of unilinearity and consanguinity, actual or supposed (Goody 1961). In political anthropology, unilineal descent associations were the focus of attention. For the purposes of this work, a lineage is a unilineal descent (matrilineal or patrilineal) association of limited genealogical scope within which everyone is able to trace their relationship to everyone else. As political structures, lineages are firmly bounded entities that demand the allegiance of their members, maintain order through the intervention of elders in disputes, are responsible jointly for the actions of their members, and provide the fountainheads from which flow the leadership and authority structures—episodic leaders, elders, councils, big men, headmen, chiefs, and heads of state—in those broad social categories that were identified as tribal and primitive state societies (Befu and Plotnicov 1962; Mair 1962). Lineages also functioned as political organizations even without the intervention of observable and identifiable leadership.

The concern with the political aspects of kinship emerged in *African Political Systems* (Fortes and Evans-Pritchard 1940). Contributors to this work identified the lineage, especially the segmentary lineage, as a territorially based political association embedded in kinship relations. To attain a clear understanding of the political aspects of segmentary lineages involved a difficult and protracted enterprise.

Segmentary lineages represented structures of government that existed without permanent, centralized authorities. They also appeared to be unstable because they were prone to segmentation and fission. Nonetheless, they functioned quite capably to maintain social order and to regulate relations within and between political communities, some of which in Africa numbered in the hundreds of thousands. The identification of segmentary lineages as political formations provided the watershed from which analyses of the political dimensions of kinship organization would flow. Although a major goal of exemplars of the functional paradigm was to understand the political structure and function of segmentary lineages in "tribal" societies, research gradually exposed the political aspects of lineages in both stateless and state formations.

THE SEGMENTARY LINEAGE

Lineages, patrilineal or matrilineal, are more or less prone to segmentation and have fissiparous tendencies. They range from associations that have no identifiable leadership to those with strong centralized leadership structures, and there is no necessary correlation between the size of lineages and their leadership structures. Some are able to mobilize lineage segments into increasingly larger units that could number in the thousands to respond to external threats and problems (Evans-Pritchard 1940; Fortes 1945, 1959, 1969; Bohannon and Bohannon 1953; Sahlins 1968, among others). But the primary political function of lineages as determined by functional exemplars was to maintain order and enforce conformity to lineage norms.

Fortes and Evans-Pritchard (1940) emphasized that even though the segmentary lineage was largely devoid of a centralized government, it was a territorial unit that regulated political relations within and between related lineages and with external political communities to whom they were not related. The ideal model of the segmentary lineage derives from the Tallensi of Ghana (Fortes 1945), who numbered in the thousands, and the Nuer (Evans-Pritchard 1940) and Tiv (Bohannon and Bohannon 1953) of the Sudan and Nigeria, respectively, each of whom numbered in the hundreds of thousands. The latter two peoples were special challenges for colonial administrators. They moved around a lot, broke apart and regrouped in response to environmental and social problems, fought with

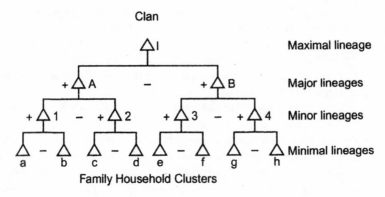

FIGURE 6.1   Segmentary lineage

other lineages in their respective societies and with their neighbors for territory, and lacked an identifiable central authority with whom colonial officials could negotiate. Neither the Nuer nor the Tiv responded well to colonial administrative control and authority. Evans-Pritchard (1940) referred to the major regulatory principle of the Nuer as a structure of "segmentary oppositions." This was later reconceptualized as a structure of "complementary oppositions" (Middleton and Tate 1958; Sahlins 1961).

The model of the segmentary lineage is characterized by unilineal descent associations, almost exclusively patrilineal, that are related through higher and lower orders of inclusion. Individuals at lower levels trace descent through a line of ancestors that extends to higher levels. With some minor variation, the levels of inclusion from most to least inclusive may be identified as maximal, major, minor, and minimal lineage segments, the latter of which are likely to be individual extended family household clusters or hamlets (Figure 6.1). The maximal segment is associated with a territory that is occupied by lower-order segments, each of which can trace descent to the maximal segment, which some anthropologists refer to as a clan. The politics internal to these segments is managed by heads of households and lineage elders, who may convene as councils that sometimes cut across levels of inclusion. But dynamics internal to the structure of segmentary lineages and the principle of complementary opposition also function to maintain order and lineage cohesion.

For example, complementary opposition is based on the idea that each level of inclusion is characterized by lines of potential segmentation (–) and unification (+). According to this principle, dissension (–) among a lower level of inclusion, such as the minimal lineage segments "a" and "b", could be resolved at the higher level of unification (+) provided by

"1". And potentially divisive problems (–) between "3" and "4", for example, could be resolved (+) by "B".

Another dimension to the principle of complementary opposition responds to potentially divisive conflict between same-level but more distant lineage segments. In this scenario, any dissension between same-level segments that are closely related will be set aside, at least temporarily, and they will unite to resolve the problem with the more distant relations. For example, if "a" has a problem with "c", then "a" may turn to "b" for help. This may then cause "c" to seek assistance from "d" and this could result in the mobilization of kin related to "1" to confront the kin related to "2." In these circumstances, because of genetic propinquity, or consanguinity, any differences between either "a" and "b" or "c" and "d" will be submerged for the duration of the conflict with the cousins of the other related segments. Hopefully, the conflict will be resolved by the intervention of peacemaking elders at levels "1" and "2", or even at level "A."

In another scenario, "d" may have problems with "e". Should either of them seek additional assistance, say "d" from "c" or "e" from "f", the possibility arises of then involving kin from "2" and "3" and, perhaps, "1" and "4" in the conflict. Theoretically, mobilization along lineage lines could escalate to include "A" and "B", which would enlarge the conflict accordingly. However, the escalation of conflict to the levels in this scenario is unlikely because it threatens to destroy the lineage. The principle of complementary opposition theoretically precludes this. It is likely that peace would be restored by the actions of elders at various levels of inclusion.

Of course, not all models work as expected. Sometimes intervention by elders at higher levels of inclusion fails. In these instances, other agents and mechanisms intervene to mediate the dispute and reestablish the functional integration of the system. Evans-Pritchard (1940) identified the Leopard-Skin Chief of the Nuer as a religious official who was able to exert sufficient influence to mediate problems when all else failed. If he failed, protracted feuds might prevail.

But even such intralineage feuds may be suspended if outsiders threaten any of the kin involved. For example, problems sometimes emerge with outsiders at lower levels of inclusion, such as if "a" and "b" expanded and occupied the land, pasture, or water sources of neighboring political communities (Evans-Pritchard 1940; Bohannon and Bohannon 1953; Sahlins 1961, 1968). In this event, serious differences between kin would be suspended until the external problem was resolved. Here again, obligations based on consanguineous propinquity prevail over internal squabbles and conflicts.

Sahlins (1961) referred to segmentary lineages, such as those found among the Tiv and Nuer, as organizations of "predatory expansion." He attributed this to their ability to expand at the expense of neighbors who were unable to mobilize allies to the same extent. Sahlins identified a decidedly processual and dynamic process. But within the functional paradigm, the unifying principle of complementary opposition and its potential to continually unite higher levels of lineage inclusion provided a classic model of a functionally integrating process.

However, you will notice the "theoretical" qualifications offered in the descriptions above. That is because not everyone is convinced that the model of the segmentary lineage and its principle of complementary opposition operate so neatly. Several anthropologists have suggested that the model represents an idealized condition, an ideology, and not an empirically determined practice (Peters 1967; Gough 1971; Holy 1979), and that the Leopard-Skin Chief was not the powerless figure that Evans-Pritchard identified. (Gruel 1971; Even 1985). There is some truth to this. Even before questions arose regarding the dynamics of the segmentary lineage, Evans-Pritchard (1951) pointed out that his representation of the segmentary lineage was an ideal and somewhat distorted picture. Subsequent research has shown that the Leopard-Skin Chief did have sufficient material power in the form of cattle and supporters and mystical and symbolic resources, such as the threat of imposing a curse, that he could resort to arbitration to resolve a dispute when mediation failed (Gruel 1971; Even 1985). Even though segmentary lineages may not have functioned as neatly as the model suggested, they did illuminate an opaque aspect of political organization that generated research and deeper insight into the political organization of kinship systems.

POLITICAL ALLIANCES

The detailed investigation of the contribution of kinship to the formation of political alliances came from an unlikely source. It was known that political alliances had been established historically in a variety of ways. But it was the application by Levi-Strauss (1963, 1969 [1949]) of his ideas to Morgan's (1870) timeless categories of cross-cousins and parallel-cousins that allowed anthropologists to probe new aspects of the political significance of marriage. As we shall see, marriage between particular categories of cousins is a good way to control resources of power and positions of influence.

Social scientists have known for a long time that marriages were often used by elites to unite potential enemies in a political alliance. But it was Levi-Strauss (1963, 1969 [1949]) who identified the more subtle intricacies of alliance formations in indigenous societies, thus expanding the understanding of the political implications of this process. Initially Levi-Strauss's models of alliance formation had little to do with political relationship. He was concerned with uncovering marriage structures embedded in unconscious models to account for the exchange of women for material goods, such as cattle, pigs, or horses, in indigenous societies. Levi-Strauss's ideas were complex and controversial, and resulted in a vast literature whose authors debated the validity of his ideas (Homans and Schneider 1955; Salisbury 1956; Needham 1958, 1962; Leach 1961; Coult 1962; Lane 1962; Livingstone 1964; Spiro 1964; Mayberry-Lewis 1965, among others). Gradually the scope of alliance theory was expanded to demonstrate that the principles of alliances established by Levi-Strauss functioned to unite potential enemies and provide leaders with strategies by which to acquire human and tangible resources in the form of allies and material goods (Salisbury 1956; Meggitt 1958; Murphy and Kasdan 1959; Fortes 1969; Fleming 1973; Clastres 1977).

Leaders who use marriages to establish alliances confront the problem of how to structure alliances efficiently. The mechanics are not haphazard. They often involve marriage to prescribed categories of potential mates. These categories ensure that a leader does not marry too far from nor too close to the primary kinship group or association of which she or he is a member. Alliances with distant political communities may be unmanageable. Those with closer political communities may be fraught with the contempt and problems that come from propinquity, such as envy and conspiracy. Alliances always are somewhat unstable, which is why rituals and symbols provide important cement to alliance formations. This is as true among the governments of contemporary state formations as it is among the indigenous societies of anthropological concern.

For example, the popular anthropological film *The Feast,* filmed in 1968, shows in detail the rituals involved in the formation of an alliance between two hostile Yanomamö villages. It also shows an exchange between a host and a guest of similar palm wood bows. This exchange has no practical value other than to cement the alliance symbolically (also see Chagnon 1992). Such rituals and symbolic exchanges are no less evident in the formations of alliance between contemporary state polities. Recall that in 1970 President Nixon visited and established relations with China. To symbolize this event—best considered perhaps as anticipatory to an alliance—he presented China with a pair of musk oxen. But that gift was overshadowed by China's reciprocated gift: They gave the United States the famous panda bears that graced the Washington zoo for years thereafter.

Even where exchange is less obvious, the symbolic richness of the marriage ritual may help to bond an alliance. In October 1997, Princess Christina of Spain married Inaki Urdangarin, a Basque athlete, in

Barcelona, the capital of Catalonia. As well as uniting a romantically popular couple, the wedding event seemed to be aimed at uniting Spain by symbolically uniting two regions where separatist sentiments run high, Catalonia and Basque. During the service, the Archbishop of Barcelona, a center of Catalan separatism, presided over the event and spoke in both Spanish and Catalan, and Basque and Catalan choirs sang praises to the union. As the Associated Press release said, "the ceremony appeared orchestrated [by Spain] to tie a love knot with [its] two most unruly regions, Basque and Catalonia" (*Austin American Statesman*, Oct. 5, 1997, p. A19).

The formation of alliances is a fundamental political process in all polities, including among nomadic hunters and gatherers. Alliances may also be formed by written treaties. These characterize relations between modern state governments. They may be established through ritual practices, such as the feasting and symbolic exchanges that cemented alliances between Yanomamö villages (Chagnon 1992) and China and the United States. But the most rudimentary and most common alliance is that established by marriage. Marriage alliances involve practices related to exogamy, cousin marriage, and polygyny. Statistics are hard to come by, but there are suggestions that leaders and aspiring leaders in indigenous societies who are most likely to adhere to prescribed marriage patterns, such as cousin marriage and polygyny, are either culturally conservative or have strong support from the culturally conservative members of their political communities (Freedman 1958; Barth 1959; Pastner 1979).

Marriage and Exogamy

The fundamental marriage rules to establish a political alliance were first elucidated by Sir Edward Tylor (1889) in his work on the significance of exogamy and by Morgan (1870) in his important study of cross- and parallel-cousins. Nineteenth-century evolutionists were not especially concerned with the political aspects of marriage. But strategic marriages make friends out of enemies, reduce potential conflict, and shore up existing intergroup relations. Exogamy and cross-cousin marriage provide mechanisms to ensure these results. For leaders and aspiring leaders, strategic marriages generate access to additional allies and supporters from whom more tangible power resources may then be gathered.

Almost all alliances established through marriage begin by adhering to the rule of *exogamy*. Exogamy establishes intergroup relationships where none existed previously because it requires individuals to marry outside the primary consanguineal units of which they are members. Sir Edward Tylor was the first anthropologist to perceive marriage exogamy as a way of avoiding intersocietal conflict. He observed that "tribes . . . had . . . the simple practical alternative between marrying out and being killed out"

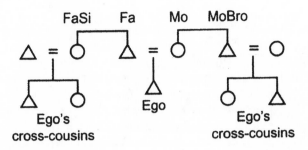

FIGURE 6.2   Cross Cousins

(1889:267). Insightful for its time, this observation overstates the matter. There is good evidence that exogamy and alliances reduce severe conflict (Fleming 1973; Podolefsky 1984), but there is also compelling evidence that they do not guarantee peace (Salisbury 1956; Meggitt 1958; Fox 1967; Kang 1979). Of course, no alliance can guarantee that conflict will be avoided and that peace will prevail.

Political alliances established through exogamy are not haphazard affairs. They usually require adherence to rules that specify categories of suitable mates and prescribe specific strategies to direct the selection of proper mates, that is, those with whom marriage confers specific political advantages. Ordinary folks may or may not adhere to the prescribed rules and strategies. Even where prescriptive marriage rules prevail, individuals have considerable latitude in selecting mates. But leaders are likely to comply with the rules. When leaders conform to the cultural values of their political communities, they enhance their legitimacy. On the other hand, leaders also are more likely to break the rules openly and challenge community values. They usually do this with the intention of changing the rules to their advantage. In either instance, the bottom line for leaders in any marriage alliance is the access it provides to resources of power. Cross-cousin marriage is a specific form of exogamy that has specific consequences for the formation of political alliances through marriage (Levi-Strauss 1963, 1969 [1949]).

Cross-Cousin Marriage

Cross-cousins are the children of siblings of different sex (Figure 6.2). Therefore, Ego's cross-cousins are his mother's brother's and father's sister's children. Cross-cousin marriage may occur patrilaterally on the father's side (marriage of a male ego with father's sister's daughter), matri-

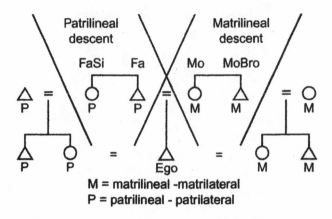

FIGURE 6.3   Marriage of Ego to matrilateral or patrilateral cross-cousins

laterally on the mother's side (marriage of a male ego with mother's brother's daughter), or bilaterally (marriage of a male ego with a cross-cousin on either the father's or mother's side). Each form of cross-cousin marriage, bilateral, matrilateral, and patrilateral, has implications for the nature of the alliance established. But the underlying principle of exogamy by which cross-cousin marriage creates an alliance between unilineal descent associations is simple. *In unilineal descent associations, marriage between cross-cousins, regardless of the type of descent, results automatically in a marriage between persons of different descent associations* (Figure 6.3). In those cases where descent associations constitute separate political communities, cross-cousin marriage establishes alliances between different polities.

Ethnographically, nomadic hunters and gatherers represent the most rudimentary societies in which individuals establish alliances through marriage. These alliances, often mislabeled as sister exchange (Figure 6.4), anticipate bilateral cross-cousin marriage (Fox 1967). Among nomadic hunters and gatherers, sister exchange occurs between categories of males and females who are designated by the societies' senior generations as potential mates. As a model, sister exchange requires males from Band I to acquire wives from Band II and males from Band II to acquire wives from Band I. Males also may acquire wives from other bands with which similar exchanges are formalized. The result of this strategy may not be explicitly political since leadership and strategies to acquire power are underdeveloped. But marriage through sister exchange results in a wide dispersal of allies, kinfolk by marriage, in different bands upon whom individuals can call for assistance (Fox 1967).

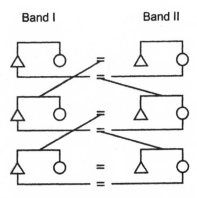

FIGURE 6.3   Sister Exchange

Where marriage between consanguineous cross-cousins is likely, bilateral cross-cousin marriage provides the most flexible way to establish an alliance. In bilateral cross-cousin marriage, leaders may marry either mother's brother's daughter or father's sister's daughter (Figure 6.5). This strategy permits leaders to negotiate marriages from which they will derive the most benefit. Such a strategy is especially rewarding in societies where unilineal descent associations are ranked hierarchically (ramages), as in some advanced chiefdoms and early state formations. In these societies, lineages that are ranked higher in the ramage probably will have control of more tangible resources than those that are ranked lower. Strategic marriages provide leaders with the means to tap the tangible resources of other associations, to enlarge their followings, and for the parties involved to consider the implication of each other's status for their mutual benefit.

A caveat to this practice is the possibility that a consanguineous cross-cousin may not exist for a variety of reasons, such as death or failure of parents to produce the needed gender. To compensate for such an eventuality, eligible cross-cousins may be identified within a culturally prescribed category of potential mates, some of whom may be fictive kin. Even if the proper relation does exist, leaders may establish and/or marry a fictive cross-cousin for strategic and tactical purposes.

Matrilateral and patrilateral cross-cousin marriage strategies (see Figures 6.6, 6.7) are practiced primarily among polities whose members trace descent either patrilineally or matrilineally. The rule of descent is not important in establishing these alliance formations. But the side on which the marriage occurs—father's (patrilateral) or mother's (matrilateral)—is

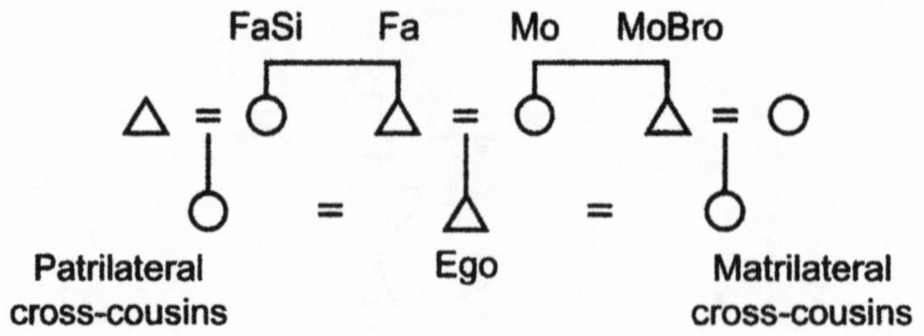

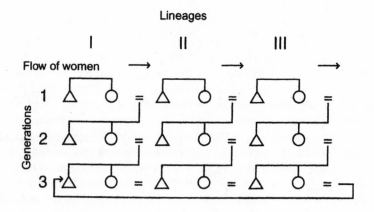

FIGURE 6.5   Bilateral cross-cousin marriage of Ego, either to FaSi's daughter or to MoBro's daughter

Lineages

FIGURE 6.6   Matrilateral cross-cousin marriage. Women flow from Lineage III to Lineage I in each generation

important. It configures the pattern and time of exchange of mates, limits a leader's marriage option to specific cross-cousins, and thereby reduces the flexibility of a leader's alliance strategy.

In the ideal matrilateral cross-cousin marriage strategy (Figure 6.6), leaders receive women from the same associations generation after generation. To cement this alliance, the kin of the associations that receive the women give something of culturally prescribed equal value to the kin of the associations that provide the women. Thus women flow in one direction between the participating associations and the culturally valuable material items flow in the opposite direction. This immediate exchange

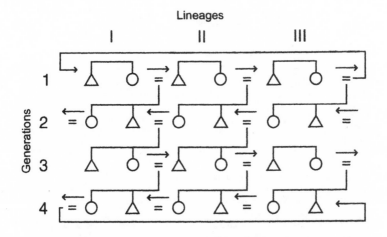

FIGURE 6.7   Patrilateral cross-cousin marriage. Women flow to the lineages involved in alternating generations

provides solidarity to the alliance and may account for why it is more common than patrilateral cross-cousin marriage.

Leaders who follow a patrilateral cross-cousin marriage (Figure 6.7) strategy marry women from the same associations in alternate generations. In this pattern, women flow in one direction in one generation and in the opposite direction in the next generation. Women are reciprocated in the process. But because the exchange of women is delayed, theoretically for years, until the next generation begins to marry, the alliance is fragile. This delay accounts largely for the infrequency of patrilateral cross-cousin marriage as a significant alliance formation.

In contradiction to the vast anthropological literature on this topic, alliance formations based on the marriages of cross-cousins are not exclusive to non-Western, indigenous peoples. Prior to World War I, bilateral and matrilateral cross-cousin marriages were common among the royal households (read descent associations) of Europe (Fleming 1973). "Marriages of state" in Europe and elsewhere are a well-recorded phenomena and a euphemism for political alliances through marriage. But the extent to which they either comply with or diverge from anthropological models of cross-cousin marriage has yet to be determined.

Patrilateral Parallel-Cousin Marriage

Parallel-cousins are children of siblings of the same sex. Compared to exogamous cross-cousin marriage, patrilateral parallel-cousin marriage is endogamous (Figure 6.8): It takes place within a patriline and requires the

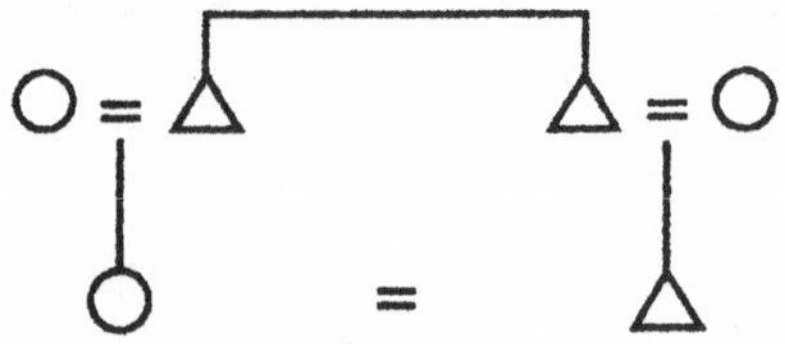

Patriline

FIGURE 6.8   Patrilateral parallel cousin marriage

marriage of a male ego to his father's brother's daughter. This pattern of cousin marriage is not very common. At least in part this is because it does not establish alliances with other descent associations.

Nonetheless, the pattern has an ancient history. It was practiced among the ancient Hebrews and others in the Near East and can be ascertained in genealogies identified by tracing the marriages involved in whom begat whom as recorded in the Old Testament. Ethnographically, the strategy is reported widely among nomadic bedouins in the Near East and across North Africa. But it also occurs among urban Arab populations in the same regions. Although this strategy denies the possibility of one patriline forming an alliance with another, it is an effective means by which a maximal patriline may retain tight control over the lineage's resources (Murphy and Kasdan 1959), such as herds among bedouins and money and property among urban Arabs.

Since patrilateral parallel-cousin marriage strengthens kinship bonds internal to a patriline and ensures that a tightly knit unity of males will control and defend the resources of their respective lineage, the strategy also suggests that all other patrilineages are real or potential enemies (Goldschmidt 1965). Patrilateral parallel-cousin marriage also conforms to the ideology of an ancient Arab proverb: "Myself against my brother; my brother and I against my cousin; my cousin, my brother, and I against the outsider" (Murphy and Kasdan 1959:20). As with the principles of complementary opposition, brothers and cousins will resolve, at least temporarily, conflicts among themselves to confront threats from patrilineages to whom they are not related. Murphy and Kasdan (1959) also suggest that the survival of this ancient structure and its attendant sentiments may impede the development of intersocietal political alliances among Arabs and bedouins in the Near East, and also may be one reason why the wish among some Arab leaders for a pan-Arab political unity has been so difficult to attain.

Anthropological analyses of alliance formations are restricted largely to the practices of indigenous peoples. A neglected area of analysis is the relationship between politics and kinship in contemporary industrial societies. Even where royal lines are not important to government, as in the United States, elite families continue to establish political alliances through strategic marriages. In the United States and other industrial societies, the powerful and influential commonly marry their own kind to provide access to and retain control over their influence, power, and resources within a predictable kinship context (Weatherford 1985, 1993; Birmingham 1990; Hertzberg 1999). This is even more prevalent in Europe, and may account for why practices identified in indigenous societies, such as alliances based on cousin marriage, were intricately interlaced with the lineages of European royalty up until World War I (Fleming 1973).

Better research is needed to determine the structure of marriage alliances in contemporary industrial societies. But there does seem to be a different ideological justification for these marriages than that which is recorded among preindustrial societies. We call it love.

Goode (1959) does not consider the role of marriage among kin of some remove in alliance formation in contemporary Western society. But he does get close to the basis of the ideology that underlies these formations in theory if not practice. Goode suggested that romantic love, whatever that elusive, poetically, and chemically charged emotion represents, emerged as a political ideology in western Europe (probably among favored bards in the court of Queen Eleanor of Aquitaine) during the transition from feudalism to capitalism that began in the twelfth and thirteenth centuries in southern France with the development of textile mills. During this transition, wealth and its accompanying power were increasingly controlled by a nouveau riche with no royal or noble bloodline pedigree. As wealth began to accumulate among the capitalist petit bourgeoisie, an ideology of romantic love began to propagate and expand among this class and the proletariat. In effect the idea of love gave the latter something to look forward to other than the wealth to which they rarely could aspire.

Today, in contemporary capitalist formations, the idea of romantic love is certainly strong, even among the elites and rich. But in practice, elites are likely to marry to protect their resources and the power they provide as much as they are for the illusion of love (Birmingham 1990). Indeed, the rest of us may be victims of one of the most insidious plots ever devised as an unconscious model by the rich and powerful and their natural allies, political leaders. Those of us, which is most of us, with little wealth and power to control are left with the illusion of romantic love as the foundation upon which to construct marriages that appear to be increasingly fragile. The rich and powerful are left with their resources, the control of which through strategic marriages may have little to do with the chemical and emotional reality of an ideology of romantic love. Who is the happiest in the long run? I leave this for you to decide.

Polygyny

Polygyny is a marriage strategy by which a leader may maximize the resource return from marriage alliances. It creates a household based on the marriage of a man to two or more women. Polygyny is not unique in the ethnographic record. In fact, it is permitted in most societies that have been studied ethnographically. However, monogamous households, composed of one man and one woman, are the most common form of household worldwide. Even in polygynous societies where gender imbalances favor polygyny, the economic realities do not allow most men to support more than one wife. The practice of polygyny therefore suggests motivations other than simple economic or lascivious considerations: they are political.

Polygyny is associated with higher-status males who tend to be the wealthy and influential members of a society. They are also more likely to aspire to positions of leadership and the prestige, status, authority, influence, and power that such positions convey. Chiefs are more likely to live in a polygynous household than big men, and heads of preindustrial states are more likely to do so than chiefs. While these men, like the fabled sultans of *The Arabian Nights* with their enormous harems, may be political leaders, heads of polygynous households who are not leaders are also likely to be their benefactors and loyalists, and, often as not, given their political economic clout, the power behind the leaders. Shrewd leaders who acquire multiple wives follow strategies to bring them more resources to enhance their political aspirations. For aspirants to political statuses and offices, polygynous alliances provide access to human and tangible resources that can translate into political power as their careers develop.

Nonetheless, polygyny can be expensive economically and emotionally. Wives may not get along. Husbands may have problems with one or more of them. Jealousies may create tensions. Children from different wives may present serious problems regarding succession to office. To mitigate these and other problems related to polygyny, men are expected to provide for each wife equally. This may or may not happen. Still, from the male perspective, multiple wives and the labor and allies they can provide may help a man improve his net material worth. To a leader or aspirant to leadership, this worth may translate into human and material power.

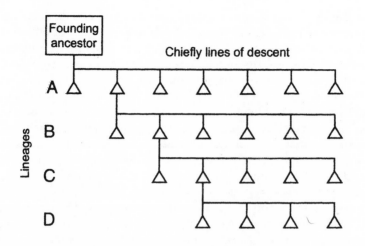

FIGURE 6.9   Ramage (also a cognatic descent association, or a conical clan)

Ranked Lineages

In the 1930s, anthropologists made sharp distinctions between lineages that were egalitarian in status and role and those in which statuses and social structures were ranked in a hierarchy and governed by strong chiefs (Kirchhoff 1959 [1955]). Kirchhoff initially identified these ranked lineages as *conical clans*. This terminology was superseded by Firth, who referred to them as *ramages* (Firth 1957 [1936]), and by Murdock (1960), who identified them as *cognatic kinship structures*. I will adhere to Firth's terminology.

A ramage (Figure 6.9) refers to a structure of *agamous, ambilocal,* and *ambilineal* descent associations, or lineages, that are ranked in a hierarchy. Each lineage of the ramage represents a polity headed by a chief, each of whom can trace descent to a common ancestor. Ramages are subject to segmentation and fission, and if one word could suggest the social and political dynamics of a ramage it would be *flexibility*, which is a product of the principles of agamy, ambilocality, ambilineality, and segmentation (Firth 1957 [1936]; Sahlins 1958; Murdock 1960; Fox 1967; Sahlins 1968).

The practice of agamy is in stark contrast to marriage principles that prescribe certain categories of mates, such as cross- or parallel-cousins. Agamy refers to a marriage rule that permits individuals to marry whomever they choose, within certain cultural limits. Ambilocal refers to a rule of postmarital residence that contrasts with rules that prescribe where the newlyweds will live [with or near the husband's kin (viripatrilocal), the wife's kin (uxorimatrilocal), the husband's mother's brother (viriavunculocal), or by themselves, separate from either side (neolocal)]. The ambilocal rules allows newlyweds to assume residence either with kin on the husband's or the wife's side or separate from each. Ambilineal descent does not necessarily preclude unilineal (patrilineal and matrilineal) descent principles. Instead, ambilineal descent permits a married couple the flexibility to choose which of their parental descent lines with which to associate. Most likely they would choose the line that most benefits a spouse's social and political ambitions. The segmentation of lineages within a ramage also allows individuals to begin other branches of the ramage, perhaps with a strategic marriage and separate household, that would support a spouse's social and political ambitions.

In a ramage, each descent association is governed by a chief who can trace his descent to the founding ancestor of the ramage. The status of the lineage and the influence of its chief may depend on his proximity to the founding ancestor. Fried refined the idea that accounts for the hierarchical status of ranked lineages by pointing out that, "The line of descent isn't simply the transgeneration tie that recedes toward the first-known ancestry . . . but the string of first born through time" (1967:126–127). Chiefs of higher-ranked lineages tend to have more authority and power than chiefs of lower-ranked lineages. In some lineages, different chiefs might have responsibilities for different aspects of critical rituals (Titiev 1944). In others they might control access to different resources (Firth 1957 [1936]).

Ordinary individuals in a ramage may never aspire to the office of chief of the association. But the flexibility and strategic choices that individuals may make in these alignments have implications for political development because they allow leaders and individuals latitude in manipulating the social and political environments to their advantage. For example, a chief may marry to acquire more resources, whereas an individual or family may arrange a marriage that permits a spouse to move up in the social hierarchy. Agamy, ambilocality, ambilineality, and segmentation begin to approximate the flexibility in kin and nonkin relations that are common to class distinctions in state formations.

The politics of kinship illuminated an otherwise vague relationship between political and social structures. At the moment, kinship analysis receives little attention in anthropology. Even British social anthropologists, who were always more interested in kinship than their American counterparts, have recently ignored it. Still, works such as Allen's (1984), which will be explored in more detail later, and lacunae in our knowledge related to kinship and power in industrial and postindustrial societies suggest that much remains to be learned about the relationship between kinship and politics in our rapidly changing world.

7

THE PROCESSUAL PARADIGM

The nominal dominance of the structural-functional paradigm over the field of political anthropology ended with the appearance of three works in the 1960s. The editors of *Political Anthropology* (Swartz, Turner, and Tuden 1966) introduced the first conceptual framework for an anthropological approach to an agent-driven politics. Two years later, Swartz (1968) edited *Local Level Politics*. He and contributors to this work expanded and refined some ideas presented in *Political Anthropology*. A year later, Bailey (1969) synthesized and reinterpreted much of what was introduced in these two works in his book *Stratagems and Spoils*. This work was a capstone for the processual paradigm.

The exemplars of the processual paradigm rejected the functional idea that sociopolitical structures, the maintenance of order, and typologies of political systems constituted the proper focus of political anthropology. Although the processual paradigm provided strategies for research and analysis of an agent-driven politics in process, neither *Political Anthropology* nor *Local Level Politics* broke totally with the functional paradigm. Instead, processual practitioners introduced new ideas by political anthropologists who were unhappy with functional interpretations of politics that contributed to the subordination of the functional paradigm. Nonetheless, some anthropologists continued to defend the functional explorations of political structures because they provided neat analytic units (R. Cohen 1970a, 1970b).

THE PARADIGMATIC BREAK

After World War II, the reconstitution of the field of political anthropology developed slowly. Through the 1950s and early 1960s, some anthropologists continued to elaborate functional typologies of political systems

(Middleton and Tate 1958; Vansina 1962). Others continued to explore how the maintenance of order contributed to the functional integration of total political systems (Gluckman 1956, 1965; Lambert 1956; I. M. Lewis 1961; Mair 1962). But other anthropologists, many of whom were students of mentors who established the functional paradigm, were busy dismantling it (Leach 1954; Southall 1956, 1965; Turner 1957; Bailey 1963; Lloyd 1965). Edmund Leach (1954), a student of Raymond Firth, was one of the first to denounce soundly the implications of the functional paradigm for political research.

In *Political Systems of Highland Burma*, Leach (1954) analyzed the conditions under which subsystems of Kachin and Shan clans in Highland Burma rose and fell in authority and power. Because of his depiction of these fluctuations, Leach's analysis was considerably more dynamic than studies done under the aegis of the functional paradigm. But from another perspective, the dynamics of Kachin and Shan political processes remained caught in an oscillating equilibrium that always resulted in another pattern of functional integration. Despite Leach's disclaimers, his work continued to demonstrate functional principles.

Victor Turner, a student of Max Gluckman and an admirer of Monica Wilson's work, developed the implicitly dialectical idea of the *social drama* in *Schism and Continuity* (1957) to explore conflict in Ndembu society. But true to the Hegelian implications of the thesis–antithesis–synthesis dialectic, the resolution of conflict in a social drama always returned the society to another state of functional integration not much different from that which existed prior to the drama.

Others also challenged the typological, time-space bounded, ahistorical, and synchronic approach that functionalists brought to the study of political systems (Southall 1956, 1965; M. G. Smith 1960; Lloyd 1965). Some attempted to break with the paradigm and develop what they argued were dynamic models. However, the models invariably established new typologies of the political organizations or systems under scrutiny (Lloyd 1965; Southall 1965). Yet some researchers were more successful in making the break.

M.G. Smith (1956, 1960), for example, argued that all politics, whether in the lineage or the state, is segmentary, that is, prone to divisions and realignments, because structures of government always stand in contraposition to each other. He also argued that the idea of government that prevailed in the functional paradigm was confused by terminological ambiguity. Instead of representing government as a structure, Smith suggested that government is a process composed of two related practices: administration and politics. According to him, the administration of government is concerned with the conduct and coordination of public business. The politics of government addresses the development and implementation of political policy. We will return to these ideas in Chapter 11.

Other contributions to a new political anthropology came from outside British social anthropology. Fallers (1955, 1965) was one of the first to demonstrate some of the negative consequences of colonial rule. He revealed how British restraints on the traditional behaviors of African chiefs placed them in an ambiguous relationship vis-à-vis their subjects. This resulted in conflict where none had existed previously. Fredrick Barth (1959) broke with the Afrocentric orientation to politics that dominated the thinking of British anthropologists. Instead he analyzed the politics of the Swat Pathans of northern Pakistan.

Barth's work was seminal because he was among the first to emphasize the dynamics of the political leader in an anthropological study of politics. He explored how constraints imposed by various social relations influenced the choices leaders make and the impact of these choices on reciprocal relations between leaders and followers. Barth's work anticipated Bailey's (1969) concerns with politics as a game involving rules that regulate the actions of agents.

By the middle of the 1950s, functional exemplars had demonstrated thoroughly how practices and beliefs in most human social structures functioned to maintain social integration and equilibrium. Eventually some criticism of the functional paradigm came from those who helped to establish it (Gluckman 1954, 1956, 1965; Fortes 1969). Gluckman (1956), in effect, exhausted the potential of the paradigm to provide new insight into the integrating mechanisms at work in human society when he demonstrated that even social conflicts, such as feuds and rebellions, resulted in social integration! Gluckman and others (Southall 1956; Murphy 1957, 1960) now began to argue that conflict, not integration, provided the proper focus for exploring political process. Because of these efforts, some say that the structural-functional paradigm actually died during the 1950s.

The emphasis that political anthropologists placed on conflict was the most definitive feature of the processual paradigm. Gluckman (1965) eventually established a useful way to distinguish practices that cause divisions in human society. He identified competition, dispute, argument, quarrel, strife, dissension, contention, fight, and the like as surface disturbances in social life. Conflict is the result of oppositions in social relations at the heart of a political system that are compelled by the very structure of the system and that result in the alteration of sociopolitical statuses and roles, but not in the pattern of these positions. He suggested that contradiction refers to the discrepant principles and practices in social relations that inevitably result in radical changes in the pattern. This concept of contradiction may not be threatening today. But when Gluckman suggested its importance for social and political processes, the implications of a communist resolution to the dialectic of the class contradiction that Marxists perceived to be inherent in Western capitalism were terribly threatening. Because notions of the dialectic and contradiction were associated with a communist argot and rhetoric that threatened the West's capitalist mode of production, Western scholars used the idea and methodology of contradiction with care, if at all.

Criticism of the functional paradigm even came from outside anthropology. Recall that the respected political scientist David Easton (1959) said that political anthropology had dubious merit because the field was invested so heavily in the study of structures and concerns that were not political, such as kinship, and that it lacked political theory. Some anthropologists agreed with this, but most did not agree with Easton's implications of the field's dubious merit. By this time, a new, processual paradigm that was conceptually more akin to the ideas of political science was lurking in the wings of the functional paradigm and about to emerge. As with the functional paradigm, the processual paradigm was a product of history.

BACKGROUND

It was not merely the reaction to functionalism that gave rise to the processual paradigm. The scholarly and political concerns of the early-twentieth-century colonial era no longer reflected the post–World War II political economic order. The former emphasis on stasis, synchrony, equilibrium, integration, and the denial of strife and conflict as political forces was largely an acquiescence of British social anthropologists to the demands of the British Colonial Office to keep order throughout the empire. Because the Colonial Office provided research funds to British social anthropologists, research suggesting anything to do with conflict or political change that might put seditious thoughts in the minds of the "natives" was unacceptable. By the end of the 1950s, the politics of empire had become unimportant. By then, British anthropologists, such as Gluckman, Bailey, and Turner, who aided in the development of the processual paradigm, no longer had to worry about the integrity of the now largely defunct British Empire. Although British social anthropologists helped to dismantle the exhausted functional paradigm, the processual paradigm was largely a response by American anthropologists to issues and challenges in local, national, and international political arenas that culminated in the turmoil of the 1960s and 1970s. At the risk of oversimplifying complicated processes, three general conditions colluded to subvert the research strategies of the functional paradigm.

The first condition related to the omnipresent dangers of the cold war and its hot spots that superseded problems in the colonies of Western governments. The protracted and culminating struggle of Viet Nam for independence from French colonial rule and, later, American aggression were important in this respect. The second condition, of which Viet Nam was belatedly symptomatic, was the gradual disintegration of the colonial empires after World War II. Emerging postcolonial societies—India, for example, in 1947 and many African nations thereafter—constituted that obstreperous political bloc commonly called then the "third world." Increasingly, third world governments gave birth to political actions, processes, conflicts, and contradictions that gradually became normative practices in the world's political arenas. Most postcolonial societies were caught in struggles over affiliation with the capitalist or communist blocs, self-determination, and cultural identity.

The third cause emanated from a post–World War II generation of suburban/urban, middle- and upper-middle-class students in higher education in the United States and other of the world's more developed nations. Around the world these students began to express, sometimes violently, their disenchantment with the perceived hypocrisy and injustice of their governments' social, cultural, political, and economic policies. Conflict swirled around issues of poverty, human and civil rights, the ideological content of higher education, self-determination, nationalism, drugs, suburban values, gender relations, sexuality, and opposition to war and the nuclear bomb. Each issue was fraught with political, economic, social, cultural, and moral implications and contradictions. As a result, they provided local, national, and international arenas within which the ideological and material interests and goals of capitalist, communist, and fascist governments and their citizens collided in the long and widening vortex of the Viet Nam war.

These three processes shared a curious political practice. Ideologically they were vehicles for the expression of opposing hegemonic agents (Gramsci 1971) who strove to inculcate the cultural values, beliefs, and identities favored by their competing regimes in different political communities over which they contested (Kurtz 1996b). In material, ideological, and practical ways, these conditions were expressed in conflicts not only at the level of national governments, but also at the local level of the quotidian practices in which citizens engaged. This is an important point because these conflicts provided a new context for ethnographic depictions of everyday, quotidian altercations among ordinary people at the local level. Such quotidian activities and conflicts among common folk have always been more attractive to anthropologists than the machinations of elites, and I will explore their political significance later.

During the 1960s, ethnographic studies by anthropologists began to reflect the political reality of the times and gave birth to the synthesis that became the processual paradigm. In the field of anthropology at large during the 1960s and 1970s, this tendency was expressed in innovative research strategies aimed at making sense out of an increasingly complicated postcolonial world. The problems of this new world—urbanization, poverty, migration, self-determination, the political economy of center–periphery relations—spawned new research orientations.

These included methodologies related to network analysis and urban studies in developing and developed nations (Bott 1955, 1957; Mitchell 1969), as well as new paradigms, such as structuralism (Levi-Strauss 1963, 1969 [1949]), cognitive anthropology or ethnoscience (Tyler 1969), and historical-cum-cultural materialism (Harris 1968, 1979), and the rediscovery of older paradigms, such as cultural evolution and adaptation (Service 1962; Y. A. Cohen 1969). Political anthropologists responded to these crosscurrents with a new paradigmatic strategy that was aimed at political conflict and consequent processes at the "local level." Their focus was on an agent-driven politics that was not necessarily embedded in the structure of government, such as the state or lineage (Swartz, Turner, and Tuden 1966; Swartz 1968; Bailey 1969).

THE PROCESSUAL PARADIGM

The processual paradigm provided anthropologists with a rich and novel perspective on politics. Its exemplars enhanced many ordinary political ideas with sharper and more insightful meaning than had existed previously. Legitimacy, support, faction, leadership, conflict, power, and other issues were composed in a diachronic framework that explored them as temporal and spatial processes. Exemplars of the paradigm replaced in word, if not deed, the synchronic, typological, and functional concerns of political structures, such as the lineage and governments. In their place they suggested methodologies that explored politics as a dynamic, agent-driven process that was concerned with team building, factional formation, and the strategies by which leaders acquired power. Instead of giving lip service to history, change, and political dynamics as was common by exemplars of the functional paradigm, processual practitioners boldly asserted that politics was a diachronic, historical process. They expanded the maximalist orientation of political anthropology to explore processes in *parapolitical* institutions other than those of kinship that are not inherently political but still engage in politics, such as universities or castes (Bailey 1960, 1968, 1977).

Exemplars of the processual paradigm made four major contributions to the field of political anthropology. First, they provided a definition of politics that emphasized process. Second, they provided a rich ensemble of concepts by which to analyze politics as process, and even, as Bailey (1969) did, showed how to participate in the process. Third, they placed conflict in the forefront of any analysis of politics. And fourth, they rejected political structures, such as governments and lineages, as the major focus for political analysis.

For processual practitioners, the proper research strategies of political anthropology considered how political processes and conflicts that were disruptive of social order led to changes in political systems. This was asserted in their conceptualization of politics as "the *processes* involved in determining and implementing public goals and in the differential achievement and use of power by the members of the group concerned with those goals" (Swartz, Turner, and Tuden 1966:7). The definition implies that political processes were fraught with conflict over the goals of leaders and supporters. The conflicts were usually resolved in favor of those with either more power or more skill in using what they had.

But as the paradigm developed, processes related to implementing public goals did not signify the antithesis of functional concerns with order. Political actions and practices of agents did not transpire without constraints. Instead they were hemmed in by rules that governed and regulated the strategies that constituted the game that leaders and other agents played for high stakes and prizes with the power at their disposal (Bailey 1969).

To establish the processual point of view, Swartz, Turner, and Tuden proceeded "to bombard the reader with political concepts and theoretical constructs" (1966:4). First and foremost was the idea of *conflict*. This was not merely an event. The emergence and resolution of conflict were construed as a process. Indeed, the concern with conflict anchored the research strategies that enlivened the processual paradigm.

The functional ideas of *force* and *coercion* remained important in political process, but they were identified as political actions that were costly in human and tangible resources. They were better used when other strategies that were less costly failed. For example, exemplars conceptualized force as a mode of support that relies on other modes of support, such as institutions of coercion. *Support* was construed to refer to anything that contributed to achieving political goals. Support could be direct or indirect. In the case of direct support, individuals explicitly provide support to a political structure or individual. Indirect support is present when individuals give support to others who then represent their concerns to still other people.

Significantly, they perceived *legitimacy* to rest on more than a shared ideology, which was a standard idea in political science. Rather, they conceptualized legitimacy as a type of support. It derived from the values held by those political agents involved in attaining political goals and those affected by them.

Swartz, Turner, and Tuden (1966) defined *power* in ways that were different from the functional notion of coercion. In one incarnation, power was a symbolic, generalized resource whose efficacy depended on the expectations of those who use, comply with, or resist it. In another case, it was a panoply of natural resources that provided direct and indirect support to those who used it. Compliance by subjects with the wishes of leaders produced *consensual power*. In contrast, *coercive power* came to the fore when compliance was not forthcoming. Depending on circumstances, any leader or authority figure could rely on either a great deal or very little consensual power. This usually existed in an inverse relationship with the coercive power at their disposal.

They also reconstituted the traditional concept of authority as the acknowledged right of some to make decisions that are binding on others; this was an *authority code*. According to this principle, those in hierarchical positions of authority and power are subject to supernatural and secular constraints and potentials on their exercise of power. The divine right of medieval European kings and the ethical values made explicit in modern state constitutions are examples of such codes. In practice an authority code is embedded in a structure of values and reciprocal obligations between leaders and supporters. If an authority code is effective, leaders have little need to use force to enforce their decisions. Instead, compliance with political decisions can rely on the ability of political leaders to influence and persuade others of their intentions. If these fail, then they might resort to force or coercion.

The political processes in which these phenomena are embedded engage a *political field*. The field is composed of those agents who are directly involved in the process under scrutiny. *Factions*, neglected structures in the functional paradigm, became part of the field. Factional conflicts engaged members dedicated to changing or displacing the organization out of which the faction emerged and other competing factions.

Political actions also take place in an *arena*. The concept of the arena was meant to provide an alternative to the functional idea of a political structure composed of individual statuses. Instead the arena referred to a temporal-spatial abstraction. This space included the agents and organizations that constituted the field involved in the conflict, which always transpired over time. It also included the repertory of values, meanings, and resources upon which agents in the field draw to help attain their goals.

Perhaps the most far-reaching contribution of the processual paradigm was the rejection of the idea of *government* as an essential feature and focus for political anthropology. This rejection provided a watershed in the anthropological perspective of politics. It set the stage for the development of an anthropology concerned with politics instead of a political anthropology that focused on political systems, functions, and structures.

Government was a defining hallmark of the functional paradigm. But exemplars in the processual paradigm attributed "no special significance to government or any other particular type of structure" (Swartz 1968:2). Instead the major research strategy of processual exemplars focused on the goal-oriented activity of leaders and their use of power as they competed for disparate goals. Processes related to public goals and the differential distribution and uses of power were considered to be political regardless of whether they occurred within or had relevance to institutions of government. That opened the door for analysis of politics in other, more mundane spheres of social existence, and for the analysis of politics related to personal ambitions and goals, either in or outside political institutions. I will return to the idea of government in Chapter 11 and recuperate it in a practice theory model that reveals its dynamic processes.

To demonstrate the dynamic quality of these concepts, Swartz, Turner, and Tuden (1966) developed a model of political process that they adopted from Turner's (1957) idea of the social drama. In other contexts this model has been referred to as a *political phase development*, an *extended case method*, and a *microhistory* (Gluckman 1965; Swartz 1968). The model of the social drama provided a context in which to demonstrate the paradigm's salient ideas. Each phase of the drama—breach, crisis, mobilization, countervailing measures and redressive mechanisms, peace—embodies in one way or another the paradigm's central ideas.

The process begins with a *breach* in the peace of social relations. This results in a *crisis* and leads to the *mobilization* of powerful forces on each side of the breach. Concern over the outcome of the potential conflict results in *countervailing measures* by leaders and others within and outside the affected political field. If the conflict continues, agents then develop and deploy *adjustive* or *redressive mechanisms*. Ultimately, *peace* is restored and normal relations among the contending parties are established.

The authors concluded that with the restoration of peace, the social, cultural, and political relations of the parties involved in the political contest would be different from those that existed previously. This is a reasonable, if not startling, conclusion. But, in effect, the process represented the resolution of a quotidian altercation. As presented it does not appear amendable to a resolution of a contradiction at the heart of the system and, therefore, does not result in qualitative change in the system. The restoration of peace seems to be the end goal of the social drama. The ideas upon which the model was based sounded exciting. But the model remained disturbingly functional. This was rectified largely by the work of F. G. Bailey (1969).

NEOPROCESS: THE CAPSTONE

Bailey (1969) provided a skillful refinement and synthesis of processual ideas. On the one hand, his work *Stratagems and Spoils* is an excellent handbook for political action. Bailey provided considerable insight into how a leader or aspiring leader (you, for example) could go about winning a political prize, Bailey's term for the political goal. On the other hand, *Stratagems and Spoils* provided a methodology for political anthropologists to explore political dynamics and processes beyond that suggested by other political paradigms. This book was also the first of several works in which Bailey (1983, 1988, 1991) exposes the humbuggery, manipulation, rhetoric, hegemonic lies, and outright deceit that politics necessarily includes if an agent is to win the prize.

The politics described in *Stratagems and Spoils* was a game governed by rules, the outcome of which could not be calculated quantitatively (Bailey claimed innumeracy and disinterest in the mathematics of game theory). Instead the game and its outcome were determined empirically, according to the framework for analysis that Bailey established. The game of politics involved five rules with variations on how they could be manipulated by the players. In general, the rules regulated the prizes to be gained, the eligibility to participate, the composition of the teams, the conduct of the game, and the handling of violations of these rules. The players and their conduct are central to Bailey's idea of politics.

The players comprised teams. These might be either *moral* or *transactional*. A moral team has a clear, established, and respectable place in the game. A transactional team is ambiguous, not well established, and lacks respect. Its goal is to replace existing moral teams in the game. Transactional teams try to accomplish this by manipulating the rules of conduct, which also limits play by moral teams.

Because of their respectability, moral teams are required to play by *normative rules* that were generally agreed on publicly and ethically. Transactional teams use *pragmatic rules* aimed at producing the best outcome, even if they involve dirty tricks. In the context in which Bailey places these variables, the game of politics exists in near perpetuity because the process of the game is, in effect, an unresolvable dialectic, although Bailey did not use the Marxist-loaded term.

The strategies of Bailey's game are framed in a model that redefines many of the ideas that first established the processual paradigm. In Bailey's model, *structure* is neither an organization of statuses nor a political field or arena. A *political structure* refers to the rules enumerated above that regulate the behavior, rights, and duties of those agents involved in the politics. Politics takes place in a social, cultural, and natural environment. The *environment*, together with political structures, constitutes the *political system.* The latter is an abstract entity that has nothing to do with states, lineages, tribes, or any other preconceived system. The *resources* essential to building power to pursue the prize exist in the environment, which, along with the structures, constrain the behavior of the players involved.

The teams also have *leaders.* Though their behavior and practices are regulated by the structure, leaders do have latitude in whether they apply rules normatively or pragmatically as they use the power available to them. The competition between the teams constitutes the dialectic that accounts for change in politics over time and space and therefore changes in the political system, the environment, and rules of the game.

For Bailey, too much political stability and integration are deadly. They cause the demise of political structures when they are confronted by teams that are more dynamic and less integrated and adapted to their environment. Although the configuration and composition of teams can and will vary, as models they assume the following baseline characteristics.

A moral team is composed of a leader who enjoys a relationship with a core of supporters who believe in the leader and what she or he stands for. The members of the team engage in complex but relatively unspecialized activities. They are, however, committed to highly focused and multiple goals, and members must accommodate themselves to the realities of these expectations. The team manifests a rigidity imposed by the normative rules that regulate their political actions. The rules require the team's actions to be aboveboard and open to scrutiny. They are on front stage constantly, and to some extent their moves are predictable. Moral teams can easily develop into bureaucracies and their politics can become rigid and stultifying.

A transactional team is composed of a leader of a body of followers and hirelings who are attached to the leader for what they can personally get out of the relationship. The goals of the team are immediate, narrowly defined, and singular. Team members are specialized in their practice, which is aimed at attaining a particular prize. The team operates behind the scenes and responds to particular situations unpredictably and flexibly. The team's behavior and tactics are regulated by pragmatic rules. It uses whatever strategy and tactic work to attain the prize. It does not have to be ethical and dirty tricks may prevail. But to help its chances for future support, the team presents a normative face when it is on stage. Transactional teams tend to be unstructured and loosely bounded networks of political agents. They approximate the idea of a faction.

The new ideas and strategies that Bailey presents provided the processual paradigm with a model for conflict and change that revealed the unending process that makes politics dynamic. Peace and cohesion were not the result of conflict. New conflict among new teams, those always in and emerging from the wings of the stage upon which the game is played, is the source and outcome of conflict. In dialectical thinking, contradictions beg resolution. And each resolution provides the basis for new conflicts, which suggests that there never really is a resolution. Transactional teams always stand in dialectical opposition to moral teams and pose a threat to them, a contradictory discrepancy at the heart of the system as Gluckman (1965) understood it. This notion is implicit in Bailey's thinking about the competition between moral and transactional teams (also see Giddens 1979).

Bailey paraphrased Marx when he suggested that unstructured networks of political actors always lurk in the wings of existing political structures, waiting to emerge and challenge the political dominance and hegemony of existing structures. Bailey's analysis of these relations and practices relates to other dimensions of the political process. One is a concern with the place of networks of human relations in the political process, and another is the place of factions in the political process.

In the terminology of network analysis, those transactional teams lurking in the wings of existing political structures represent action sets (Mayer 1966). For Bailey, action sets are the unbounded or loosely bounded networks of political agents that constitute political factions. Factions are those fluid and flexible networks of transactional relations that strive to destroy the organizations that birth them and establish themselves permanently as moral teams in the political arenas of their society.

MUDDLES IN THE MODEL

The processual paradigm was not without problems, such as the implicit functionalism in its "dynamic model" of the social drama. Some of its other dynamic concepts, such as the political field and political arena, were ambiguous and difficult to apply. The ideas of political field and arena sounded exciting, but their practical application was fraught with methodological difficulty. The temporal and spatial structure and size of the field and arena and their identification and priorities were easily analyzed in small-scale, institutionally less complex societies. It was difficult to apply the ideas of field and arena in institutionally complex situations where local-level, urban political fields and arenas overlap with other venues and levels of political organization at state and federal levels (Kurtz 1973). Attempts to clarify the field and arena (Swartz 1968) muddled the model more, and they continued to be used in a variety of ways, often interchangeably. Today, if these ideas are used at all, they exist as metaphors for structures that are difficult to objectify.

As we saw in Chapter 4, authority structures and leaders, not power, are the proper focus of legitimacy. To argue as Swartz, Turner, and Tuden

(1966) did that legitimacy is a kind of support and that power is legitimate unnecessarily muddles the idea of legitimacy. It is true that the authority of leaders and agents rests on the support of others. But power cannot be legitimate apart from the authorities who have and use power. Power simply exists as resources whose use by leaders, wisely or unwisely, influences the support upon which they rely and the legitimacy of their status as leaders.

In the processual paradigm, the study of factions was supposed to lead to the nexus of political action and conflict (Swartz, Turner, and Tuden 1966; Swartz 1968). This did not happen. Some authors, Bailey for example, used the idea creatively to analyze various political processes. But even Bailey's idea of the faction as a transactional team did not become salient in the thinking of political anthropologists. As Bujra (1973) pointed out, the promise of factions for political analysis was short-lived and the analyses in which political anthropologists engaged were not much enlightened by the idea of factions.

There are reasons for this. In part it was because discovering types of factions, a functional practice, became more important than exploring their political dynamics (Nicholas 1965, 1966). Even more important, factions simply were not as dynamic an element in political processes as they were initially thought to be. The excitement they created, and still can as they did among archaeologists looking for the key to social and cultural change (Brumfiel and Fox 1996), is not borne out by their importance in political processes. Bailey suggests that factions become important players in the political game only when they become permanent competitors for power, that is, moral teams dedicated to more lasting and durable goals. Too often they fade as the immediate goals that motivate their organization in the first place quickly fizzle out.

There were omissions in the study of politics by processual practitioners, but this is not a serious grievance. Recall that any paradigm selects some issues for analysis and rejects others. Nonetheless, the processual paradigm largely ignored the role of kinship in political process. To a significant degree, this reflects the different orientations of British social and American cultural anthropologists. The British were fascinated by the complexity of kinship structures and attentive by necessity to their prevalence in the colonies. American political anthropologists always were and continue to be less fascinated by the study of kinship. In part this was because, as noted, by the 1960s, when the processual paradigm originated, most of the problems related to kinship had been resolved.

Finally, the hallmark idea of conflict in Swartz, Turner, and Tuden's (1966) interpretation of the processual paradigm incorporated too much and was too general. Gluckman was correct to make distinctions between surface disturbances of social life, conflicts, and contradictions to identify practices that cause divisions in human societies. But his idea of conflict is not what conflict meant to many processual exemplars.

I consider Gluckman's (1965) surface disturbances of social life to be *quotidian altercations*. At one level, such altercations represent the ever-present, nagging problems that persist and recur in day-to-day living, which Gluckman identified as competition, strife, quarrels, fights, and the like. At a more intrinsic level, quotidian altercations may also involve leaders in recurrent issues and events that have deeper and more fundamental roots in a political community and that, as leaders work them out, result in "peace" but not much change in the structure of relations. Processual exemplars did not comply with Gluckman's idea of conflict as social oppositions at the heart of a system to account for changes in sociopolitical statuses and roles. Instead, processual exemplars relegated conflict to the quotidian altercations that imbue everyday life, and these altercations do not necessarily result in significant change in political statuses and roles.

But they can under certain circumstances. If their effect is joint, cumulative, and long-lasting, they may evoke changes in statuses and roles because under these circumstances they approximate the spatial and temporal aspects of political conflict. Curiously, Bailey (1969) rarely uses the term conflict. Still, his analyses come closer to Gluckman's framework than to most other processual exemplars.

Despite the emphasis that the processual exemplars placed on conflict, their analyses were quite functional. Gluckman's ideas of conflict and contradiction had deeper methodological implications for political process, and they were largely ignored by processual practitioners. Along with the idea of quotidian altercation, conflict and contradiction as driving forces in political evolution are explored more fully in Chapter 10 in the topic of the evolution of politics.

8

THE PARADIGM OF
POLITICAL ECONOMY

Of the paradigms that direct research in political anthropology, political economy is the only one that comprises a separate social science. A social science of political economy can be traced at least from eighteenth-century thinkers such as Adam Smith and Adam Ferguson [some begin with Aristotle's distinction between family and state economies (Beard 1957)] and into the mid-nineteenth century. At that point, political economy bifurcates between a radical Marxist political economy and conservative classical (A. Smith 1804 [1759], 1904 [1776]) and neoclassical (J. Mill 1844; J. S. Mill 1848) political economies. As a result of Marx's ideas and reactions to them, the development of political economy thinking is a consequence of the century-long debate that social scientists in general, including anthropologists, have carried on with the ghost of Karl Marx.

At the core of that debate was Marx's radical critique of political economy thinking at the time. Over the last one hundred and fifty years, the basic concern of political economy has remained the same: How human labor engaged the production, distribution, and consumption of material goods to satisfy human needs and wants. Until Marx, these concerns were largely ahistorical, idealist, supportive of capitalist economies, and, except for their functional implication for societies integrated through political economic relations, devoid of a unifying theoretical orientation. Marx added a historical dimension to try to account for change, especially the evolution of capitalism, and theoretical formulations to address the material relationship between economics, power, and ideology that transformed political economy into a critique of capitalism (Donham 1999).

The basic idea of political economy today remains the same: How work satisfies human needs. And in anthropology the paradigm retains a largely Marxist methodology. However, the theoretical emphasis has shifted considerably. Much of the explanation for political economic processes and relations remains grounded in a materialist discourse. But a neo-Marxist research strategy situates ideology, an idealist power resource, as a material force in political economic relations. Exemplars of this neo-Marxist methodology argue that ideology becomes corporealized as a material force through the actions of political agents who are in effect created, defined, and reproduced ideologically (Gramsci 1971; Laclau 1979; Laclau and Mouffe 1985; Godelier 1988; Donham 1999). This neo-Marxist methodology is embedded in a cultural Marxism or, synonymously, in a Gramscian perspective that subordinates the explanatory power of the economic base to political forces embedded in the ideological superstructure.

The paradigm of political economy in political anthropology has a complicated history. To understand it, we need to understand problems raised in nineteenth-century neoclassical and Marxist political economy thinking, as well as how problems from these orientations were developed in the anthropology of political economy. Because of its curious history, the political economy paradigm remains the most holistic, multidimensional, multifaceted, and theoretically diffuse of the paradigms of political anthropology. Exemplars of the paradigm explore political economic relations from theoretical formulations that are material and idealist, epistemologically ethnographic (relativist) and ethnological (cross-cultural), and, in some instances, independent of and, in others, deeply embedded in economies of dominant Western societies.

POLITICAL ECONOMY

Classical and neoclassical economic theory (A. Smith 1804 [1759], 1904 [1776]; J. Mill 1844; J. S. Mill 1848) shared many ideas, with some modification, of course. Its exemplars established capitalist, free market economies as the basis for political economic theory, assumed that the economy operated independently of social institutions, believed in the universality and beneficial power of the market, and sought "natural" laws related to the market and the organizations of labor involved in satisfying human wants through the production, distribution, and consumption of material goods. Along with the continual insemination of capitalism with a Calvinist work ethic, the received political economy theory contended that *most* people had a "natural propensity to work, truck, barter and exchange" (Smith 1804 [1759] cited in Giesbrecht 1972:69) in their own self-interest. Reminiscent of the recent "supply side" economic practice and ideology of the Reagan administration in the United States, some political economy theory argued that the poor were "naturally" slothful and decided that extreme motivations were necessary to ensure their labor. When William Townsend urged repeal of the English Poor Laws in 1786 that guaranteed subsistence as a traditional social right, he argued that the "natural" force of fear of hunger was the most efficacious inducement to get the impoverished to work (Polanyi 1944; LeClair and Schneider 1968).

Neoclassical economic theory increasingly became differentiated from classical theory. Gradually its exemplars assumed that certain aspects of an economy were a given and therefore needed no explanation. Among these were presumptions that markets and scarcity were universal features of the economy and, since human wants also were thought to be insatiable, that scarcity required individuals to economize by making rational, value-laden decisions dedicated to overcoming structural constraints that impeded sufficiency. Eventually, in the latter nineteenth century, these ideas conduced the modern concept of the "economic man" dedicated to maximizing gain and profits (Veblen 1953 [1899]; Giesbrecht 1972). True to the positivist formulations of economic theory at the time, neoclassical economic theory determined that history was irrelevant to economic theory, and ignored any relationship between economics, power, and ideology (Donham 1999).

Marx did not break totally with neoclassical economic theory. He agreed, for example, that individuals make rational economic choices (Donham 1999). But Marx did upset nineteenth-century philosophy and social theory when he challenged two among many of their hallowed assumptions. First, he challenged the idealist assumption that the "Spirit" force of the Hegelian dialectic was the determinant for the organization of human society. And second, he challenged Auguste Comte's positivist law of statics, which held that the proper study of the human condition should emphasize the functional relations of that condition and not the laws of dynamic social change.

Marx countered with two of his own assumptions. He purposefully denied the primacy of the law of statics and introduced his own ideas of the cause of dynamic social change. One argued that it was the "mode of production" of material life and neither a "spirit force" nor human consciousness that determined the social, political, and intellectual conditions of human life. Marx's idea of a mode of production established a relationship between the social relations of production, the forces and means of production, and surpluses in labor value and material (Marx 1970 [1859]). In the second he asserted that it was not the circularity of Hegel's thesis, synthesis, antithesis dialectic that reflected change in the human condition. Instead Marx argued that it was the ongoing attempt to resolve the *contradiction* between the material forces of production and the social relations of production that generated social change. This contradiction emerged as capitalists gradually usurped total control of the means of production and relegated artisans and craftspeople to the status of wage laborers. Rhetorically this contradiction referred to the class war between workers and capitalists that Marx thought to be imminent. The negation of social classes and the state was the ultimate goal of the non-capitalist utopia that Marx envisaged.

Marx challenged the existing neoclassical theory with sufficient anti-capitalist rhetoric to have his ideas pushed out of mainstream Western social science thinking until they became less threatening, nearly a century later. Today in the emergent capitalist world order, his ideas seem relatively harmless, even though many of his prognostications have been remarkably accurate. The unchecked free-trade flow of commodities, labor migrations, the spread of capitalism, intense competition between capitalist enterprises, the increased gap between the rich and the poor, persistent social and economic crises, booms and busts, and the development of wealthy nations through the impoverishment of others were all predicted by Marx.

Marx tried to account for these processes in a body of complementary ideas that emphasized the powerful influence of the material conditions of human life, dialectical contradictions, modes of production, and the subordination of the ideological superstructure to the determining influence of the economic base. Today most of these ideas are politically benign. Still, some, such as the importance Marx placed on the economic base over the ideological superstructure, continue to generate debate.

POLITICAL ECONOMY AND ANTHROPOLOGY

The paradigm of political economy in anthropology is now a derivative largely of Marx's ideas. But while an anthropological political economy was developing that relied on the ideas of Marx, another was developing among exemplars whose ethnographic interpretations ignored, rejected, and avoided Marx's ideas. The political economy that helped to establish the paradigm in political anthropology derives more from this latter body of thought. Exemplars of this orientation, the substantive approach to political economy, accepted Marx's ideas only gradually. It is the topic of the next section.

Today the discipline of anthropology, more than any other social science, has defined itself through its opposition to capitalism. That does not mean that exemplars of an anthropological political economy were fellow travelers in disguise. It means that some anthropologists were sufficiently preconditioned by anomalies in their data to accept Marx's ideas as a basis for their research agendas. These data began to reveal much of what Marx had presaged to be a result of the centuries during which capitalist nations expanded and through colonial and imperial policies subordinated to their economic advantage those people who became the objects of anthropological research. Marx's ideas simply provided alternative explanations for the extant social formations of anthropological subjects than existing ideas. And political economy provided the paradigm best suited to these agendas and explanations.

In anthropology a Marxist political economy developed largely in response to the influence of neoclassical economic ideas. Because of their traditional focus on non-Western "exotic" societies, anthropologists rejected the idea that economic principles operated independently of social institutions (Malinowski 1961 [1922]; Polanyi 1957). It was ethnographically obvious that markets were not universal. But a long debate emerged in the 1960s regarding the universality of market principles in human economic practice (Polanyi 1944, 1947, 1957; Dalton 1961; Cook 1966; LeClair and Schneider 1968). Some anthropologists argued that principles related to market exchange were universal in human economies. Others argued that markets were peculiar only to capitalist societies. Anthropologists found ethnographic evidence that human beings were not endowed with a "natural" proclivity to work. Instead, anthropologists attributed a Zen-like attitude to the world's least complex societies that provided an illusion of affluence in the absence of most things (Sahlins 1972). Finally, anthropologists used Marx's ideas to rectify the failure of neoclassical theory to account for any relationship between power, economics, ideology, and the construction of human state and stateless formations (Leacock 1954; Wolf 1959, 1982; Wolf and Hansen 1972; Nash 1979; Taussig 1980; Mintz 1985; Donham 1999).

An anthropology of political economy that relied on Marx's ideas to address these concerns emerged in the 1940s through the research presented in *The People of Puerto Rico* (Steward et al. 1956). Contributors to this work argued that the social construction of Puerto Rican society was an epiphenomenon to a long history of capitalist penetration and exploitation. As was common in the social sciences at large at that time, any overt expression of Marx's ideas was guarded or disguised. In this instance, anthropologists argued that their research was concerned with culture history (Wolf 1956; Roseberry 1988). As Marx's ideas gradually came to be perceived as less of a threat to Western capitalist hegemony, other ideas provided methodologies for a variety of political economic approaches that attempted to explain the historical organization of contemporary human society and culture. As in no other dimension of anthropological endeavor, political economic theory in anthropology became entwined with that of other social sciences—history, political science, sociology, political economy—and provided a distinct interdisciplinary flavor to political economic analyses. Two of these approaches stand out.

In the first approach, exemplars of dependency and world systems theory concluded that developed and less-developed nations were structurally linked historically, both to modern colonial empires and, in the Mediterranean, to those of Ancient Greece and Rome. They argued that developments in the world's economic centers resulted from their exploitation of societies on the peripheries of their zones of influence and of peoples, such as peasants, within their own nations. This resulted in the underdevelopment of peripheral societies and their economic dependence on the developed centers (Frank 1967, 1969; Wallerstein 1974; Roseberry 1988). Other researchers established this process among early non-Western civilizations, such as those in preconquest Middle America (Feinman 1996; Carmack, Gasco, and Gossen 1996). Still others tried to account for the social and political organizations of peripheral societies, such as Sicily, as a result of their status as a periphery to the powerful Mediterranean centers, such as Greece and Rome, for over two millennia (Schneider and Schneider 1976).

In the other approach, exemplars developed the idea that modes of production could cause social and political change. They argued that in some instances, modes of production accounted for the development of stages in social evolution as a result of complex relations between technology, economics, politics, and social organization. A goal here was to account for the evolution and dominance of the capitalist mode of production. Others sought to account for the articulation between modes of production in extant political economic systems as a way to understand the different routes from one mode of production to the capitalist mode (Terray 1971; Godelier 1978; Meillasoux 1981; Bloch 1983; Roseberry 1988).

Most exemplars separated the political economy of world systems and mode of production theory. But the two approaches are not necessarily exclusive. Wolf (1982) rejected the idea of the evolution of modes of production. Instead he showed how the spread of a capitalist mode of production beginning in the sixteenth century impacted on non-Western societies that relied on precapitalist modes of production and subsequently relegated them to positions of inferiority and dependency.

Most recently, anthropologists with neo-Marxist proclivities have subordinated the power of material forces in Marx's economic base to the power of ideas in the political-ideological superstructure, but without necessarily succumbing to the Marxist dictum that equated culture with ideology. Some thinkers follow an independent path in this regard (Wolf 1999). But in general, the neo-Marxist revision of political economy follows two paths: a path of cultural Marxism and a Gramscian path. They are not mutually exclusive and differences in the work of exemplars of these paths are a matter of emphasis. As noted previously, I think they are generally synonymous, since the relationship between culture and ideology is central and formative to both paths.

Exemplars of cultural Marxism (Nash 1979; Taussig 1980, 1987; Godelier 1988; McDonald 1993a, 1993b, 1999; Donham 1999) owe much, directly or indirectly, to the humanistic Marxism of Raymond Williams (1977) and to Marcus and Fischer's (1986) critique of the ethnographic method. Of these works, those by Taussig (1980, 1987), Nash (1979), and Donham (1999) are the best known. Each used an interpretive, cultural analysis that emphasized the role of ideology in shaping the relations of production of societies on the peripheries of the world capitalist system. Taussig and Nash interpret these relations in capitalist mining and plantation enterprises in South America. Donham uses an analysis of the current status of Marxist theory to interpret them in practices related to the reproduction of inequality in Maale villages in Ethiopia. In each case, individuals involved in these enterprises used ideological constructions grounded in traditional and contemporary symbolic formations to provide themselves with, on the one hand, a mode of resistance and, on the other, an accommodation to their exploitation.

The Gramscian path derives from the writing of Antonio Gramsci (1971) (and is sometimes also referred to as neo-Marxist). In anthropology, Gramsci's ideas empowered an extensive body of writing that is centered largely around his idea of hegemony. Only a small portion of this literature relates to political economy. Most Gramscian anthropologists use hegemony as it is interpreted by Raymond Williams (1977) and others, and not by Gramsci (Kurtz 1996b). But, curiously, Gramscians who address political economic concerns are truer to the idea of hegemony as it was formulated by Gramsci (Carstens 1991; Kurtz and Nunley 1993; Kaplan and Kelly 1994; Kurtz 1996b). In whatever way exemplars account for hegemony, they articulate ideas related to hegemony and culture to understand political economic processes.

These diverse orientations account for the richness of the political economy paradigm in political anthropology. They also add to the complexity of the paradigm. Unlike any of the other paradigms of political anthropology, political economy continues to develop, gain in influence, and provide ideas that penetrate other political paradigms, such as political evolution. The influence of the paradigm developed only gradually as its practitioners overcame the general prejudice in anthropology against Marx's ideas. This history is explored next.

POLITICAL ANTHROPOLOGY AND THE PARADIGM OF POLITICAL ECONOMY

A paradigm of political economy specific to political anthropology has not existed as I will develop it below. As it has been traditionally presented, political economy in political anthropology differs little from that which is characteristic of the anthropology of political economy

(McGlynn and Tuden 1991). I conceive of a political economic paradigm for political anthropology that differs from its more inclusive disciplinary and anthropological counterparts in specific ways.

To begin with, it is narrower in scope and more specific in focus. It does not address global processes represented by categories such as dominant political centers and subordinate economic peripheries, grand schemes based on contradictions between elements inherent in modes of production to account for change, or generalized articulations between different modes of production. These are the concerns of its more inclusive counterpart. The paradigm does address change, some of which is qualitative and large scale, such as the evolution of political society (Fried 1967). But the most telling distinction is the attention the paradigm gives to how political agents—leaders and others—enter and influence these processes through their acquisition and manipulation of economic and ideological instruments of power as they pursue political goals. These agents may be as specific as a Melanesian big man and Chicago ward boss or as categorical as big men and a city government. The paradigm in political anthropology explores how the political practices of agents may result in social and cultural change (Gramsci 1971; Giddens 1979).

In general, the fundamental ideas that constitute the paradigm in political anthropology remain concerned with how the production, distribution, and consumption of economic resources satisfy human needs and wants. But, because of its Marxist bias, exemplars of the paradigm in political anthropology emphasize different elements of this interest than do their counterparts. For example, Marxist political economic theory stressed the political economic importance of production through the idea of the mode of production. The earliest dimensions of the paradigm in political anthropology ignored production to such an extent that production was relegated to insignificance in anthropological thinking on economic matters at large until well past the middle of the twentieth century. Instead, exemplars emphasized the role of economic distribution in political economy.

The emphasis on the role of distribution came to anthropology through the work of the economic historian Karl Polanyi (1944, 1947, 1957). Polanyi skirted Marx's ideas and offered alternatives. He stressed the functional importance for socioeconomic integration of systems of economic distribution involved in the practices of reciprocity and redistribution. Reciprocity referred to patterns of exchanges between status equals. He defined redistribution as the distribution among a political community by its political authorities of resources provided to those authorities through taxes, tribute, appropriations, and the like. He ignored any consideration of production as a determinant force in creating these goods or in human affairs generally.

The posture that he and other social scientists adopted regarding Marx's ideas may have been due to a genuine anti-Marx bias. It also may simply have been a prudent reaction to the weight of the social and political atmosphere exuded by the House Un-American Activities Committee, loyalty oath requirements, and the fear of being dubbed a communist or fellow traveler. But Marx's ideas resonated among a generation of anthropologists who emerged in the mid-twentieth century. The following paraphrase of comments on economics by an anthropology professor of mine in the late 1950s connotes the extent to which ideas of production were subverted in anthropological thinking to functional considerations of distribution.

This professor said that the production of goods in primitive societies is simple. People make what they need out of the material at hand. Distribution is complex because it entails complicated systems of reciprocity and redistribution (he provided definitions here). These processes are important because they function to maintain the social integration and cohesion of primitive societies. In complex modern societies, the process is reversed. Production becomes complex because of the complicated fabrication networks that are involved in producing even the simplest commodity. Distribution, however, is simple. The finished product is conveyed to a store where one only has to go to purchase it, and economic integration is attained through market principles.

In practice, a discourse that presaged the political economy paradigm in political anthropology flowed through much of the paradigmatic literature of political anthropology parallel to Marx's influence in anthropology. Functionalists talked about the economic privileges that accrued to state governments because of their right to tax and otherwise acquire economic resources (Fortes and Evans-Pritchard 1940). Processual exemplars conceptualized power as the control of material resources, however they were obtained (Nicholas 1966, 1968), and distinguished strong from weak leaders based in part on the "credit" they have with their followers and their constant efforts to increase that credit through exchanges of goods and services (Bailey 1969). Exemplars of political evolution attempted to account for the emergence of power and authority from the episodic authorities of hunters and gatherers to state governments as a result of the redistribution function of political leaders and polities (Sahlins 1963; R. M. Adams 1966; Fried 1967). By the middle of the twentieth century, the closest relationship of the paradigm to a Marxian political economy was V. Gordon Childe's (1946, 1951a, 1951b) contribution to explaining political evolution in archaeology.

Redistribution undeniably represents a political economic relationship that has implications for relations of power and authority. But it is largely overlooked in the current discourse on political economy in political anthropology. Disregard of the idea of distribution obfuscates how the political economy paradigm of political anthropology was merged with Marx's ideas.

The paradigm of political economy emerged formally in political anthropology when Dalton (1961) appropriated the ideas of Polanyi (1944, 1947, 1957). Dalton wanted to sharpen the distinction between an economic anthropology based on practices of anthropological subjects and ethnographic empiricism and economics based on the presumed universality of neoclassical economic theory concerned with economizing, scarcity, rational choice, and market principles. Dalton attempted to introduce Polanyi's views into a specific anthropological context that separated market economies from "primitive" economies.

Polanyi (1944, 1947, 1957) argued that existing economic theory was relevant to contemporary market economies only. To establish an economic anthropology he distinguished between a *substantive* and a *formal* approach to economics in anthropology and asserted that there was no necessary connection between the two. Polanyi identified substantive economics with "tribal" and "archaic" societies. In these societies, people satisfied their material wants without the benefit of markets through interchanges with their natural and social environments. He identified formal economics with market-based Western economies and assumptions of neoclassical economic theory. He then emphasized forms of economic integration provided by reciprocity, redistribution, and market exchange. Polanyi associated reciprocity and redistribution with the economies of "tribal" and "archaic" societies. Markets were exclusive to contemporary Western societies (LeClair and Schneider 1968).

Polanyi's view of the economics of "tribal" and "archaic" societies appealed to many anthropologists, but not all, and his ideas generated a rash of theoretical criticism (LeClair and Schneider 1968). Throughout the 1960s and 1970s, anthropologists associated with substantive and formal economic methodologies engaged in an intellectual internecine feud to claim the high ground of economic thinking in anthropology (LeClair and Schneider 1968). By the 1980s, through merger and inbreeding, the distinction had largely vanished and was replaced by an alternative and less polemical economic anthropology.

In and of itself, the debate over economics in anthropology had little to do with political economy. But the idea of economic distribution provided an entree to political economy in political anthropology that initially avoided Marx's ideas, but that also gradually became attentive to them. At the time, the economic ideas of Karl Marx were still presumed to be loaded with revolutionary rhetoric and intention. Polanyi's explanation of the integrative power of systems of distribution and market exchange provided alternatives to any consideration of the dynamics of production and its insinuation of Marx's ideas of change triggered by forces in the modes and means of production and their consequent class contradictions. As these ideas were explored in the paradigm of political evolution, the question of how the resources to be distributed got there in the first place gave rise to insights into the fundamentals of political economy in anthropology: How and why do people produce resources above the basic per capita level of biological necessity?

In the following sections I will consider the political economy of political anthropology in three contexts. One shows how Polanyi's idea of redistribution came to incorporate ideas of production. Another explores how Marx's idea of a mode of production related to politically directed economic practice. The third uses a neo-Marxist, or cultural Marxism/Gramscian approach, to consider the role of ideology in political economic processes.

DISTRIBUTION AND PRODUCTION: FRIED

Morton Fried's (1967) *The Evolution of Political Society* is a classic analysis of political evolution. It also was a precursor of Marxist analysis in political economic theory. At a time when Marx's ideas were just becoming acceptable in American anthropology, Fried used some, albeit gingerly, to analyze the political economic relationship between political leaders and social and political organizations and the evolution of stratification from egalitarian through ranked to stratified societies.

Fried defined egalitarian and ranked societies in terms of the status positions that each provided for occupancy by political leaders. Egalitarian societies had nonexistent or weak leaders because all available statuses are equal and could be occupied by anyone in the society. In ranked societies, fewer status positions are available for occupancy and individuals—leaders—competed for these scarce positions. Stratified societies are characterized by an unequal access to available resources. Nomadic hunters and gatherers and some "tribal" societies qualified as egalitarian because of their lack of institutional complexity and political underdevelopment. Ranked societies were organized along lines of kinship—lineages and clans—and big men and weak chiefs prevailed as political leaders. Stratified societies were institutionally complex and dominated politically by strong and centralized chiefdoms and state governments. The evolution of these political formations resulted, on the one hand, from various, well-documented forces of change, such as population growth, technological change, warfare, and slavery. On the other hand, Fried suggested that manipulations by political leaders of economic distribution and production also stimulated social and political evolution.

In addition to emphasizing political evolution, Fried was also concerned with the social and political integration of egalitarian, ranked, and stratified societies. As a result, his version of political economy relied heavily on Polanyi's ideas of reciprocity and redistribution to account for the political integration of each type. But he also couples Polanyi's ideas with some of Marx's to account for qualitative change in sociopolitical relations. The result is a curious melange of functional and evolutionary forces based on Marxist and non-Marxist ideas.

Fried uses the idea of means of production to account for the lack of social and political differentiation among egalitarian societies and their reliance on reciprocity to satisfy their needs. He also subordinates production to the significance of distribution in accounting for change. Instead of expanding the idea that control over how the means of production influenced the social relations involved in production, Fried suggested that systems of distribution related to reciprocity and redistribution ultimately resulted in unequal access to the critical material resources necessary for survival.

At the time, in the 1960s, Fried was correct in emphasizing the relationship of leaders to the distribution of material goods. Marx's ideas were just becoming popular in American anthropology and, for those committed to a substantive role for economics, as Fried was, Polanyi's ideas had more purchase. Also, the ethnographic record emphasized the role that leaders play in redistributing goods much more than it did their role in promoting the production of those resources. Fried's emphasis on distribution instead of production reflected the problem that anthropologists had in coping with political processes from a Marxist perspective.

But Fried also must be credited with opening the door in the political economy of political anthropology to the importance of economic production in the evolution of social stratification. He does this by addressing the very fundamental basis of Marx's means and modes of production: How the social labor—work—that is essential to production is stimulated. Fried suggests that political leaders become powerful by stimulating people to work and produce material goods above the minimal level of biological necessity. Yet curiously, he restricts his analysis to the practices of big men and weak chiefs. Nor does he account for the power that leaders acquire as a result of the production of surpluses that they may appropriate to their own political ends. Instead, true to Polanyi's substantive approach, Fried attributes political power to the role of leaders in the redistribution of goods in the form of sumptuary feasts and potlatches. He bypasses the fact that the production of material goods precedes their distribution, and much that constitutes political power comes from controlling and acquiring the means of production by which goods are made available for distribution in the first place.

When Fried addresses stratified societies, production dissolves as a force in the creation of centralized leaders and economic structures that sharply distinguish rulers from the ruled. Instead, he relies on those presumed forces, the sometime "prime movers" of evolution (which I refer to as the *genetic pulse* of change and discuss in Chapter 9), such as slavery, population growth, and technological change, to account for inequality based on the ambiguous idea of unequal access to resources. From the perspective of a Marxist political economy, inequality derives from the usurpation of the means of production by more centralized and differentiated political economic structures. Fried does not develop further the idea that someone, usually leaders and/or their agents, is deeply implicated in the control of or influence over the material forces of production, while others, usually lower classes, are involved in the daily work of production.

Distribution is a necessary part of political economic processes. But political control and influence over the production of commodities are better gauges of how leaders acquire the power. Redistribution becomes important to the extent that political leaders and agents are able to deploy resources of power strategically and tactically to their own political ends. Wolf's use of the idea of a mode of production brought Marx's ideas more clearly into the political economy of political anthropology.

MODE OF PRODUCTION: WOLF

Marx identified several generalized modes of production that lacked historical or ethnographic verification, such as the feudal, Germanic, capitalist, and Asiatic. Others have added many more, such as lineage and domestic modes of production (Terray 1971; Sahlins 1972). Not all modes have equal explanatory value. Some have been rejected outright.

Eric Wolf (1982) brought the idea of modes of production forcefully into anthropological thinking on political economic processes. He identified a mode of production as "a specific historically occurring set of social relations through which labor is deployed to wrest energy from nature by means of tools, skills, organization, and knowledge" (1982:75). Marx, in contrast, believed that modes of production represented evolutionary stages or levels (Marx 1970 [1859]; Bloch 1983). Wolf rejects this idea, but he does suggest three modes of production that have historical and general anthropological utility: capitalist, tributary, and kinship.

The *capitalist mode of production* emerged on the stage of world politics in the sixteenth century with the expansion of European colonialism. The result was the creation of organizations of labor and markets in the colonies to support the industrial capitalism of the European nations. It developed fully in the eighteenth century. The social relations of production that develop in a capitalist mode are marked by the individual's lack of control of the means of production. In the capitalist mode the means and instruments of production are owned and controlled by capitalists and others are required to sell their labors to capitalists at the market rate established by these same capitalists.

The *tributary mode of production* is associated with political communities ruled by centralized organizations of power and authority characteristic of strong chiefs and the governments of early state formations. In the tributary mode, individuals retain control of the instruments and means of production. But they are required to work and produce for governments, government agents, or others who are obligated to governments in some fashion, such as feudal lords and merchants who provide goods for production. While people have to produce more to satisfy the tribute demands, they continue to control the means of production, although others appropriate the results of their labors.

The *kinship-ordered mode of production* relates to stateless societies, such as hunting and gathering, horticultural, and pastoral political economies whose political communities are nomadic or seminomadic. In these societies, production is embedded in social relations among people related through filiation and descent. Each individual in the context of his or her prevailing kin group or association controls the existing means of production and, as Fried pointed out, political leadership is weak or nonexistent.

For Wolf the utility of the concept of a mode of production is "its capacity to underline the strategic relationships involved in *the deployment of social labor by organized human pluralities*" (1982:76, emphasis added). The idea of social labor as an organization is central to Wolf's conception of a mode of production. Yet there is still considerable ambiguity regarding who deploys social labor and what constitutes an organized human plurality.

Presumably the social labor inherent in a mode of production represents an "organized human plurality" deployed in production by "controllers." Wolf refers to these controllers as a "kinsman, chief, seignorial lord, or capitalist" (1982:74). In a political economic context, these are political leaders, agents, governments, or others, such as capitalists, who are intricately interconnected with structures of political power and authority. Wolf does not make enough of the fact that in the capitalist mode the control of the technology and energy systems that constitute the means and instruments of production also represents control of considerable material political power (R. N. Adams 1975).

Others who have analyzed work as a social phenomenon render the relationship between leadership and those engaged in production more direct than Wolf suggests, but not necessarily in the context of a mode of production (Applebaum 1987; Kurtz and Nunley 1993; Kurtz 1996a). They do make clear that work and social labor are directed by leaders who are more than distant abstractions or mere workmates of the labor force.

These leaders, or controllers, impart values, skills, and models of work that are appropriate for the culture in which the work transpires. Above all the leaders inculcate their aims and those they represent into the aims of the organized plurality (Applebaum 1987). In this rendering, the directive force of the political practice of leaders is critical, but not necessarily in the materialist context that Wolf emphasizes. Instead, those who hold to this position emphasize the importance of ideology in a neo-Marxist framework to account for the fundamental political economic problem of why people work more and produce more than they need for survival.

CULTURAL MARXISM: McDONALD

Taussig (1980, 1987) and Nash (1979) are perhaps the most cited of those anthropologists who apply a cultural Marxism to problems in the overarching political economy of anthropology. Their work is methodologically profound and anthropologically attractive. It is conducted in fashionable experimental and pastoral ethnographic modes (Marcus and Fischer 1986; Clifford 1988) and probes deeply embedded, culturally "exotic" practices by which exploited peoples resist capitalist domination. But their work does not fit the paradigm of political economy in political anthropology. Furthermore, the attention it has received obscures other political economic analyses in cultural Marxism that, while less exotic and perhaps therefore less appealing to anthropologists, are equally profound and conducted in the political economy of political anthropology.

McDonald (1993a, 1993b, 1994, 1995, 1996, 1997a, 1997b, 1999) has developed an extensive literature in the cultural Marxism of political economy in political anthropology. Much like Taussig and Nash, McDonald explores how the impact of capitalist forces of production shapes the culture and social organization of oppressed people who, in McDonald's case, are small-scale dairy farmers in central Mexico. Taussig and Nash explain the resistance and accommodation of the objects of their research through interpretations of pre-Columbian and catholic religious symbols. McDonald analyzes how Mexican dairy farmers respond to capitalist forces that emanate from the North American Free Trade Agreement (NAFTA), the General Agreement on Tariffs and Trade (GATT), and neoliberal economic policies of the former PRI (Revolutionary Institutional Party) government of Mexico. Like Nash's workers, these farmers are fully aware of the forces they confront. But unlike the workers of her research, it is unlikely they will be able to make a cultural accommodation to them. Instead, most will likely succumb to a social Darwinism that is all too common in emerging global capitalist agriculture (Hanson 1990) and many will go bankrupt.

McDonald's work explores political and cultural power, ideology, and conflict through the voices of leaders—presidents of Mexico, aspirants to the presidency, local caciques, political bosses, heads of milk cooperatives, and farmers—and frames their politics in the context of powerful concepts. McDonald (1999) uses Foucault's (1991) concept of governmentality to account for how the practices and rhetoric of government leaders in political economic processes are drastically transforming Mexico's rural economy. From Baudrillard (1983) he appropriates the idea of the simulacra as signs detached from reality to account for much of the political discourse related to political economic processes in Mexico (McDonald 1993a). He explains the vicissitudes in Mexico's political economy as a result of the government's neoliberal policies fostered by NAFTA and demonstrates how the simulacra of governmentality are formed where the forces of production and neoliberal economic policies intersect with affective political myths and symbols. Unlike other political economic analyses, McDonald also has practical recommendations regarding how to situate anthropology as a policy-oriented discipline that may better inform people of the impact of political economic forces. McDonald's work shows that the practical and applied dimensions of anthropology are compatible with anthropology's emphasis on "exotic" and romantic frames of reference.

GRAMSCIAN POLITICAL ECONOMY: KURTZ

Recall from the earlier discussion of political power that a political ideology essentially refers to ideas that justify the exercise of power and serves to mobilize people for action around a system of beliefs. Perhaps the most preeminent concern of a polity is how to infuse their political community with an ideology of work that asserts that the production of goods above minimal levels of survival is for the common good. An ideology of work is not a usual topic of political economic concern. To philosophers and social scientists who shaped the framework of political economy in a Western Europe that was under the influence of Calvinism, any question regarding why people worked seemed to be redundant. Everyone worked, or was expected to, and apparently always had. Recall that classical economic theory even posited that human beings had a "natural" proclivity to work. Those who did not appear to be so disposed, such as the poor and colonized "others," were shamed and chastened both religiously and politically.

Still, even though work is universal, the ethnographic record reveals that not all human populations work equally hard or long. People in stateless societies left to their own devices will work sufficiently to satisfy their needs and wants for subsistence and rituals and no more. Their production of more than is necessary for survival does not seem to be a natural, biological, or spiritually induced behavior. Therefore, why people begin to produce surpluses of goods above levels necessary for survival is a question lurking at the very core of the political economy of political anthropology.

Orans (1966) and Harris (1959) posed the problem of surplus production quite succinctly. Orans wondered why people work harder and longer in state formations than people in stateless formations even though the production apparatus of state formations tends to be more efficient. Harris wondered why people surrender a portion of the result of their labor to a ruling class. How people are motivated to comply with these practices and expectations can be explained in two ways.

Very commonly, anthropologists and others account for why people produce goods that underwrite the power of leaders by blaming it on the singular practice of political coercion. Certainly history shows an incontrovertible use of coercion by governments to gain political ends. Yet Fried (1967) attributes the politically induced motivation to work in stateless formations to cajolery and rhetoric, not coercion. Even in state formations there is reason to doubt the exclusivity attributed to coercion in stimulating production (Lowie 1927; Gramsci 1971; Service 1975; Godelier 1978; Kertzer 1988; Kurtz and Nunley 1993). An alternative to explaining the production of gross surpluses as a consequence of coercion is to account for it through the work and practices of political and cultural agents engaged in *hegemonic culturation* (Kurtz 1996a) to induce an ideology of work among the people of their political communities.

Hegemonic culturation is a political process that relies on Antonio Gramsci's (1971) ideas of hegemony and culture to provide an alternative explanation to coercion for political economic processes. The common idea of hegemony refers to the domination of one state government over another through force and coercion. Gramsci (1971) redefined hegemony as an "intellectual and moral leadership" that is directed by political and cultural agents and posed it in opposition to political coercion. Hegemony is neither an alternative to nor a negation of coercion. At times coercion may be a necessary practice and may complement hegemony. But a hegemony through which agents attempt to change the cultural practices by which a political community habitually does things is less costly and more effective in the long run (Gramsci 1971). To account for these cultural changes Gramsci also put a different spin on the concept of culture than is common in anthropology and cultural studies. He defined culture as "the exercise of thought, the acquisition of general ideas, *the habit of connecting cause and effect* . . . enlivened by [political] organization" (Gramsci 1917, cited in Cavalcanti and Piccone 1975:44; emphasis added).

Simply put, hegemonic culturation refers to the changes induced by a political community's leadership in the perception and understanding of their subjects regarding why they should do something, such as work more. The union of the ideas of hegemony and culture in the concept of hegemonic culturation (Kurtz 1996a) provides a dynamic to explain political economic relations between rulers and ruled and accounts for an ideology of work that does not rely on recourse to coercion.

The belief in the intrinsic value of work becomes a core principle in the articulation and well-being of a political community and its leadership, the production apparatus of the society, and the goals of the leaders. Disruption of this production potential is a major concern of all leaders. Their power, authority, and legitimacy depend largely on the gross surpluses produced by their political communities. An ideology of work that supports these dependencies provides a government an inexpensive and efficient means to ensure the continuation of its political community's apparatus of production and its own political integrity.

Hegemonic culturation also helps to explain why and how cultural ways of doing things through habitual understanding of cause and effect in cultural agency come to appear to be the naturally occurring practices (Kurtz 1996a). Indeed, hegemonic culturation creates the political dynamics by which leaders attempt to inculcate their ideas into the thoughts and practices of the people, mold their culture, and mobilize their energies to comply with and work for the goals of the leaders, a major one of which is a sound political economy based on the predictable labors of their political communities. A central focus of hegemonic culturation in the formation of this economy is the production of a gross surplus of material goods above the minimal level of per capita biological necessity. This is because surpluses above minimal survival requirements do not disperse freely through a political economy to everyone's benefit. Rather, such surpluses are mobilized in institutions related to leadership structures and become a critical part of the reserve of political power upon which leaders depend. They are used by leaders to enact policies, underwrite lifestyles that frequently are sybaritic, aid their followers, and take care of their political communities in times of crises, an altruistic act to be sure. But benevolence is also a political act. Recall that benevolence is one strategy by which leaders help to ensure the legitimacy of their authority and the structure of the political offices they inhabit (Kurtz 1984).

In the process of creating a productive political community, political leaders also try to mold its culture so that the practices and beliefs of its members are in lockstep with the values and goals of the leadership (Kurtz 1996a). The result of this practice is a political culture that is acceptable to the community's leadership. A major political economic goal of a leadership is to produce and reproduce the culture of a political community that is in accord with the leaders' values.

A hegemonic formation of this nature may be desirable to the leadership of a political community, yet it is impossible to acquire fully. Contradictions in human and environmental relations ensure that. From the perspective of political theory, it is not even desirable. Without the conflict induced by contradictions that express different interests and goals among leaders and between leaders and their communities, there would be no change. Such a world cannot exist. The outcome of the dialectical and hegemonic relations of political economy is represented in the paradigm of political evolution. As we will see in the following chapters, the political economy paradigm in political anthropology provides a research strategy for exploring the importance of hegemonic processes for political evolution (Kurtz 1979; McGlynn and Tuden 1991).

9

THE PARADIGM OF POLITICAL EVOLUTION

Neo-evolution and Political Organization

POLITICAL EVOLUTION: POLITICAL SYSTEMS AND ORGANIZATIONS

Political evolution is a metatheory that attempts to explain qualitative changes in political systems and organizations as they are revealed in the increased complexity of social and political organization. Political evolution was not a major concern of exemplars of nineteenth-century cultural evolution. It is largely a by-product of research related to the general and specific neo-evolutionary concerns that emerged after World War II and reformulated the thinking of nineteenth-century evolutionists (L. White 1949, 1959; Steward 1955; Sahlins and Service 1960). Since World War II, anthropologists have developed the paradigm of political evolution to try to account for the qualitative changes in three related evolutionary processes: (1) the differentiation and specialization of political roles and institutions; (2) the emergence and centralization of political authority and power in those roles and institutions; and (3) the role that political organizations and agents play in the functional integration of increasingly specialized, diversified, and stratified political communities (Fried 1967; Y. A. Cohen 1968; Kurtz 1979; McGlynn and Tuden 1991; P. B. Roscoe 1993).

Anthropologists explore these processes in two ways. In the first and most common, they use a materialist approach that considers the rela-

133

tionship among forces such as technology, energy, and environment and practices such as redistribution that drive evolution and the increased complexity of sociopolitical systems (Service 1962; Fried 1967; Y. A. Cohen 1968). That is the topic of this chapter. In the second approach, they try to account for the role that political agents play in political evolution as it is expressed in the nucleation and density of political communities and the centralization of power and authority of leaders in those communities. This concern has received far less attention and is less well developed (P. B. Roscoe 1993). Most commonly, exemplars of political evolution subordinate the practices of political agents to the material forces and processes that drive evolution. The evolution of an agent-driven political evolution is the topic of Chapter 10.

There is a caveat to the evaluation of these evolutionary processes. The idea of political evolution does not imply that there has been an unbroken line of political evolution from prehistory to the present. Eric Wolf makes clear that "the societies studied by anthropologists are an outgrowth of the expansion of Europe and not the pristine precipitates of past evolutionary stages. . . . All human societies of which we have record are 'secondary,' indeed often tertiary, quaternary, or centenary" (1982:76). As a result, the ethnographic record does not support the argument that tribes, for example, evolved out of hunters and gatherers, chiefdoms out of tribes, and so forth. However, the archaeological record does support this process, and archaeological data increasingly have influenced our understanding of political evolution. Instead of providing temporal depth to political evolution, the ethnographic record shows only the political structures of societies at the ethnographic moment when anthropologists recorded their data. Nonetheless, exemplars of the paradigm of political evolution believe that the ethnographic record is sufficient, despite mischief, exploitation, and cultural dislocations by Western colonial powers, to extrapolate the probable forms of political organization that were characteristic of human societies and to depict those forms in a hierarchy from least too most differentiated, specialized, centralized, and politically integrated.

For example, the "great Kalahari debate" of the 1970s and 1980s developed over the origins of the contemporary Bushmen (Kurtz 1994b). When Lee (1982), an authority on the Bushmen, suggested that nomadic hunters and gatherers such as Bushmen represented the original condition of humankind, Wilmsen (1989) provided evidence that contradicted this presumption. He argued convincingly that the ethnographic Bushmen are an epiphenomenon of nineteenth-century colonial expansion in Southwest Africa and that their current adaptation to the Kalahari is in fact quite different from that of their ancestors of a century or so ago. Nonetheless, the episodic leadership of the ethnographic Bushmen does comply with evolutionary theory regarding what their political organization should be like under their current foraging adaptation.

Anthropologists who reject sociocultural evolution find much that is wrong with the assumptions upon which the theory rests. Many reject the idea of evolution utterly. Exemplars use the theory to develop hypotheses of the human condition that need to be tested, reconsidered, and refined. They infer political evolution from the empirical ethnographic data base of sociocultural anthropology. From these data, different research strategies can be applied to seek the regularities in the evolution of political organizations. In one strategy, hypotheses of political evolution are generated that may then be evaluated deductively and ethnologically, that is, comparatively across representations of cultures in ethnographic space and time. Y. A. Cohen (1969), for example, evaluated hypotheses regarding the relationship between sexual practices and social control in a sample of state formations.

In another strategy, data may be extrapolated from the ethnographic record to develop a typology of a particular type of society that reflects an evolutionary process. For example, Claessen (1978) used data from a sample of twenty state formations to develop an evolutionary model of these formations. Others researchers, such as Service (1962), Fried (1967), and Y. A. Cohen (1968), used ethnographic data to develop typologies of political evolution from least to most complex formations of political integration. These typologies are the best known and oldest representation of sociocultural evolution (see also Morgan 1963 [1877]; Goldschmidt 1959; Lenski 1966; Peacock and Kirsch 1973). Typologies represent attempts by anthropologists to bring order to the plethora of relative data that comprise the ethnographic record and to depict the predictable range of functional regularities in social, cultural, and political structures and behavior of their types. The nature of these types is an issue of contention in anthropology.

Fried, for example, questioned the significance of Service's typology of bands, tribes, chiefdoms, and states when he challenged the validity of the type identified as a tribe. Fried wrote, if "I had to select one word in the vocabulary of anthropology as the single most egregious case of meaninglessness, I would have to pass over 'tribe' in favor of 'race.' I am sure, however, that 'tribe' figures prominently on the list of putative technical terms ranked in order of degree of ambiguity" (1967:154). Anthropological conceptualizations of the tribe give credence to Fried's criticism. Sahlins (1968), for example, includes in the idea of the tribe all the types of societies that anthropologists have labeled between nomadic hunters and gatherers and state formations, and that includes chiefdoms. Gluckman (1965) goes even further and includes nomadic hunters and gatherers and some states in the tribal category.

Service (1971), who listed the tribe as a phase in evolutionary theory, committed a rare act of scholarly courage. He conceded Fried's criticism of the idea of the tribe instead of defending his own ideas to the death, and went even further in recommending the destruction of his entire model. Service also recommended that both band and tribe be abolished in favor of the single type, egalitarian society, and that chiefdoms and primitive states be identified as hierarchical societies and archaic civilizations.

Considerable evidence now demonstrates that the ambiguous social and cultural configuration that passes in the anthropological literature as a tribe is a secondary phenomenon. It results from the breakdown of more organized and coherent polities under the impact of the expansion of Western colonialism and capitalism (Fried 1967; Helm 1967; Service 1971). This is corroborated by archaeological evidence from at least one area of the world. In Mesoamerica, the archaeological record of pre-Columbian societies does not reveal physical evidence of any social formation that approximates that of a tribe (Sanders and Price 1968). And long before anthropologists were paying much attention to the impact of Western colonial powers on those peoples that we think of today as post-colonial, Service (1971) presented an eloquent argument on the consequences of that impact. He concluded that evolutionary stages presumed to represent primordial, pristine conditions of humankind cannot be extrapolated from the ethnographic record. This is the same argument that Wolf (1982) used to reject the evolution of modes of production.

Despite arguments over different evolutionary types, exemplars of the paradigm agree on the spheres of social activity that comprise social systems. A social system is made up of spheres of social activity that are played out in political, economic, religious, kinship, legal, and other institutions. Sociocultural evolution is revealed in qualitative changes in those institutionalized spheres of activity. In reality the spheres are all interrelated and can be separated only for purposes of analysis. However, the political sphere of social activity is, arguably, different from the others. To an extent that is not common in the other spheres, political agents, leaders, and governments purposefully acquire and use power to pursue public and private goals. Even more distinguishing, in no other sphere do clearly defined political agents attempt to expand and vertically entrench their power and authority into all other social institutions with the specific intention of influencing human practices, ideas, and changes in those institutions.

Religious institutions may appear to emulate these processes, but they are rarely independent of political institutions. Religious leaders often serve the sources of political authority that try to entrench their interests throughout the institutions of their political communities. Yet it is true that religious leaders may challenge political leaders and attempt to place themselves in positions of political-religious power to create their own hierarchies of control. To co-opt these strategies, political leaders in more complex social formations often become priests and sometimes gods, and proceed to govern with divine sanctions and power. Religious practitioners and institutions are almost always subordinate to, if not tools of, political leaders. Because these leaders attempt to entrench their values and ideologies in all other institutions, it is appropriate to refer to political evolution under the broader rubric of sociopolitical evolution. In practice, the only thing that distinguishes the paradigm of political evolution from the paradigm of twentieth-century neo-evolution is the centrality that exemplars of political evolution give to the role of political organization to account for evolution.

Finally, exemplars of the political evolution paradigm also appropriate and synthesize ideas and constructions from other paradigms to help explain political change. They appropriated the functional idea of a system to explore holistically how political formations, such as chiefdoms, emerge, change, and yet function to retain the integration of increasingly differentiated political systems. From the political economy paradigm, they borrowed materialist ideas related to economic process embedded in production and redistribution to account for political changes. Ideas from the processual paradigm have not been used much to account for the evolution of political systems. However, the next chapter will consider how ideas from both the processual and political economy paradigms can help to account for the role of the political agent in political evolution.

CAUSE AND EVOLUTION

The question of what causes sociopolitical evolution pervades the paradigm. Anthropologists have attributed cultural evolution to a variety of forces, some of which are internal (population growth) and others external (warfare) to a political community. Some use single factors to account for movement from one stage to another, such as the idea that the managerial requirements of large-scale irrigation works gave rise to the state (Wittfogel 1957). Others point out that political evolution is a product of a combination of internal and external factors (Claessen 2000). This idea has been influential in accounting for the evolution of state formations (Carneiro 1970; Service 1971, 1975; Claessen 1978). Multiple-cause models may be more elegant than single-cause explanations, but at best they establish a primacy of factors that precludes others falsely, as though they do not matter. At any evolutionary moment, some factors may be dominant and others subordinate. Yet this does not mean that the subordinate factors cease to give impulse to qualitative change.

The essential point is that no single cause or specific set of causes impels political evolution. Service's assertion, "Down with prime movers!" (1971:25), resonates with good reason. The causes of evolution vary across ethnographic space and time. They are situational, contextual, and contingent. To account for the plethora of potential forces that may move evolution, I suggest that we think of them as embedded genetic pulses that are always at work in human societies to some degree in one form or another.

THE GENETIC PULSE

The genetic pulse refers to those material and sometimes mental forces of evolution, such as warfare, technology, psychological predispositions, population growth, and religious ideologies. The impact of the genetic pulse on evolution is real, although its component forces do not have equal impact on evolution. As noted, they also are historically and ethnographically situational, contextual, and contingent.

The idea of the genetic pulse asserts that no single force moves evolution. Instead, sundry forces are always at work at any given historical moment, and at any historical moment some forces will be more important than others. But none works to the exclusion of others. And political organizations, more than other institutions, respond to these forces, if for no other reason than to try to control them. Still, other factors do influence the forces of the genetic pulse.

It is unlikely that all such forces will be on center stage of any drama that drives change. They are likely to be fomenting in the wings of the existing social and political organizations, like the butterfly of chaos theory who can create a storm next month in New York by stirring the air with its wings in Beijing today (Gleick 1987). Political evolution is likely to be most dynamic where existing and identifiable social structures and organizations that constitute a level of political integration are blurred and in a state of flux, where the rules of political life are indeterminate, and where more complex sociopolitical configurations have not yet emerged fully out of preexisting ones. This condition is represented in the figurative interstices, the political limens such as might exist between big men and chiefs, egalitarian and ranked societies, or moral and transactional teams. In the interstices of ideally modeled polities and political communities, dominant leadership and power relations are ambiguous, unformulated, nascent, yet always astir. It is in these ambiguous, interstitial contexts that the interaction among a variety of dialectical and hegemonic forces creates the intermittent, arhythmic genetic pulse that drives political evolution (Marx 1970 [1859]; Bailey 1969; Donham 1999).

There are caveats to the driving forces of the genetic pulse. Theoretically the pulse will continue to evoke general political change if the social, cultural, and physical environments permit. But in some cases the forces may be impeded by resistance from political communities and polities that have attained a functional equilibrium with their environments and cultures. Impediments that may thwart the impact of the pulse could exist anywhere—in persistent marriage practices, values that support infanticide, an encysted political economy, technological stagnation, a materially impoverished environment, superstition, and so forth. Diverse factors and practices may inhibit change, occasionally for long periods of time, until some event that often appears benign and unnoticed, such as a slight alteration in technology, leadership, relations with neighboring peoples—the fluttering wings of a butterfly—triggers one or more forces of the pulse. If there are no overwhelming constraints, these forces of change will continue, albeit at different speeds, and political organization will move toward centralization.

Political leaders represent one beat of a genetic pulse. But theirs is a formidable thump, for their decisions are more likely than those made in other spheres of human activity to stimulate the forces of the pulse and evoke a positive feedback loop. The evolution of political leadership reveals the extent to which leaders incrementally affect almost everything that transpires. They divide meat from a hunt among the people. They stimulate production. They resolve disputes and punish wrongdoers. They influence how people think and what they think about. They regulate marriage, initiate environmental and technological changes, break up empires, decide to wage war, restructure religions and their dogmas, decide what art is acceptable, and send people to their deaths, among other things.

The ideological rhetoric of some contemporary political wags in the United States and elsewhere asserts that government needs to get off the backs of the people by reducing taxes and dispensing with regulations on business. The evolution from less complex political organization to more centralized governments suggests that this will never happen. Government has been climbing on for too long. Instead, depending on their motivating ideology, governments are likely to only relax the pressure on their citizens' backs until, given the power available to them, they are able to impose themselves someplace else, over what people can read, view on television and in the cinema, or do in the privacy of their bedrooms.

BACKGROUND

The earliest model of political evolution by an acknowledged anthropologist, if not a full-time professional, was developed by Lewis Henry Morgan (1963 [1877]). Morgan drew upon the nineteenth-century idea that the evolution of human societies was an epiphenomenon linked to several lines of progress. Progress to Morgan had two dimensions. One included the accumulation of inventions and discoveries. These accounted for the quantitative aspect of evolution. In the other, progress was reflected in the unfolding, the differentiation and specialization, of human institutional relations out of a psychic unity common to humankind. This accounted for the qualitative component of progress.

Curiously, Morgan is the only anthropologist to attempt to account for the evolution of distinct political organizations. He was only partially successful. In *Ancient Society* (1963 [1877]) he described both an "organic series" of political organizations and their related stages of "government power." For Morgan, the most rudimentary level of political organization included societies in a state of thinly disguised anarchy with a class division based on gender. Subsequent political organization included gens (lineages), phratries (clans), tribes, confederacies, nations, and states. The forms of government power that were loosely articulated with these political organizations evolved through three stages of power. The first was expressed in a council of chiefs. The second included a council of chiefs plus a military commander. And the third added to the second an assembly of the people. Political organization culminated in state formations established in a territorial framework characterized by classes based on private property.

Morgan's work became unacceptable to anthropology and Western scholarship partly because his ideas became tainted with Marxist ideology and revolutionary rhetoric. But they also suffered from a prejudice by British anthropologists who hammered his writings out of print, not because they didn't use his ideas, but because they resented ideas introduced from America (Engels 1942 [1884]). The political evolution paradigm did not recover until after World War II. In the course of reintroducing evolutionary thinking into anthropology, Leslie White (1949, 1959) carried Morgan's political ideas to a final and, still for some, unpopular conclusion. White argued that the victor of the next war would be the heir to the "movement toward ever larger and larger political units [and have] sufficient power and resources to organize the whole planet and the entire human species within a single social system" (1949:388–390). As we saw in the study of political economy, more detailed analysis of sociopolitical evolution had to wait until Marx's ideas were "cleansed" of their revolutionary rhetoric.

This occurred in the 1950s. Around the time of the centennial of the publication of Charles Darwin's *The Origin of Species*, works began to appear that were sympathetic to sociocultural evolution (Steward 1955; L. White 1959; Goldschmidt 1959; Sahlins and Service 1960). Through the 1960s and 1970s, anthropology experienced a revival of interest in cultural evolution. An important component of this revival was renewed interest in political evolution and concern with how political organizations culminated in powerful state formations (Fried 1967; Y. A. Cohen 1968, 1969; Carneiro 1970; Service 1971, 1975).

Evolutionary models suggested by Service (1962, 1975), Fried (1967), and Y. A. Cohen (1968) have been especially influential in understanding political evolution. Service established a typology that included bands, tribes, chiefdoms, and eventually states. Fried developed a model of egalitarian, ranked, and stratified societies. Cohen suggested an evolutionary scheme based on levels of sociotechnological adaptation that he related to hunting and gathering, horticultural, pastoral, agricultural, and industrial societies. Each of these exemplars tries to account for the emergence and integration of increasingly diversified and stratified political communities. Each also suggests that the political sphere of activity is central to the evolution of the entire social formation with which the polity is identified.

Service: Bands, Tribes, Chiefdoms, and States

Service provided one of the most popular and commonly used evolutionary schemes. He appropriated Steward's (1955) idea of levels of sociocultural integration to establish the evolution of bands, tribes, chiefdoms, and states (Service 1962, 1975). Anthropologists and others—even those who shun evolutionary theory—refer to these types to identify ethnographic societies. Construed as levels of integration, each type represents a functional taxon that is presumed to represent the predictable range of social organization associated with the type, some of which also have subtypes. For example, Service divides bands into patrilocal and composite types and categorizes tribes into lineal, cognatic, and composite formations.

Increased efficiency in food production provides the driving force of change in Service's model. The undifferentiated and unspecialized social organization of band societies is related to their nomadic reliance on wild plants and animals for subsistence. The social organization of subsequent types is the consequence of the increased efficiency and skill of their populations in domesticating plants and animals and in producing surpluses of food. These production strategies lead to larger and denser sedentary populations that are more differentiated and specialized in their social roles and institutions, including their political organization.

Although Service introduced new ideas of social structures that went beyond those identified in *African Political Systems*, his typology relies heavily on functional ideas regarding politics. Bands and tribes are largely devoid of discernible political structures. Political organization and practices in bands are infused in the total social structure, whereas those related to tribes are conterminous with their kinship structures, especially the lineage. In addition, the tribe especially is organized around sodalities, or nonresidential associations, such as clans, secret societies, or other voluntary associations that have some corporate political functions and purposes. One might deduce from these criteria that bands are indeed the "peoples without politics" of the structural-functional paradigm (Hoebel 1949b; Sharp 1958).

Chiefdoms and states, on the other hand, are distinguished by increased social inequality and the presence of multiple "centers"—leaders and governments—that coordinate the economic, social, and religious activities of their political communities. Chiefs and heads of state occupy permanent offices, subsidize productive activities, and represent the elite level of a ranked hierarchy of political agents. Chiefs also engage in and manage the redistribution of goods and resources aimed at integrating the political community, but they lack the force of law to back up their decisions. States are distinguished by civil laws and centralized governments, the latter of which use law to back up their threat or use of force against dissidents in their political communities.

Service's model is composed largely of a hierarchy of functional types and primarily demonstrates the organizational principles that contribute to the integration of each type. In fact, his major concern is with the organizational correlates of these types: sodalities in bands and tribes, centers of redistribution in chiefdoms, and governments and laws in states. Sociopolitical evolution is inferred from the increased complexity of each type in the hierarchy, which Service suggests correlates to changes in subsistence activities and settlement patterns. Still, Service is clear that each type is not necessarily an evolutionary consequence of preceding types because the ethnographic representations upon which his model rests do not depict pristine conditions. Instead they depict social formations that were created largely by the expansion and exploitative practices of European colonial powers.

Fried: Egalitarian, Ranked, and Stratified Societies

The Evolution of Political Society (Fried 1967) remains a classic text on political evolution and political economy thinking. With its emphasis on the evolution of social stratification, it also is one of the earliest political works with a Marxist bias, although in other ways, as we saw earlier, it is distinctly non-Marxist. Fried's political systems are calibrated to egalitarian, ranked, and stratified taxa. Even though he does not use the terms bands, tribes, chiefdoms, or states, his model correlates to these systems.

Bands and some tribes are egalitarian, tribes with leaders are ranked, as are chiefdoms, which also may be stratified, as are all states.

As we saw in Chapter 8, Fried used rough measures of access to positions of social status to account for the hierarchy depicted in his model. In egalitarian societies, valued status positions are open to anyone who can occupy them. They are more limited in rank societies such that some people with sufficient talent will be excluded. Stratified societies are based on unequal access to resources to those who are qualified. The status hierarchy that Fried established correlates to the increasing socioeconomic distance between rulers and ruled, a representation of sociopolitical hierarchy, and increased control over greater resources by hierarchical political agents. Fried explains the evolution of these formations in terms of economic manipulations by political leaders and the relationship of societies to their environments.

He points out how leaders who are the equivalent of big men and weak chiefs in egalitarian and some ranked societies strive to harness resources by cajoling and pleading—a rudimentary hegemonic culturation—to induce their political communities to work and produce more. Fried suggests that weaker leaders intuitively, or reflexively in the case of particularly perspicacious leaders, sense the importance of having political communities produce more, even if the people themselves are not especially compliant. He argues that the production of surpluses is fundamental to the emergence of leaders, and that the ranked society is based on leaders' abilities to stimulate production and command any surpluses. Stratification is a clear result of the peoples' unequal access to the resources generated above minimal survival levels, which the leaders then control.

But, like Service and other evolutionary thinkers, such as Sahlins (1960, 1963), Fried also makes redistribution central to the emergence of stronger leaders. Redistribution may be a clear indication of the control that leaders acquire over resources. Yet political economic processes of distribution—reciprocity and redistribution—are functionally aimed at the integration of the society and cannot be the cause of any explanation of political evolution. The unequal access to resources by which Fried distinguishes ranked and stratified societies can develop only by an alteration in the relationship of political agents to their political communities' means of production. Fried hedges on this dynamic in favor or the non-Marxist idea of redistribution.

Y. A. Cohen: Levels of Sociotechnological Integration

In Y. A. Cohen's (1968) scheme, the central force of evolution derives from the adaptation of human populations to their environments. Adaptation to Cohen refers to the relationship of a population to its habitat as a result of the energy—wild or domesticated plants and animals, fossil fuels, and the like—they harness with their technology to make survival possible. Cohen's theory builds from ideas borrowed from several sources.

Like Service, Cohen borrowed Steward's (1955) idea of levels of integration. He also adopts from Goldschmidt (1959) and Lenski (1966), with slight modifications, the evolutionary typology of nomadic and sedentary hunting and gathering, horticulture, agriculture, herding, and industrial societies. Cohen follows L. White's (1949, 1959) and Goldschmidt's (1959) arguments that evolution is a consequence of the efficiency by which a technology harnesses increased amounts of energy. Because of his emphasis on energy and technology, Cohen redefines Steward's ideas and suggests that his evolutionary taxa represent levels of sociotechnological adaptation.

These levels of sociotechnological adaptation may be an unlikely place to seek the answer to political evolution. But Cohen argues that the functional distinction between a stateless and state polity (Fortes and Evans-Pritchard 1940) is crucial to the direction that a population's adaptation takes and the social, cultural, and political configurations that emerge. In stateless societies, which include all hunters and gatherers and some horticultural and pastoral societies, the physical environment provides the terrain to which they adapt as they harness available energy resources with the technology at hand. Cohen then anticipates Wolf's (1982) kinship mode of production and argues that the production of resources is central to the organization of social relations in stateless societies. This is because production is accomplished through institutions of kinship that control the technology and energy systems that produce the necessary resources to meet minimal levels of survival. As we saw in the paradigm of political economy, any surpluses are controlled and redistributed by leaders.

In contrast, state formations create the environment to which their populations must adapt. This is because states employ rational and future-oriented centralized planning in making decisions that influence almost all other spheres of social organization. State formations, which include societies with intensive levels of horticulture, some pastoral societies, and all agricultural and industrial societies, exert control over the political community's technology and energy to ensure that the production of resources results in gross surpluses above minimal levels of survival. States mobilize the power and authority in secular and religious institutions and replace kinship institutions as the decision making agent in control of the society's production apparatus. Through its tentacles of control, the "state" becomes, in effect, the environment to which its population must adapt.

This adaptation is neither benign nor automatic, because it is always manipulated to accord with state goals, decisions, and values. Much of Cohen's perception of state political practice derives from Wittfogel's (1957) emphasis on the coercive ability of the state's political authority and power. In short, although Cohen eschews this terminology, state political institutions assume increasing influence, much of it coercive, over the means of production and thereby the relationship among a society's technology, energy systems, and sociopolitical configurations.

POLITICAL DEVOLUTION:
REALITIES AND ANOMALIES

Explanations of the devolution of sociopolitical systems exist in inverse proportion to those of their evolution. But political devolution is important and has theoretical and practical implications for understanding political processes. Political devolution is in practice sociopolitical devolution. It results in the simplification of the institutions of a political community and sometimes the political communities of an entire region. Devolution requires more robust theory than that which exists.

In ethnographic and ethnohistorical contexts, political devolution is largely the result of acculturation, an idea that was introduced to account for the consequences of the relations and exchanges between indigenous peoples and Western Europeans that began in the sixteenth century. Initially acculturation referred to a benign process of the exchange of cultural traits that was induced by the meeting of two cultures and resulted in the increased similarity of the two (Kroeber 1948 [1923]). But acculturation was never a benign process.

By the 1960s, acculturation was understood to be a brutal, worldwide process of colonial domination and exploitation that resulted in the unnecessary deaths of more indigenous people than will ever be known, and the simplification and disappearance of indigenous societies whose complexity and place in the great scheme of world history we have only recently begun to understand, and will never know fully. In many places, especially in the New World, Western diseases were the primary cause of population decline. Soldiers, missionaries, and colonial policies simply aided and abetted in these catastrophes (Bodley 1982, 1983). In other places, such as Africa, the possession of more deadly weapons of war by European armies and colonizers hastened the population decline.

For example, in Oceania, indigenous populations declined from 3.5 million in 1552 to 2 million in 1939 (Oliver 1958). Slavery, as well as disease, was also deeply implicated in the decline. In some areas of Africa, the brutal use of European military technology caused changes in social formations. Recall from Chapter 5 how Fortes and Evans-Pritchard (1940) were criticized for accepting the apparent demographic anomaly that the populations of African state formations were often smaller and less dense than those of stateless societies. More trenchant analyses that later considered the impact of the British force of arms in conquering areas of Africa and the consequences of indirect rule proved the anomaly to be anomalous. Powerful African kingdoms, such as the Zulu, who resisted the British with their own military forces were decimated by British weaponry. "Tribal" populations that did not always contest their domination through warfare, such as the Nuer, but practiced passive forms of resistance or guerrilla warfare, survived better. Still other African societies, such as the Tallensi (recall that they were one of the classic examples of the segmentary lineage system), were dispersed after they were defeated early in the twentieth century and their population decimated. Anthropologists recorded these ethnographic realities only later (Skinner 1964; Stevenson 1965).

The indigenous populations of the New World were ravaged by European pathogens on an unprecedented scale. Following the Spanish conquest of the Aztecs in 1520, the Indian populations of Mexico declined from an estimate of 27 million to 1 million in 1605, a span of only eighty-five years. As a result, urban state polities were decentralized. Cities devolved into towns, towns into villages, and many villages disappeared (Wolf 1955; Gibson 1966; Burkhart and Gasco 1996). In South America in the Amazon basin, Indian populations declined from 10 million to 1 million over the seventy years (1530–1600) following the Spanish incursion (Clastres 1977). The social and political organizations among contemporary Indians are sufficiently diverse, atypical, and marked by curious cultural survivals to support the contention that they are remnants of political communities that were once nucleated, dense, politically centralized, and part of another major cradle of civilization (Levi-Strauss 1961 [1955]; Martin 1969; Carneiro 1970).

In North America, Native Americans also suffered dramatic losses from disease vectors. As the fur trade swept across the continent from the Atlantic to the Pacific Coast in the seventeenth and eighteenth centuries, European pathogens preceded far ahead of the expanding colonial populations. The decimation of indigenous populations involved in this trade and elsewhere has probably badly skewed our understanding of the sociopolitical organization of American Indian polities before the European invasion. Those polities on the East Coast of North America are a case in point.

Native American populations on the East Coast of North America prior to the European arrival have been described ethnographically as tribes and chiefdoms. Yet John Smith used the English word "king" to refer to the werowances of Virginia and claimed that his enemies falsely accused him of courting Powhatan's daughter Pocahontas so that he might make himself a "king" by marrying her. The point is that Smith and other Europeans, such as conquistadors who used similar terms in Spanish to identify American Indian leaders in Middle America, recognized by their European experience the trappings of kingship. Since many New World and Old World societies were not socially and politically as different as we have been led to believe, references to "Indian kings" by people on the scene suggest an equivalency with European kings in form and function that ought to be accepted as fact (Vincent 1990; Lemay 1991; Barker and Pauketat 1992; Kehoe 1992). This means that the "tribes" who were later mobilized under leaders such as Pontiac and Tecumseh to evict or at least halt the advance of Europeans were remnants, composite organizations of previously more politically centralized entities whose populations had declined because of European-borne and introduced diseases.

Historical accounts of political devolution also exist. They suggest causes that were largely political economic in nature. Feudal periods in Japan and Europe, for example, shared similar characteristics of devolution and recovery (Bella 1957; T. C. Smith 1959; Ganshof 1961; Bloch 1964; Trevor-Roper 1965). In each case, the political power and authority of kings were undermined and then appropriated by the lords and nobles of landed estates that the kings themselves granted. Centuries of warfare usually ensued as the lords of these estates vied for domination. Eventually, centralized authority and power were reestablished and centralized leaders and governments acquired independent resources as they gradually appropriated the power and authority of the lords of the estates. In Japan this led to the development of a single national government in 1861. In Europe it resulted at different times in the organization of the modern nations and states that, after centuries of internecine wars, are now evolving into an even larger political entity, the European Union.

The collapse of Western European empires after World War II and the Soviet Union in the late twentieth century resulted in the emergence of a plethora of local state formations, many of which continue to struggle for national unity. Yet these political changes have also complemented the slow but steady emergence and influence of supranational government structures and agencies. These supranational political and military structures include NATO (North Atlantic Treaty Organization) and the United Nations. Supranational legal institutions include the International Court of Justice (otherwise known as the World Court, located in The Hague, in the Netherlands) and international tribunals, such as Criminal Tribunals for the Former Yugoslavia, East Timor, Cambodia, and Iraq. The tribunals presage an International Criminal Court to prosecute war criminals for crimes against humanity. Legal precedent for the function of this court derives from the Nuremberg laws, which were established to prosecute Nazi leaders following World War II. Some think that the plethora of independent state formations that have emerged from the demise of European colonies and the collapse of the Soviet Union confute a general political evolution toward a centralized world government to which independent polities will gradually surrender certain political and economic powers. This is another anomalous anomaly that history will prove to be incorrect.

10

THE PARADIGM OF POLITICAL EVOLUTION

The Evolution of Politics

Traditionally and because of methodological proscriptions that privilege material and mental prime movers over human agents as a way of explaining cultural evolution, anthropologists have subordinated the human agent to a passive and reactionary relationship to material and mental forces in evolution. Anthropologists are likely to argue that the "individual is not a prime mover" (Sahlins 1960:392) and that the study of cultural evolution is concerned with populations and institutions, not individuals (Y.A. Cohen 1968). In political anthropology, this orientation is expressed in the evolution of political organization, the topic of the last chapter.

There are good scientific reasons why individual organisms should not be considered as a force in biological evolution. But there is no good methodological reason why the role of the sapient, praxis-oriented, political agent should be excluded from consideration as a force in political evolution and, by extension, social evolution in general. In an idea-rich and novel paper, P. B. Roscoe (1993) suggested that practice theory (Bourdieu 1977; Giddens 1979; Ortner 1984) provides the theoretical foundation by which to insert the agent as a primary force in political evolution.

Prior to Roscoe's paper, perhaps the last really cogent argument for the role of the agent as a force in social evolution was made by the philosopher William James over a century ago. He wrote:

> social evolution is a resultant of the interaction of . . . the individual deriving his peculiar gifts from the play of physiological and infra-social forces, but

bearing all the power of initiative and origination in his hands; and . . . the social environment, with its power of adapting or rejecting both him and his gift. Both factors are essential to change. The community stagnates without the impulse of the individual. The impulse dies away without the sympathy of the community (James 1956 [1897]:232; cited in Lewis 1993:129).

Evolutionary thinking lost credibility in anthropology just about the time that James made his perceptive observation, and it took a half a century to recover. During the first half of the twentieth century, Western anthropologists either did not read or misrepresented Morgan's writings, sometimes purposefully (Engels 1942; Harris 1968; Fortes 1969; Bloch 1983). Instead of developing more fruitful evolutionary methodologies as happened after World War II, Western anthropologists abandoned evolutionary thinking.

During the revival of the evolution paradigm that began in the 1950s and 1960s in American anthropology (L. White 1949, 1959; Steward 1955; Sahlins and Service 1960), evolutionary theory was recuperated in a generalizing, positivist anthropology that largely excluded consideration of the human individual as a force in change. Roscoe says politely that the role of the agent in political evolution is dimly sketched. In this chapter I will coruscate the role of the agent in evolutionary change.

ROSCOE AND PRACTICE THEORY

As we saw in the last chapter, exemplars of the theory of general political evolution fashioned various linear evolutionary schemes by manipulating different genetic pulses. The political dimensions of those schemes represent a transition from the weak episodic leaders of nomadic hunters and gatherers to the powerful centralized governments of nucleated and densely populated state formations. Regardless of how these schemes are plotted, exemplars of political evolution subordinated the practices of leaders to circumstances over which they were presumed to have little control and explained political evolution as a functional response to the need to maintain order. As a result, the role of the agent simply has not been properly situated to account for sociopolitical evolution. But a theory of the agent as a driving force in the evolution of politics is congruous with the theory of political evolution. To establish the agent as an evolutionary force requires a different reading of the ethnographic record.

Anthropologists who argue that populations and institutions are the proper focus for evolutionary analyses (L. White 1949,1959; Sahlins and Service 1960; Service 1962, 1971; Y. A. Cohen 1968) forget that institutions are defined by the social statuses that individuals' hold and the roles they play in those institutions (Linton 1936), and that individuals are neither inert nor passive elements in the dynamics of institutional change. From the perspective of practice theory, the ethnographic record needs to be examined to ascertain the creative responses of leaders at all levels of social integration to problems they confront and the impact of these confrontations on sociopolitical change.

The concept of practice is social science jargon for what people do in all contexts that involve human action. When practice was resurrected as theory, it was embellished with the role of power and conflict in political relations (Bourdieu 1977, 1990; Giddens 1979; Ortner 1984). The incorporation of power and conflict in a practice theory that was distinctly political suggested a way to account for how political practices might cause evolutionary change. The placement of politics at the center of practice theory focused on how agents used power to attain public and private goals in conflict and competition with other agents, much as anthropologists in the processual paradigm suggested.

Roscoe adds to practice theory the powerful idea that the political practices of agents are the major motivating factor of political evolution. For Roscoe, political evolution is characterized by the increased centralization of agents' political power and the increased nucleation and density of the population of political communities with which the agents are affiliated. Roscoe uses ideas derived from practice theory to argue that the practices of political agents exist in a recursive relationship with the social structures of their political communities (Giddens 1979; Bourdieu 1977). The result of this relationship is a centralization of political power in the hands of agents who use that power to cause political communities to become increasingly nucleated and densely populated. To develop this theory, Roscoe elaborated on and made adjustments to Giddens's (1979) concept of *structuration.*

Structuration (Giddens 1979) embodies the idea that social structures provide the medium for and are the outcome of the practices of agents who respond to contradictions within those structures. As contradictions emerge in the social structures of political communities, the responses of agents change the communities' social structures as well as the structure and organization of their political agents. Giddens refers to the competition between agents that triggers structural change as a *dialectic of control.* He argues that this dialectic represents the attempts by agents to balance the tendency for political communities and individuals to seek autonomy from political control at the same time they depend on it to respond to problems beyond their control.

Roscoe suggests the idea of the *effectiveness of control* to supplant Giddens's dialectic of control. Roscoe contends that the contradiction between autonomy and control is balanced better and with less conflict by the effectiveness with which agents use power in their relationship with their political communities. In short, the effective use of power by agents helps to promote the centralization of their power, reduce individual autonomy, and cause political communities to nucleate and increase in density. The effective use of power also results in fewer social and political problems.

In addition to linking action and structure as forces in evolution, practice theory also embraces *time* (Bourdieu 1977; Giddens 1979). To complement time, Roscoe adds the dimension of *distance.* Time refers to that temporal span over which the creative practices of agents reproduce and transform structure qualitatively. Evolution is, after all, a temporal process. Distance helps to account for the amount of time that political agents are able to practice their politics. Simply put, there is a covariance among the distance leaders have to travel to respond to the problems of a political community, the time they have to practice politics to meet those problems, and the nucleation and density of political communities. The factors of time and distance influence the amount, kind, and effectiveness of political practices in which agents may engage and, therefore, the significance of their practices for political evolution.

Roscoe argues that practice theory provides a better methodological solution to account for political evolution than materialist theories that rely on linear relations of cause and effect. According to him, practice theory incorporates structural, functional, and individual-centered theories in a methodology that incorporates the recursive relationship between agents' political practices and the social structures of political communities to account for evolution. Roscoe presents a convincing argument that the centralization of power in political agents and offices results in a political evolution characterized by communities that are increasingly densely populated and nucleated.

As powerful and elegant as Roscoe's theory is, it remains untested. Roscoe does not demonstrate how the political practices of specific agents, such as chiefs or big men, account for general political evolution. As a result he does not enlighten us regarding how the practices of political agents result in the nucleation and density of political communities. Nor does he clarify how conflict and competition over power contribute to nucleation, density, and political centralization. Roscoe does not provide the necessary methodological tools to establish clear and meaningful human agents and the specifics of the practice in which they engage. Thus Roscoe's ideas are only powerfully suggestive, at best (Kurtz 1993).

Still, because of their import, Roscoe's ideas provide the basis in the following discussion to demonstrate in a very general way how agents' political practices may activate sociopolitical evolution. A first step toward this goal is to recall the obvious: Political agents engage in politics. As obvious as this may be, it is important. If the political practices of agents are the motive force of political evolution, then it is necessary to depict the specific politics that those practices engage in different levels of social integration and modes of production, identify the factors to which these politics relate, and determine how the pursuit of the public and private goals results in the nucleation and density of political communities.

A terse refinement to the theory of practice suggests that political evolution is the result of the *evolution of politics*. This refers to the unfolding of goal-oriented practices by agents who are increasingly differentiated and specialized and committed to developing, aggregating, and using political power to pursue those goals. This reconstitution of the theory of practice imputes a recursive relationship between political agents, their political practices, the variables that drive those practices, and the consequences of their politics as they are revealed in various ethnographically depicted political communities.

THE EVOLUTION OF POLITICS

There are two caveats to the relationship between the evolution of politics and political evolution. First, the idea of the "agent" is too inclusive to be meaningful. Political agents come in a variety of forms, and they are not equally relevant. The political agents who are important to political evolution are those leaders or aspiring leaders of polities who represent and are empowered to act on behalf of a political community or the constituency of such a community. Because of their power and authority, leaders have the capacity to make things happen. Most agents either do not have this capacity or lack it sufficiently to make any difference in evolution. In this analysis I use "leader" to refer to those agents who have the power to make things happen.

Second, although the archaeological record supports a general evolution from nomadic hunters and gatherers to state formations, the ethnographic record does not represent the social evolution of fossilized societies from the Stone Age to the present. Nor does it portray the culture and social organization of human societies much before the beginning of the compilation of the ethnographic record in the nineteenth century. By that time, the "primitive" societies that provided the basis for that record were seriously reconfigured owing to the exploitation of Western European colonial governments that had begun to spread around the world in the sixteenth century (Service 1971; Wolf 1982).

Nonetheless, there are only so many ways that political communities can organize socially and politically to cope with problems of survival. Despite social and cultural distortions due to Western expansion, the ethnographic record is a representation of the possible and probable sociopolitical organizations of which human societies are capable.

Methodologically, therefore, the ethnographic record may be construed as a model of *the range of probable sociopolitical organizations* in which human populations have existed and of the practices inherent in an evolution of politics.

A practice model of an agent-driven political evolution also requires a statement about the elements that drive political evolution. Recall that the practices of political leaders and the problems to which they respond are not as infinite and complicated as might appear. As Occam's razor suggests, the best theory of practice will rely on the fewest and simplest factors to account for the centralization of power and authority and the nucleation and density of political communities. A practice model will eschew the multiplicity of idiosyncratic variables that cultural relativism brings to such an endeavor. Instead, practice theory will account for political evolution by relying on the cross-cultural regularities and recurrent elements in the recursive relations between leaders and structure.

For example, there is the presumption in political evolution that each level of social or technological integration (Steward 1955; Y. A. Cohen 1968) represents a predictable range of sociocultural variation. That means that the organization and political practices of leaders will be similar in similar political communities. This can be demonstrated in different ways. Big men, episodic leaders, chiefs, and heads of state represent polities that operate in political communities that, respectively, share similar technologies, energy systems, and social organizations. But in an evolutionary methodology it is also difficult to distinguish the organization of political communities and the practices of political leaders in those interstices where political polities and communities that represent one mode of production or level of integration segue into another. For example, in the interstices between big men and chiefly polities, or chiefdoms and inchoate state formations, powerful big men are not appreciably different in form and practice from weak chiefs, and the practices of powerful paramount chiefs do not differ much from those of heads of state of early inchoate state formations.

Only a few factors are necessary to demonstrate how the evolution of politics relates to political evolution. But such an analysis must also account for the recursive relationship between these factors, the political leaders involved, and, most importantly, the *effectiveness of their control.* The factors are not mutually exclusive and become more complicated and intertwined in more institutionally complex societies. They can be subsumed under seven categories, five of which were discussed previously. These include the *genetic pulses* to which leaders respond creatively to help drive evolution (Chapter 9); the *quotidian altercations* that birth the day-to-day problems that leaders need to resolve to maintain social order(Chapter 7); *political power* in the form of the resources that leaders control (Chapter 2); the *political economy* that leaders manipulate to their advantage (Chapter 8); and *hegemonic culturation* by which leaders strive to inculcate their political communities with their ideologies and values (Chapter 8). The remaining two variables, *contradictions* and *political praxis*, are introduced below.

Recall (Chapter 7) that Gluckman (1965) introduced the idea of a contradiction in political anthropology to divert anthropologists from functional thinking and to account for change. He identified contradictions as those relationships between discrepant principles and processes in social structure that must inevitably lead to radical change in the pattern of a society's social positions. Callinicos's (1988) idea is more precise and gets to the critical nexus of the discrepant principles that lead to radical change. He identifies a contradiction as those discrepant principles and practices in human societies that are characterized by two or more entities that are constituted by virtue of being integral and mutually interdependent features of a social structure and have the potential for conflict by virtue of their opposing relationship in the social structure. Depending on the culture and complexity of a political community, contradictions may represent oppositions in kinship, ethnicity, caste, gender, the supernatural, descent, culture, class, religion, or ideology, and may exist in the context of any institution. Some are centrally important in the structure and organization of a society, such as the relations of production in capitalist models of production.

According to Hegel's and Marx's dialectic, change comes about through the negation of contradictions and the automatic emergence of new contradictions. Today the idea of negation has little credibility in dialectical thinking (Murphy 1971; Marquit, Moran, and Truitt 1982; Kurtz 1994a). Contradictions are more likely to become residual or remain dormant as other oppositions supplant or usurp their influence. Those that perdure and frustrate attempts at resolution will diminish over time to struggles that emanate from quotidian altercations. Perhaps the most fundamental, perduring, and universal political contradiction is the dialectic of control that Giddens (1979) identified as the discrepancy between the autonomy of decisionmaking and action at the local level of political communities and the practices of leaders who, at all levels of authority, work to usurp that autonomy.

A political praxis refers to the union of theory and practice that leaders use to direct how they create, reproduce, and deploy power, and the strategies they develop to pursue their projects and respond to problems in their political communities. Leaders' praxes—effective leaders have more than one praxis—also impute intent and motivation to their practices. Some practice theorists suggest that agents' actions are unconscious and motivated by structural forces, such as discourses (Bourdieu 1977;

Foucault 1979; de Certeau 1984). Certainly there are events and issues that are beyond the control of agents that influence their practices. But leaders are not likely to succeed without clearly defined projects and thoughtful strategies and tactics on how to accomplish them. Skillful leaders do not develop their praxes haphazardly, on the conditions of the moment. They are nurtured during their apprenticeship and reinvented during their careers. Skillful leaders learn to anticipate problems and confront them with praxes designed to make their control effective and to reproduce and augment their power. Leaders who try to operate without a political praxis are likely to be inept (Kurtz 1994b).

PRACTICE AND THE EVOLUTION OF POLITICS

In practice theory, as in the theory of general evolution, political evolution is characterized by the gradual nucleation of increasingly dense populations and the centralization of political authority and power. But unlike general evolutionary theory, practice theory does not subordinate leaders to forces beyond their control. Instead it implicates them directly in political evolution. In practice theory, political evolution is an epiphenomenon of the *evolution of politics* and is revealed first in the practices of episodic leaders in nomadic hunting and gathering societies. The universal attributes of leaders (Chapter 3) and the idea of the "political person" who seeks power (Chapter 2) provide points of departure to explore the creative and recursive relationship of leaders to the structures of their political communities, their environments, and the genetic pulses with which they interact and influence.[1]

But there are caveats to this proposition. They reside in the nature of the environments of political communities and the material and symbolic attributes they make available to leaders to respond to environmental constraints and potentials. Sociopolitical evolution is largely the product of efforts by people to free themselves from constraints imposed by environments that are at once physical (Y. A. Cohen 1968) and sociocultural (James 1956 [1897]). Each of these environments provides potentials and opportunities, as well as constraints, on political practice. The constraints on practice are especially important in accounting for the evolution of politics in political communities with weak leaders, such as episodic authorities and big men.

Ideas related to the role of innovation in culture change (Kroeber 1948 [1923]) may not be fashionable today, but they help to demonstrate the previous caveat. Nearly two centuries ago, long before anyone imagined an anthropology to study change, Mrs. [Mary] Shelly, the author of *Frankenstein or the Modern Prometheus*, observed that "Invention . . . does not exist in creating out of void, but out of chaos" (n.d.:14). Simply stated, the more disparate material and symbolic traits that are available to a political community and its leadership, the more likely is the potential for agents to put these traits together creatively and provide increasingly novel ways to respond to environmental constraints. Leonardo da Vinci had drawn viable plans of airships and underwater submersibles that could not be constructed in the sixteenth century because of the things that would not be discovered or invented for another four hundred or more years. The evolutionary potential of the practices of leaders in environments that are less materially rich, such as episodic leaders of hunters and gatherers, is considerably less than the evolutionary potential of the practices of the governments and heads of state of irrigation civilizations. Phrased in practice theory, the paucity of material things available to leaders in less complex political communities, especially hunting and gathering bands, impedes their ability to challenge their environmental potentials creatively, constrains the time they have to practice politics by requiring them to be food producers first and political agents second, and creates such distance between small, dispersed bands that it inhibits the potential for leaders to centralize and nucleate their political communities.

These constraints are mitigated by the nature of leadership. The evolution of politics suggests that leaders, whether they be episodic, big men, chiefs, or heads of state relative to the structure and size of their political communities, are abundant commodities in the political marketplace, and that their motivations differ in degree only. Individuals who assume the obligations of leadership are the "doers" of the society. They are psychologically predisposed to lead and are ambitious at least for the status and prestige of leadership. But because they are politically more perspicacious than those they lead, they are sensitive to the fact that leadership can provide something more than status and prestige. In political terms that something is power.

EPISODIC LEADERS

Episodic leaders of hunting and gathering bands exist along a continuum of political power from weakest to weak.[2] In some bands, leaders are almost nonexistent and households manage their own affairs. In others they are more influential and may indulge in different spheres of competence, such as hunting, curing, or lore. The fissiparous social organization of band society limits leaders' power and their effectiveness of control.

The hallmark of episodic leadership is the lack of long-term planning. The practices of episodic leaders are dedicated by necessity to immediate goals that are largely redundant: where to move next, how best to conduct a hunt, or how to resolve a quotidian altercation. Despite these im-

positions on their effectiveness of control, within the constraints and potentials available to them, episodic leaders rely on directing praxes to develop strategies to acquire and use power, manipulate the economy, and
inform band members of the value of their ideas in a variety of ways.

When something needs to be done in band society, as in political communities at large, most individuals abrogate their responsibility. Some
may move away. But eventually one or more episodic leaders with the required skills emerge in response to the need. The hunt is organized, consummated successfully, and the meat is distributed equitably. The community is organized to confront a quotidian altercation that threatens the
social order. The dispute is resolved. The decision is made where to move
next. If an adequate leader is not available to direct these matters, or
should the band disagree with one who is, band members resolve the
problem among themselves.

Episodic leaders cannot bring much power to bear on their practices.
Material resources are not abundant and ideational resources are hard to
develop because of the strong egalitarian bias in band societies and the
impermanency of band organization. To acquire and reproduce resources
as political power, leaders cultivate what resources are available.

Episodic leaders have supporters, if only among consanguineous and
affinal kin, although some or all of them are likely to be scattered at any
given moment. They also have some access to rudimentary tangible
power, if only momentary, such as the meat from a hunt, of which they often influence the distribution. Their involvement in the redistribution of
food provides leaders a chance to demonstrate their concern for the well-
being of the band, acclaim the value of those individuals who worked
harder in the hunt, enhance their own prestige, and expound their values
to the band.

Hegemonic culturation and gentle persuasion are politically inexpensive ways for episodic leaders to inculcate the values, beliefs, and practices they deem to be important, such as a precocious ideology of work
and community responsibility that may increase the availability of tangible resources. A typical and subtle way for them to impel this hegemonic
impetus is to demonstrate by deed and action the work that they hope
others will emulate and to convince them that its consequences might result in more abundant feasts, rituals, and ceremonies or otherwise serve
the common good. Even if there is no appreciable increase in material resources, through their actions episodic leaders may increase their status
and prestige. Members of a community who choose not to follow the
leader are free to ignore him and go their own way.

As inceptive as these practices may be, they suggest that episodic leaders have some idea of the advantages to be gained from the control of resources. Leaders are not utterly subordinate to exigencies beyond their

control. Instead, they try to implant desirable behaviors in the potentially fertile ground of their political communities (James 1956 [1897]; P. B. Roscoe 1993). The extent to which communities accept their ideas helps to change their relationship to their community, predispose the community to change, and increase the effectiveness of the control of episodic leaders.

Episodic leaders can begin to reap political advantage, that is, power, as a result of altering the relationship of bands only where the environmental potential for the transition permits. Under these conditions, leaders may help through cajolery to alter genetic pulses concerned with technology to promote the cultivation of foodstuffs, a potential source of tangible power, which also leads to increased population nucleation and density. Alteration in the pattern of social and political relations may evoke the status of big man and increase the resources available to them, albeit incrementally, for weak big men do not differ much from strong episodic leaders.

BIG MEN

Big men are often referred to ethnographically as *primus inter pares*, or first among equals. They are ascribed this appellation because weak and some typical big men are indistinguishable in their communities, possess no emoluments of prestige, as a praxis build only short-lived political coalitions, do not pass their status to heirs, and can be rejected and replaced by their political communities at any time. From a practice theory point of view, the status of *primus inter pares* is a mystification of a political reality.

Big men may appear to be like everyone else in their political communities. However, their status, praxes, and politics elevate them above their communities and evokes the fundamental and permanent contradiction between leaders and led, autonomy and control. Even the political practices of weak big men place them in opposition to their political communities and other big men and create practices and tensions that are not characteristic of episodic leaders.[3]

Big men are the first leaders of polities who have a discernible effect on the factors that induce evolution. The weakest are associated with political communities that may be small and semisedentary, rely primarily on hunting and gathering, and use horticulture to supplement their foraging. The strongest dominate nucleated and densely populated, intensively horticultural societies. In between are the typical big men who live in loosely nucleated but relatively dense political communities that rely primarily on extensive horticulture and some foraging for subsistence (Y. A. Cohen 1968).

The practices and praxes of big men along the political continuum from weak to strong leaders show a decided change in the effectiveness of control and their ability to plan activities. Even the weakest big men have praxes aimed at augmenting their power and changing sociopolitical relations within and between political communities to their advantage. The effectiveness of big men's control—there usually is more than one—is likely to be represented by their different capabilities and practices, such as generosity, feast giving, redistribution, oratorical skill, sorcery, warfare, peacemaking, curing, and the like. Mediation of quotidian altercations is an important function.

The concern of functional exemplars with resolving quotidian altercations internal to a political community is a fundamental political goal of any leadership. Mediation of disputes is one of the first services that a weak big man provides to his community and may be the reason for a political community to allocate that status. Resolving these altercations is also important to the evolution of politics. A secure social order sets the stage for the nucleation of populations that would be difficult if people are driven apart by social unrest. Relative peace allows relations with other political communities and evokes specialized big men, such as ritual and war leaders and peacemakers. If big men do not have to expend disproportionate time and political capital resolving quotidian altercations, they can redirect their praxes to projects that garner more power and authority over larger nucleated political communities.

Recall that an important factor that legitimates "status leaders" and "officeholders" (Chapter 4) is a sound economy. Increased economic production is one response to the political and hegemonic practices and influence that big men begin to exert over their political communities and the potential of genetic pulses in their environment. Big men may not be able to adjust a genetic pulse to their advantage, as state governments can when they intensify irrigation (Wittfogel 1957; R. M. Adams 1966). However, a reasonably secure social order provides a fertile social environment for hegemonic culturation by big men to encourage technological efficiency, more work, and increased production. These forces may not automatically accelerate the nucleation and density of political communities. But the recursive relationship that big men have with their communities and genetic pulses can provide conditions that allow them more time to refine their praxes, practice politics, and increase their political power.

Big men, even weak ones, are notorious manipulators of their political economies. Most big men acquire resources through the goods that their community provides them as recognition, at least in part, for their own services, such as resolving quotidian altercations. To retain their status, most big men must redistribute these resources as the authority code of the communities requires. Redistribution is a strong social integrator, a potential nucleating force, and a legitimating factor of big man status. The basic rule of redistribution requires big men to comply with demands by community members for material items to replace ones that are lost, broken, or otherwise desired. Although typical and strong big men appropriate some of the goods for their own use, weak big men often are the poorest members of their communities because they are required to redistribute more than they receive.

Nonetheless, weak big men do have praxis-based agendas, such as trying to stimulate the people of their communities to work and produce more. But with the limited power at their disposal, they find it difficult to acquire resources beyond what they themselves produce. To continue to hold the status of big man and its attendant prestige and potential for power, they must give away on demand much that they produce. Yet even weak big men engage in the fundamental practices that distinguish the big man type of leadership. They are generous with what they accumulate and have oratorical skills that others lack. To keep up with demands on their resources, weak big men manipulate the political economy in ways that are better developed by the politics and praxes of typical and strong big men. Even so, weak big men have some power in the form of both tangible and human resources that derives from the material and affective credit they have with supporters.

One of the first steps that big men take to build material power is to establish credit with some individuals and try to place others in debt. By clever manipulation, successful big men acquire more benefactors than creditors to provide them the resources with which to sustain their economic redistribution and its nucleating potential. Benefactors are likely to be links in a wider system of planned trade, exchange, and polygynous marriages that big men try to turn to their advantage. For typical big men and, even more, strong big men, these ties extend beyond their local community and integrate and help to nucleate a larger number of people in their sphere of political influence.

Other resources come as big men influence production hegemonically by encouraging their communities to produce more. The surplus material goods that big men control allow them to appropriate some for their own use to provide largesse that obliges support later and to extend credit more deeply through chains of economic relations. Unlike weak big men, who are more debtors than creditors, typical and strong big men have more credit, hegemonic potential, and political power at their disposal.

Although weak and typical big men and some strong big men operate in communities that are patrilineal and patrilocal, an inordinate number of strong big men practice their politics in matrilineal societies, as do many chiefs and heads of state. Big men cannot alter much the descent and postmarital residence patterns of their communities. But social structures do influence the consequences of their practice (Allen 1984). As the stakes in the power game increase, so too does the potential for big men to take risks, to see what they can get away with that will enhance their status and prestige, and to centralize their power. This is especially likely where social and cultural conditions are amenable, such as in nucleated political communities whose social structure consists of matrilineal descent and patrivirilocal postmarital residence (Allen 1984).

Patrilineal and patrivirilocal social structures facilitate the transition of authority in a male line of descent and can result in strong leaders. But patrilineal descent also requires close kin to compete for political power. Matrilineal descent complemented by patrivirilocal postmarital residence, a pattern that is more common than the better-known matrilineal-avuncuvirilocal residence pattern of the Trobriand Islanders, establishes conditions that evoke strong big men and voluntary political associations, such as secret and age-graded associations (Allen 1984).

The political economic praxes of big men dedicated to wheeling and dealing and power plays attain their highest development among matrilineal–patrivirilocal societies. This happens because matrilineal descent and viripatrilocal residence distribute males and females among different political communities over a wide area and induce competition for political power and authority in political communities that are inhabited largely by unrelated adult males. Some males succeed as big men and exert influence beyond their political communities. They are at the apex of exchange relations with subordinates who also have subordinates, each of whom is a client indebted to someone above them. Subordinates to a powerful big man can call upon their subordinates for help to meet demands from the big man. Such deep links of political economic obligation to strong big men make their sources of power more predictable and secure. And social and real distance from competing kinsmen allows big men to display more aggressive behavior.

Strong big men begin to coerce others with whom they have some difference. But more important to the evolution of politics is the change in pattern and the contradictions that these politics invoke. Strong big men are also complemented by voluntary associations that provide political alternatives and challenge the power of big men (Allen 1984). Where contradictions emerge, politics becomes more complicated. Political practices of big men that respond to these changes presage practices that begin to distinguish chiefs from big men (Allen 1984).

CHIEFS

Chiefs represent the first leadership structure that responds meaningfully to the contradiction between local autonomy and political centralization

(Giddens 1979). To respond to this and other contradictions, chiefs develop praxes to build power, centralize the effectiveness of their control, and engage in practices that are planned to facilitate the nucleation and density of populations that mark political evolution. The most important impetus for chiefly practices that encourage political evolution derives from the change in succession that replaces status leaders, such as big men, with officeholders who are chiefs.[4]

Exemplars of general evolution distinguish chiefly polities from big men polities primarily because of a sharp break in the rules of succession. Chiefs, unlike most big men, can transfer their status through inheritance to an heir. How the idea of a political office developed is not clear, but chiefs certainly did not seize their power and prerogatives as some suggest (Earle 1991).

The office is likely to have emerged as the result of strong big men taking the risk of transferring their power and authority to heirs and then relying on the abrogation of reaction by political communities to ensure the transfer. If heirs who immediately succeed the initial heirs can also transfer their power and authority, the office of chief becomes secure. When later incumbents are challenged by competitors but the existence and legitimacy of the offices are not, political offices are infallible.

The emergence of the abstract idea of a political office assumes paramount importance in the evolution of politics because all political power and legitimate authority reside and are centralized in the office. Leaders acquire access to that power and authority by virtue of their incumbency in the office. The existence of the office endows chiefs with a preexisting base of centralized power that gives an edge to their effectiveness of control beyond anything big men could hope for. Access to that power alters the recursive relationship of chiefs with their communities. It allows them to forge long-term plans and develop praxes to meet future exigencies and expand the powers of the office in ways that impel political evolution as the politics of big men could not.

Because of the preexisting centralization of their power, chiefs can plan and make decisions that promote the nucleation and density of their political communities in different ways. Chiefs may decide to absorb refugees from wars or famine, or adopt adults and children of communities they have defeated in war. When they enter into marriage alliances, they may require some of the bride's kin to reside (or be hostage) in their community. In polygynous marriages this can add substantially to the density of a chiefly polity. Strong chiefs may extend claims to neighboring land and those who reside on it, or extend their authority and protection to communities without chiefs or whose chiefs are less powerful. In areas that are prone to warfare, chiefs may stimulate technological improvements, such as terracing, which may also nucleate people in defensive communities. Chiefs who expand trade with other chiefdoms may bring people together to facilitate the production or appropriation of goods involved in the trade. Or chiefs may decide to confederate their political communities in response to more powerful chiefdoms or other confederations with whom they are in competition. Warfare and/or trade may increase the nucleation and density of the confederacies. Even weak chiefs govern political communities that are more nucleated and denser than those of most big men. Nucleation and density on this scale allow chiefs more time to practice their politics, extend their effectiveness of control, and augment their power.

Allies, lands, trade, technology, and warfare (providing one wins) are all additional sources of chiefly power. Where conditions permit or demand, shrewd and skillful chiefs parlay their existing power into a positive, political economic feedback loop. Additional power allows them to oversee and subsidize technological developments and improvements in the genetic pulses that influence evolution, such as terracing, drainage, fallowing, or irrigation. Strategic marriage alliances may bring under their control and influence other influential men, benefactors, and loyalists who can in turn contribute to their power. Anticipating the practices of heads of state, strong chiefs may invoke rights of eminent domain and claim unused or conquered lands for themselves, and then require corvée service from their political communities to work them. The control of trade routes provides chiefs a larder of political economic power, centralizes their authority, and makes them independent of others.

Chiefs have another edge in the evolution of their politics that big men lack. As a result of the hegemonic culturation in which big men engaged, chiefs inherit apparatuses of production in which populations are preconditioned to work and produce surpluses above minimal levels of biological necessity. Absolved of the need to create these apparatuses from scratch, chiefs are free to stimulate work and production hegemonically, sometimes coercively, and manipulate economic surpluses to their political advantage. A surplus of economic resources allows chiefs to plan for undertakings such as warfare, technological change, or sumptuary feasting.

As with big men, according to general evolutionary theory the major political economic function of chiefs, and upon which their power rests, is their control of the redistribution of their communities' resources. But redistribution involves other motivations. Weaker chiefs may use feasts to reaffirm and integrate their relationship with their political community. Stronger chiefs are more likely to use lavish feasts, or potlatches, to place others in debt, establish more credit upon which they may draw later, and, in general, bring potential benefactors under their orbit of control and influence.

Warfare between big men polities is likely to be ritualized and dedicated more to providing diversions from the tedium of day-to-day life than the conquest and appropriation of others' resources. Warfare between chiefly polities may also fill leisure time, but it is likely to be more politically motivated, purposefully stimulated by chiefs, and internecine. Losers are subject to the appropriation of their lands, trade routes, warriors as slaves, and tribute, each of which become independent sources of power for victorious chiefs.

But the domination by strong chiefs of potentially recalcitrant dependents and disruption of economic production, or decrease in the potential for production, can also create uneasy relationships that may stress the resources of victors in war. Practices that promote the nucleation and density of political communities require chiefs to make decisions that alter their recursive relationship with their communities and others. Chiefs who make wise decisions may significantly increase their power and centralize their control. Bad decisions, or events beyond their control, such as a change in trade routes that decreases their access to resources, may be detrimental to political evolution and cause a chief to lose power and become subordinate to another chiefly polity.

When a stronger polity can convince a weaker polity to accept subordinate status, perhaps in a confederation against more distant confederations, each polity may gain. The stronger chiefs acquire territory, people, and resources to add to their power. Subordinate polities avoid conquest, retain some power, and may actually increase it through successes of the confederacy in warfare. Confederations and alliances establish stability within and between chiefly polities that alters recursive relations between chiefs and communities. Some chiefs delegate authority to others to help govern subordinate polities. This enables them to extend the effectiveness of their power and authority horizontally over subordinate communities in their sphere of influence and entrench their effective authority vertically in their social structures. An increase in the scale of chiefdoms and the power of chiefs creates additional contradictions to which they must respond.

The existence of the office of chief creates an abundance of contradictions in rank, class, and power between chiefs and their competitors, chiefs and their political communities, and chiefs and other polities. In addition to the secular power vested in the political office, the office acquires other powers that add still more contradictions that help to trigger political evolution. The political office becomes imbued with supernatural, symbolic, and ideological power that incumbents can develop and bring to their political projects. Supernatural powers insert another dynamic into the recursive relations of chiefs and their communities, the effectiveness of their control, and the evolution of politics.

Political communities are not likely to care much if their chiefs claim access to external sources of power, such as lands acquired through warfare that will be worked by slaves or defeated peoples as part of a levied tribute. But chiefly polities that do not possess developed apparatuses of coercion have to worry about a diminished effectiveness of control and an increase in quotidian altercations if they try to levy taxes, demand corvée service on their private estates, and otherwise appropriate resources from their political communities. Since most chiefs lack coercive mechanisms to force people into compliance, they reciprocate for these services by redistributing some of the resources they accumulate to their political communities through ritual feasts and ceremonies. Chiefs who can augment their larder of material power with supernatural power can mystify and hegemonically increase the effectiveness of their control and reduce altercations.

Many stronger chiefs are believed to have supernatural power to make good things happen—the rains come to break a drought—and to make bad things go away—a plague of locusts. They can infuse their spirit into other objects, such as plants and animals. Anyone who defiles these objects also defiles the chief. When supernatural powers become invested in the office, chiefs acquire rights to supernatural sanctions that complement their secular sanctions. In effect, transgressors who are able to avoid secular sanctions can expect supernatural retribution.

In some instances, when chiefly polities begin to approximate state formations, chiefs may assume a divine status and intervene with supernatural forces to support their authority. But when priests become a separate and specialized category of religious practitioners, a new, powerful, political agent and significant contradiction is inserted into the driving force of the evolution of politics.

Priests do more than validate the legitimate authority of leaders through the presumed supernatural forces at their control. They are important sources of ideational power and hegemonic motivation in chiefly practice. When they work on behalf of chiefs, priests intercede with the supernatural to motivate people to action—planting, harvesting, fighting, trading—and impose supernatural sanctions for noncompliance. But priests may also challenge the legitimacy of existing political structures and try to subordinate them to religious authority and supernatural power. This is not a major concern in chiefly polities, but it can be an issue in state formations. In chiefly polities, priests are more likely to complement the apparatus of power and effectiveness of chiefly control to which political communities become subject in the course of the evolution of politics.

Exemplars of general evolution explain the evolution of chiefly polities as a response to genetic pulses, such as technology, warfare, population growth, and trade, and explain political leaders as epiphenomena to the genetic pulses that emanate from their environments. A practice theory interpretation of ethnographic data suggests that the evolution of leaders' politics and the effectiveness with which they use their power are powerful and to some extent alternative impetuses to political evolution. The evolution of politics births increasingly complicated contradictions that stimulate radical change in the pattern of sociopolitical relations that the politics of big men began to elaborate on the foundation provided by the episodic leaders of hunters and gatherers. The governments of state formations represent the culmination of the implication of political practices for political evolution. State formations are the topic of Chapter 11.

NOTES

1. The model of political evolution is based on ethnographic depictions of the political practices of episodic leaders, big men, and chiefs. I will create a brief annotated bibliography from which data on those practices were extrapolated. Each example of the practices of these leaders is a distillation of overlapping and redundant data. Citation of these data would clutter the text unnecessarily and require ethnographic descriptions that are not compatible with the aims and intentions of this work.

2. Weak leaders exist among the BaMabuti (Turnbull 1962), Washo (Downs 1966), and Bushmen (Lee 1982). They are largely nonexistent among the Gosciute Shoshoni (Steward 1938, 1943). Because the Shoshoni live in the Great Basin of the American West, where food is scarce for long periods of time, they scatter and each family forages on its own. Leaders emerge among the Bushman, Washo, BaMabuti, and other foragers to organize hunts, direct rituals and ceremonies, and manipulate the distribution of food. They may reward those who conform to band values and deny equal shares to recalcitrants (Service 1979). Leaders have support from affines and consanguineous kin among the Iglulik Eskimo (Damas 1968) and the Tiwi (Hart and Pilling 1960), the latter of whom also have stronger episodic leaders. The Tiwi's environment on the coast of northern Australia was rich in foodstuffs and permitted larger, more sedentary populations. Tiwi leaders controlled resources, such as access to foodstuffs and women, and behaved in ways that approximated the Melanesian big men to the north.

3. The description of weak big men comes from South America, among the Kalapalo (Basso 1973), and in a more generalized context from Clastres (1977). Neither Basso nor Clastres use the term big man. Rather, they describe practices that subscribe to the big man model, especially the fundamental practices that distinguish big men: generosity that may be required to such an extent that it impoverishes the leader, oratorical skill, alliances through polygyny, mediation, and hegemonic exertion upon people to work and produce more. The leaders they describe also have little power and limited authority and, like episodic leaders, do much of the work that needs to be done themselves.

Typical big men are represented by the Kapauku (Pospisil 1963), Kaoka speakers (Hogbin 1964), Gururumba (Newman 1965), Dani (Heider 1970, 1979), Chimbu (Brown 1972), Jalé (Koch 1974), and many others. In addition to the traits that characterize weak big men, typical big men develop obvious strategies to integrate larger numbers of people into their sphere of influence who can then help them in their quest for power. They attract supporters through success in warfare, by forging relations through alliances, exchanges, and trade, and by giving feasts to demonstrate their status and to humiliate rivals.

The Siuai (Oliver 1955) are an example of those Melanesian societies that are matrilineal and patrivirilocal (Allen 1984), although postmarital residence among the Siuai is both matri- and patrilocal. The practices and organization of Siuai big men approximate those of chiefs. Siuai big men belong to lineages that are ranked in a hierarchy, demand deference, coerce others by imposing supernatural and secular sanctions, and sponsor ritual feasts that are designed to depose rivals and alter power relations. Through marriage alliances, shrewd exchanges, and trade relations, Siuai big men integrate benefactors and others from farther afield and, to some extent, even nucleate large numbers of people under their influence.

4. In chiefdoms, the practices that drive the evolution of politics, such as nucleation of political communities, increases in chiefs' power, and strategies to centralize it, are complex and commingled. For the sake of parsimony, I merge these factors to some extent in the following references.

Among the Huron (Trigger 1969) and in Panama (Helms 1979), trade relations helped chiefs to increase their power and nucleate political communities under their influence. Extensive terraces provided defensive networks that brought people together under Kachin chiefs who fought to control trade routes (Leach 1954). Confederation under the direction of chiefs helped to account for nucleation and power building among the Huron (Trigger 1969) and the Iroquois (Morgan 1901 [1851]), who also, along with some African societies, adopted adults and children into their communities (Mair 1962) and absorbed refugees from war and famine. Some African chiefs required the kin of brides to reside in their communities (Mair 1962), but marriage alliances were common to almost all chiefs. Nucleation and power building by claiming the lands of others transpired among chiefs (rajas) of northern India (Thapar 1984), Konyak Nagas (von Fürer-Haimendorf 1969), Kachin (Leach 1954), Alur (Southall 1956), and Swat Pathans (Barth 1959). The Alur (Southall 1956) and Konyak Nagas (von Fürer-Haimendorf 1969) also expanded their spheres of influence by exporting their chiefs to neighboring societies. Losers in war forfeited lands to the winners among the Konyak Nagas (von Fürer-Haimendorf 1969), Kachin (Leach 1954), Iroquois (Morgan 1901 [1851]), north Indian rajas (Thapar 1984), Panamanian chiefs (Helms 1979), and Swat Pathans (Barth 1959). Sometimes lands were not appropriated, but rather warriors on the losing side became slaves to winning chiefs, as on the Northwest Coast of North America (Ruyle 1973) and in Panama (Helms 1979). Supernatural sanctions in one form or another were important sources of power among chiefs in the Trobriand Islands (Weiner 1988), north India (Thapar 1984), and Tikopia (Firth 1957 [1936]). James Gibb provides a graphic demonstration of these powers in his easily accessible film from the 1970s on the Kpelle of Liberia, *The Cows of Dolo Ken Paye.*

11

ANTHROPOLOGY AND THE
STUDY OF THE STATE

The state does nothing.

—Professor M. Estellie Smith, 1988,
International Congress of Anthropological
and Ethnological Sciences, Zagreb

The state represents a topic of special interest to anthropologists. Neither archaeological nor sociocultural methodologies by which anthropologists study the state constitute a paradigm. Instead, anthropological analyses of the state cut across all the paradigms of political anthropology, except the processual. Exemplars of the processual paradigm largely ignore the state as a unit of study. For them, the state simply provides a receptacle within which to analyze local-level political processes. Exemplars of the other political anthropology paradigms focus on the state *per se* and its internal and external relationships.

Traditionally anthropologists studied precapitalist, preindustrial, non-Western states from their origins five to six thousand years ago up to the present. Increasingly over the last two decades, anthropologists have included socialist and capitalist industrial and postindustrial states in their studies. As a result, anthropologists have made three substantive contributions to the literature on the state in the social sciences and humanities.

First, anthropologists have provided a body of theory to account for the origins of states. This takes place largely but not exclusively in an evolutionary framework. Second, they have identified different kinds of states that have existed from their inception to the present. These studies may also have an evolutionary bias, but they usually result in functional typologies of state formations and vary widely. Third, and most important, anthropologists have contributed to understanding and explaining the internal and external dynamics of state formations as they have existed over the last several thousand years, in particular, those early, non-Western, preindustrial, precapitalist state formations mentioned above. These will be the major concern of this chapter. Aspects of the historical background to the study of the state will be incorporated in the analysis.

THE ORIGIN OF THE STATE

From the inception of anthropology in the nineteenth century and through the declining interest in the last quarter of the twentieth century (Harris 1977 is an exception), many anthropologists were dedicated to discovering the origin of social and cultural phenomena. Of these phenomena, only a concern with the origin of the state persists. This is because the appearance of the state provided a watershed for political practice that had an impact on world societies unlike any other. The state at its inception was represented by the most powerful centralized government over the most nucleated society invented by humankind. The governments of these early states attempted to entrench their politics and ideologies vertically into all the institutions that comprised their political communities, as governments still do. They expanded horizontally at the expense of the autonomy of neighbors, as powerful states still often do. The persistent concern with the origin of this political behemoth is ancient.

Aristotle (384–322 B.C.) was perhaps the first to be aware of the significance of the state (*polis*) for the human condition. He attributed its origin to the increasing amalgamation of villages into ever-larger formations that became the state (Aristotle 1943). In anthropology, Morgan's (1963 [1877]) materialist methodology was the first approach to the evolution of the state. With rare exception, such as Geertz's (1980) idealist depiction of the "theatre state" in nineteenth-century Bali, this methodology persists. But Morgan was not concerned with the evolution of the state per se. He perceived it to be a correlate of civilization. He was more interested in the social implications of the evolution of private property. This latter idea attracted the attention of Marx and Engels and they make much of it in considering the evolution of the state (Engels 1942). P. B. Roscoe's (1993) exposition on practice theory in political evolution is the most recent to try to account for the origin of the state. Most origin theories fit into one of four theoretical categories: voluntaristic, coercive, synthetic, and political.

Voluntaristic theories argue that people come together and create a state for their common good. The classic philosophical treatise for this proposition is Jean-Jacques Rousseau's idea of the social contract. In anthropology, Lowie's (1927) voluntaristic theory suggested that the state emerged out of different associations that superseded kinship and neighborhood organizations and provided other functions that related people across territorial units, such as religious or police services. The ideas of the historian Karl Wittfogel (1957) were important in anthropology because of the research they provoked on the relationship between irrigation and the evolution of the state. According to Wittfogel, farmers who were struggling to support themselves on small-scale irrigation works saw an advantage in setting aside differences and merging their villages into a larger political organization, the "hydraulic" state, to administer irrigation on a larger scale. Simply put, according to Wittfogel, hydraulic states emerge in response to managerial demands of large-scale irrigation works.

Coercive theories deny the role of enlightened self-interest in the origin of the state. The most common coercive theories attribute the origin of the state to the conquest of one polity by another. For Oppenheimer (1975 [1914]; also Ibn Khaldun 1967 [1377]) this happens when nomadic pastoral peoples conquer settled agricultural populations. For Y. A. Cohen (1969) it happens in two ways. In one it occurs when one stateless society among others conquers its neighbors and unites them into an *incorporative state.* In the other it occurs when a distant, technologically advanced state usurps the autonomy of a stateless society or societies and creates an *expropriated state* where none existed previously. We will return to these state formations later.

Two major synthetic theories account for the origin of the state. One builds on the ideas of environmental circumscription and is ecological in nature (Carneiro 1970, 1987). The other is Marxist and political economic in nature. Each includes elements of coercion. And like other synthetic theories they are linear. Each event triggers another that moves toward the appearance of the state.

Carneiro's (1970, 1987) theory is based on the premise that states emerged in environments that were circumscribed by deserts, mountains, or oceans from which populations found it difficult to move. These conditions existed in areas where the earliest states are known to have emerged in prehistory, such as the valleys of the Tigris–Euphrates, Indus, Yellow, and Nile Rivers in the Old World, the lacustrine Valley of Mexico and river valleys in the South American Andes in the New World, and some islands in Oceania. Carneiro's theory relies on the articulation of contingent factors related to resource diversity, population growth, technological change, social evolution, and warfare. The theory depends on a diversity of natural resources and a source of plentiful water in a circumscribed environment as the minimal conditions for the process to occur (also see MacNeish 1964, 1967; Service 1975).

A synthesis of these ideas suggests that the process begins as hunting and gathering societies increase in size and begin to compete for access to resources. As population increases, so does the efficiency of the technology. Foragers gradually give way to horticultural tribes, different ones of which have access to different resources. Demand for these resources stimulates conflict and trade. But increases in population continue to stress the resources, trigger technological innovations, and give rise to incipient agriculture. Some societies become weak or typical chiefdoms. But as the resources are stressed even more by larger populations, competition escalates and warfare ensues. Tribes and weaker chiefdoms decline in number and amalgamate through conquest or defense into larger, more powerful chiefdoms. Eventually extensive irrigation agriculture develops to feed growing populations and some chiefdoms evolve into states by either amalgamation or conquest. Once states emerge, their governments fight for political dominance in the region.

The Marxist theory of state origin relies on a dialectical process and merges ideas of Marx and Engels with Morgan's regarding private property (Marx and Engels 1970 [1932], written 1845–1846; Marx 1888 [1848]; Marx 1964 [1858]; Morgan 1963 [1877]; Engels 1942 [1884]; Bloch 1983). According to this theory, the state appears conterminous with the appearance of classes. Critical to Marxist theory is the presumption of the existence of a lineage (*gens*) that was egalitarian in gender and other statuses, an increase in the amount of available property, and the growing suppression of women.

In this theory, classes develop as people work out the contradiction between private and communal property. Accordingly, men begin to claim private ownership to property. Gradually their acquisitions negate the communal ownership of property by lineages. The lineage declines as men establish monogamous households to provide discrete male heirs to whom they can transfer their property. As a result of monogamy, women are relegated to a subordinate and exploited status. Their previous economic and social functions are suspended and replaced with service to their husbands and sexual reproduction. The ownership of private property and the creation of the monogamous household restructure society into a system of classes, ergo the origin of the state, in which control over the means of production is appropriated by upper-class elites. The subsequent exploitation of lower classes provides the basis for the Marxist identification of the state as an instrument of coercion in the service of the ruling, exploiting class.

Gailey (1987) develops this theory with sufficient particulars in a contemporary context to transform the synthetic nature of the theory into a political theory of state origin. She brings a "Marxist-feminist" approach to the ideas outlined above to account for the transition in Tonga over three hundred years, from about 1650 to the present, from a chiefdom based on cognatic descent associations (ramages) to a class-stratified state formation in the nineteenth century. Gailey uses the appropriate abstractions of the theory—state, class, gender, and the like—to generalize the process. But she also identifies and describes the specific practices of chiefs, missionaries, colonial officials, and others that relegated women and men to lower status. Despite resistance, legal, religious, and ideological strategies wielded by elites and outsiders altered the political economy and destroyed the multiple productive roles that women filled in the society. Kinship relations declined in importance and women were relegated to positions of inferiority both productively and reproductively to accommodate the emerging social stratification and state organization that resulted in the Kingdom of Tonga.

The most explicit political theory to account for the origin of the state was suggested by P. B. Roscoe (1993; also see Lewis and Greenfield 1983). As we saw, practice theory is suggestive but lacks ethnographic verification. Later I will continue the analysis of the evolution of politics that began in Chapter 10 to account for an origin and dynamics of the state.

STATE TYPOLOGIES

Typologies have two major scientific values. First, they allow scientists to make sense out of chaos by bringing order to disparate empirical data. Second, typologies also provide "theoretical models" and independent variables of varying explanatory power against which to test reality. In anthropology, typologies are usually a product of evolutionary theory, and this is true for political anthropology. But as we saw in Chapter 5, the "typological approach" in political anthropology attained notoriety in the functional paradigm.

The fundamental typological contribution of functional exemplars was the distinction between state (type A) and stateless (type B) societies (Fortes and Evans-Pritchard 1940). This distinction fomented a proliferation of typologies of states that were largely African, descriptive, laden with detail, functional, and of little explanatory power regarding cause and effect (Vansina 1962; Lloyd 1965; Southall 1965). As the paradigm lost credibility, "butterfly collecting" (Leach 1961) of this purely functional sort ceased. But typologies with more or less explanatory power for the study of the state continue to appear, and the distinction between state and stateless societies continues to provide a general distinction for anthropological analyses.

Claessen (1978) provided the most recent state typology. Although it is functional, as typologies tend to be, it has considerably more explanatory power than other functional typologies. He argues that "early states" are not automatically complete formations. His project was to determine the point at which a state formation becomes a "full-blown, or *mature* state"

(Claessen 1978:22). To account for this, Claessen relied on data from twenty "early state" societies "grouped around a number of *key* concepts (e.g., territory, sovereignty, stratification, etc.)" (1978:537). He decided that categories of key concepts bunched incrementally and correlated to stages through which states passed: inchoate, typical, and transitional, the latter representing the mature early state that verges on a modern state.

Fried (1960, 1967) drew a typological distinction between pristine and secondary states. The idea of the pristine state identified those states that arose *sui generis* out of stateless formations uninfluenced by any preexisting model of the state. Pristine states emerged in those environments that Carneiro (1970) identified as environmentally circumscribed (the Tigris–Euphrates, Indus, and Yellow River valleys, the lacustrine Valley of Mexico, river valleys of the Andes Mountains, and some islands in Oceania). Fried attributed their emergence to the interaction of a variety of factors, such as population growth and warfare. All states that emerged subsequent to the five areas identified above, such as Tonga, Pharaonic Egypt, or the United States, were secondary states.

As noted earlier, Y. A. Cohen (1969) identified incorporative and expropriated states. This typology is one of the least known. But of all state typologies it has the most explanatory power. Cohen provides generalized explanations for their origins. The incorporative state occurs when, in a region where a number of societies are culturally, linguistically, and technologically similar, one conquers the others and forges them into a state. Expropriated states are created when a technologically advanced and politically more powerful state from far away creates a state where none existed previously. This formation was commonly a product of the expansion of imperial and colonial powers, especially those that expanded worldwide after the sixteenth century.

Of these two formations, the incorporative state has attracted the most attention of anthropologists, and practice theory accounts better for the origin and political consequences of the incorporative state than Cohen's generalized coercion hypothesis. I will use practice theory below to explore the third and major anthropological contribution to the study of the state, the dynamics of state organization.

THE DYNAMICS OF STATE ORGANIZATION

In the broadest sense, the dynamics of state organization refers to the complex relationships that account for the origin of the state, internal structural changes thereafter, and the consequences of these changes and relations with other societies for the development and expansion of state formations since their inception. Anthropologists continue to contribute to the dynamics of these processes, as in their analyses of state terror. And they continue to explore the dynamics of state formations through all the theoretical orientations they bring to their projects.

The most comprehensive anthropological study of the state was initiated by Henri J. M. Claessen. He enlisted colleagues from around the world to contribute to six volumes dedicated to exploring aspects of "early states." The first to appear was *The Early State* (Claessen and Skalník 1978). Subsequent works included a follow-up analysis entitled *The Study of the State* (Claessen and Skalník 1981) and topics related to its evolution and decline (Claessen, van de Velde, and Smith 1985), dynamics and economics, respectively (Claessen and van de Velde 1987, 1991), and ideology (Claessen and Oosten 1996). A plethora of books and articles in different languages have spun off these studies and complement other works on the state (Geertz 1963, 1980; Fried 1964, 1967; Krader 1968; Y. A. Cohen 1969; Service 1975; Lewis and Greenfield 1983; Patterson and Gailey 1987; Thapar 1984; Foucault 1991, among others). Despite the copious literature on the state, the *vertical entrenchment of the incorporative state* (Y. A. Cohen 1969) is one aspect of state dynamics that has not been given the attention it deserves. That will be my focus in the following.

However, because of the vast body of work on the state and the emotion that the idea of the state evokes, the very idea of the state remains ambiguous (Kurtz 1993). To explore the significance of the vertical entrenchment of the state in a practice theory model requires another conceptualization of the state that privileges the idea of government, and not the state, as the source of political power and agency.

State, Government, Nation

A problem that pervades the study of the state is the predilection of social scientists at large, but anthropologists in particular, to anthropomorphize the state as a synecdoche for political agency. Ronald Cohen's conjured image of the state as "the most powerful organizational structure ever developed in the history of the planet [because] *it literally moves mountains and redirects rivers and . . . has on occasion sent untold thousands, even millions, to their deaths*" (1979:1, emphasis added) is characteristic of this synecdoche. It is a dramatic pronouncement. It is poor methodology. It muddles and obfuscates the source of political agency. Professor Estellie Smith's observation in the epigraph to this chapter that "The state does nothing!" provides a more accurate depiction of state agency. But recall in the analysis of power (Chapter 2) Radcliffe-Brown's cogent comment. He identified best the real source of state agency when he asserted, "There is no such thing as the power of the state; there are only, in reality, powers of individuals—kings, prime ministers, magistrates, policemen, party bosses and voters" 1940:xxiii). Allocating political agency to human agents where it belongs and not to an anthropomorphized abstraction referred to as the state provides different insight into the origin and dynamics of early and later state formations, their governments, and the nations they rule. This endeavor requires sharper definitions of state, nation, and government than currently exist.

Years ago, Titus (1931) accounted for 145 definitions of the state; in 2001 there is still no agreement on a definition (Kurtz 1993). The concept of the state is elusive, but it is not beyond conceptualization. To apply once again Occam's razor, the best idea will be that which relies on the fewest but most universal features of the state.

Ronald Cohen (1978) contends that it is impossible to establish a set of traits that apply to more than just a few states. This is not so. There is one universal diagnostic of the state that provides a key to defining it and explaining state agency: the political office (Parsons 1964; Weber 1964 [1947]; Kurtz 1993). Recall that the political office emerged when status leaders were able, without resistance from the political community, to transfer their personal power and authority to an heir, which in time assured a heritable source of power and authority. Contrary to Cohen's belief, the political office represents a universal criterion of the state.

A state may be defined profitably as a structure of interlocking abstract offices that are vested with specific powers and authorities. Formally the structure of offices that constitute the state is characterized by a hierarchy. At the apex of the hierarchy is a single office. This office is occupied by the head of state (which occasionally may be shared by more than one person) and is endowed with three distinct and specialized powers and authorities that were not inherent in the office of chief. These are concerned with command of the armed forces, execution of the laws, and management of the revenues (Gibbon 1897; Mair 1962; Polanyi 1966; Y. A. Cohen 1969; Kurtz 1993). Compared to the powers in preindustrial states, the powers in modern states (such as the United States and other modern democracies) may not be as singular and sharply defined, partly because such governments are subject to a system of checks and balances. But the offices of president of the United States and governor of the various states that comprise the republic (or their equivalents elsewhere) still retain considerable control over the armed forces and national guards, have authority to commute criminal sentences and pardon offenders, and possess veto power over budgets. All other offices in the hierarchy are subordinate in power and authority, at least theoretically (feudalism is an exception), to the office of head of state. These offices comprise the hierarchical bureaucratic structure of the state.

Despite the reservoirs of power and authority vested in them, the offices of state are inert abstractions, mere niches for the incumbents of government. The political agency that anthropologists so commonly attribute to the state is in reality a product of the incumbents of the offices of state and constitute the government of a state. This does not mean that the concept of the state is meaningless. The state is an entity, *de facto* initially and subsequently, in modern times, *de jure*, in whose name incumbents of its offices practice politics. Today incumbents of state offices may be legally liable for crimes committed in the name of the state, and extant incumbents may be held accountable to rectify sins of their predecessors and indemnify those who suffered as a result of their policies (Kurtz 1993). Some think of the state as a mask that conceals real sociopolitical relations and practices (Abrams 1988; McGlynn and Tuden 1991). In reality, it is an abstraction whose mystification is the result of the ritual, rhetoric, and practices of political agents (Bloch 1978, 1985).

Functional exemplars defined government as a static political structure (Fortes and Evans-Pritchard 1940). But the dynamics of government becomes a process when incumbents engage in the business of government, which is administration and politics (M. G. Smith 1960). Administration refers to the practices of government agents who are concerned with the conduct and coordination of public business. The politics of government is dedicated to the use of power by political agents to implement policy and attain public and private goals (M. G. Smith 1960). The administration of government is directed primarily at the affairs of the nation that a government rules. The politics of government applies to relations internal to the nation and to relations with state governments elsewhere. The idea of government agency provides a sharper and more accurate depiction of the agency that can send millions to their deaths than Ronald Cohen's idea of state agency.

The state does not send people to their deaths. Specific incumbents of government may do so, such as judges, generals, executioners, and the heads of state. And it is not the state but agents of government in modern and early states that carry out the goals of government in the spheres of social activity that make up human society. Consider some of the following generalized practices of early and later governments.

In the economic sphere, government agents collect taxes, are licensed to conduct international trade on behalf of the government, and manage the national treasury. In the legal sphere, agents such as police, legislators, special pleaders, and judges enact laws, punish criminals, and define the social structure of a nation by determining the legality of forms of marriage, such as polygyny, and conditions of divorce. In the realm of technological development, government engineers and technicians oversee the development of projects, such as irrigation works, dams on rivers, monuments, and nuclear power plants. Regarding the environment, government agents determine land use and manage national parks. In the political-legal sphere, judges and local head men appointed by government regulate land tenure, rights of eminent domain, voting procedures, and the time and conditions of succession to offices. In the religious sphere, priests often are incorporated into the government's bureaucracy to conduct the rituals and ceremonies that ensure the protection of government by God or the Gods, to invoke the Gods' help in time of war and during other problems, and to bless their nations. In some cases priests may serve as heads of state and direct government through divine authority. To lump specific agent-driven practices under the trope *state* obfuscates the complexity of government and muddles research into the dynamics of politics.

The special administrative and political powers that governments bring to political practice, what Foucault (1991) refers to as *governmentality*, directly affect populations that inhabit political communities known as nations. A nation represents a society within a more or less firmly demarcated territory that is inhabited by nucleated political communities composed of populations that are occupationally specialized, differentiated, and stratified socially and economically. The idea of the incorporative state, with modification to account for the roles of government agents, provides a vehicle to continue to explore how practices related to the evolution of politics account for the origin and dynamics of incorporative and other state formations. However, it is important to remember that even though incorporative and expropriated state formations emerge from different causes, once an expropriated formation attains independence from colonial domination its government often goes through a process of incorporation similar to that of early incorporative formations. I will pay most attention to the idea of the incorporative state, because it represents the type of state that has attracted the most attention of anthropologists and is most amenable to critical analysis by practice theory.

The Evolution of Incorporative State Formations

P. B. Roscoe (1993) identified political evolution as the centralization of political power and authority and the nucleation of increasingly densely populated political communities (see Chapter 10). According to practice theory, political evolution is the result of the recursive relationship that political leaders have with their political communities and the struggle by leaders to control and resolve effectively the contradiction between the autonomy of local communities and political centralization. Political evolution was driven by the power that leaders and political agents used to maintain order and resolve quotidian altercations, alter the influence of the genetic pulses in their environments, manipulate their political economies, hegemonically inculcate desirable cultural values and an authoritarian ideology, and resolve contradictions that are internal and external to their political community.

The evolution of politics may drive the qualitative transformation of polities toward increasing centralization and nucleation. But once a chiefly polity crosses the threshold to a state formation, the evolution of politics does not generate a qualitatively different polity, as occurred when chiefdoms evolved from big men polities or states from chiefdoms. After the appearance of the state, political evolution accounts only for the appearance of more powerfully centralized and nucleated state formations, all of which share the same basic structure of government offices. Minimally this will include the office of head of state, an immediate council, war leaders, and select minions at the local level to whom the head of state delegates authority, such as collecting taxes. As governments build their political power, they elaborate the basic offices of government and try to extend government control over the nation and, where their power permits, neighbors.

Regardless of the array of theories that anthropologists use to explain the origin of the early incorporative, preindustrial, precapitalist, non-Western states that attracted their attention, the appearance of the incorporative state is, fundamentally, a product of warfare. But from a practice theory point of view, warfare is not a generalized occurrence in a linear progression of synthetic events toward statehood driven by abstract genetic pulses. War is the result of conscious, goal-oriented decisions made by chiefs who have much to gain (or lose) as a result (Lewis and Greenfield 1983).

Even though a variety of factors may provide motives for warfare, such as competition over scarce resources, the appearance of an incorporative state formation is the result of the decision of a chief and his war leaders in one society to embark on or continue a war that results in the conquest of immediate neighbors. At some point in the war, the victorious chief steps over a political threshold and becomes the leader of a politically centralized polity that only since the sixteenth century has been identified as the state. Once over this threshold, the chief, now head of state, and his incipient bureaucracy are responsible for governing relatively densely populated political communities that were already highly nucleated as the result of the evolution of chiefly polities. The task that this new state government confronts is how to weld these communities into a nation and elaborate the offices of government to rule it. This is largely accomplished by the vertical entrenchment of government authority and power.

The political practices that Wittfogel (1957) attributes to despotism provide the basis for Y. A. Cohen's model of the vertical entrenchment of the state or, as conceived here, the government of the state. Recall that Wittfogel explained the emergence of the state as a result of farmers deciding to unite to manage large-scale irrigation works. After presenting that idea in his book *Oriental Despotism: A Comparative Study of Total Power*, Wittfogel launched into an analysis of the Asiatic mode of production and the corresponding despotic "Oriental" regimes that he believed were birthed by these waterworks. Wittfogel's work was not value-free. His purpose was to demonstrate that the Soviet Union was a form of Oriental despotism and to relate it to the terror tactics he identified with an Asiatic mode of production (Krader 1975; Hindess and Hirst 1975; Ulmen 1978; Claessen 2000).

Many of the practices that Wittfogel associates with "Oriental despotism" are part of the government politics and praxes of every state, and do not always denote a despotic government. Still, even the most benevolent and legitimate state government will confront some social categories that it perceives to be threats and that it might try to subvert through despotic practices. To extrapolate the semiotics of Foucault's (1991) idea of "governmentality," the mentality of governments often borders on paranoia. To be otherwise in politics is to be insane (see Chapter 3). In every state formation, other political organizations are always lurking in the wings of existing governments waiting to prove that they can govern better. Under these conditions, the mentality of governments that occupy the offices of state induces political and administrative practices that can result in despotism. The extent to which governments are despotic depends on the degree of their legitimacy and state inchoateness. Governments that are less legitimate and rule more inchoate states are more paranoid and more likely to resort to terror to reduce their inchoateness.

The Political Dynamics of the Vertical Entrenchment of Government

The model of the vertical entrenchment of government authority does not apply in every detail to every incorporative state formation. No model has universal application. But the practices of vertical entrenchment are remarkably consistent across those formations that are characterized by the governments of inchoate incorporative state formations.[2]

Y. A. Cohen (1969) identifies the incorporative state as the ruling body of an incorporative nation. It is more accurate to speak of an incorporative government as the ruling body of an incorporative nation. In state formations, the relationship between government and nation is recursive and dominated by the dialectic of local autonomy and centralized control (P. B. Roscoe 1993). The contradiction is never resolved fully, but theoretically it is most severe in incorporative nations. To understand the development of the incorporative state and its government, it is essential to understand the nation with which government has a peculiar recursive relationship.

Incorporative governments inherit from previous chiefly polities communities that are already highly nucleated, densely populated, and preconditioned through hegemonic pressures to an ideology of work. Incorporative governments expand and intensify these processes. Increased nucleation and density create a problem of scale and a different recursive relationship between governments and their nations.

A nation is a political community that is made up of groups of people who are geographically contiguous and at the same level of cultural development. In an incorporative nation the dominant, ruling class and subordinate classes rely on similar economic foundations, share comparable cognitive orientations and notions of cause and effect in nature, speak the same or similar languages, share idioms regarding kinship and community organization, and are ethnically homogeneous (Y. A. Cohen 1969). As a result of these proximate features, the social distance between rulers and ruled is slight and the resistance of some to the domination of others is likely to be more intense. Since governments require a pronounced degree of social distance from those they rule (Lenski 1966; Kurtz 1984), an incorporative government adopts measures to establish that distance and extend its rule. To fend off resistance by local groups to this strategy, the government of an inchoate incorporative state formation attempts to entrench its authority vertically in all spheres of institutionalized social activity and into the practices of the people that make up the nation. To do this, government practices alternate as conditions require between the application of force and hegemonic culturation in its recursive relationship with the nation. During a government's vertical entrenchment phase, the use of force is more dramatic and attention getting, and it can be effective, although it is also likely to be costly. The effectiveness of its control in welding together a nation is likely to be accomplished better and with less cost if, through its hegemonic culturation, it is successful in inculcating an ideology and practices that the government desires (Kurtz 1996a). But there is no necessary correlation between the ideology of a government and its political practices.

For example, the structure and organization of the offices that housed the governments of the Aztecs, the former Soviet Union, Nazi Germany, and the United States were not much different except that the offices of the latter three governments were more elaborate. But the validating ideology by which each government justified its politics and attempted to convince the nation of its right to rule differed considerably. Yet, in the realm of practices concerned with coercion and even terror, the political practices by which these governments entrenched their power and authority were not all that different. Each used force and coercion to gain its ends when it felt necessary to do so. Human sacrifices by priests of the Aztec government, the slaughter of dissidents in the Soviet Union, the extermination practices of the Nazis, and genocidal policies of the governments of the United States against American Indians and the incarceration of Japanese citizens in World War II differ in degree and not kind. Governments decide on the political practices that result in their vertical entrenchment. That is why it is imprecise to speak of the entrenchment of the state.

The vertical entrenchment of the governments of incorporative states is largely a natural history of the increasing influence of the praxes of state governments over the personal practices of their citizens and the nation's institutions. The vertical entrenchment of the power and authority of governments complements their legitimation (Chapter 4). But legitimation involves a reciprocity between governments' practices and citizens' compliance (Kurtz 1984) that is not necessarily expected by governments as they pursue their vertical entrenchment.

The praxes by which government agents pursue their vertical entrenchment is insidious. Governments initiate policies and practices across a broad social front. Most people in early incorporative nations are not aware that changes are taking place. Some changes may happen quickly. Other changes may transpire over generations. But over time, the traditional interests and rights of the people, such as control over their sexual practices and the integrity of their lineage structures, are subverted and gradually transformed by government controls (Y. A. Cohen 1969). Often people are not aware of these transitions until it is too late to resist meaningfully or, because of successful hegemonic culturation, they are too comfortable in the new political environment to do otherwise than comply.

The vertical entrenchment of governments is based on two overlapping and complementary political strategies. One is aimed at developing the political economy upon which the power of governments fundamentally rest. The other strategy is dedicated to securing their power and survival. Some incorporative governments isolate themselves for varying periods of time through some form of closed-door policy from external political arenas. Most do not have this luxury. But for those that do, this space gives governments time within which to establish some critical preconditions that increase the effectiveness of incorporative strategies.

The government of an incorporative state moves quickly to install trusted local-level leaders and headmen to whom the head of state has delegated some authority and power. Some of their delegated duties ensure the survival of government, such as disposing of quotidian altercations, reporting local discontent, quelling rebellions, and, in general, maintaining social order. But they are necessary for the success of other practices that are more distinctly politically economic, such as collecting taxes, assigning corvée service to citizens, and confiscating the properties of malcontents and undesirables. These local leaders are also largely responsible for the hegemonic culturation of the government's ideology. The constant reaffirmation of government values is a politically inexpensive way to ensure the survival of the government. Taken together, these strategies create a social and physical environment within which government can influence and control the nation's political economy.

Taxes are collected in both kind and service, and are expanded considerably from those extracted in chiefly polities. Taxes taken in kind provide resources directly to the national treasury for use on government projects. Corvée service is important to build and maintain the technological infrastructure of the nation and the political economy upon which government relies. Through corvée service, people are obliged to work the lands their government expropriates in conquest and confiscation as its own private resource base. Corvée labor builds roads to connect nucleated populations, move troops to frontiers to meet external threats, and move goods to market, within which government agents may set prices, ensure fair exchange, and maintain order (Kurtz 1974). Governments use corvée labor to build and maintain irrigation works or terraces or to maintain other technologies of the political economic infrastructure, such as the estates of the ruling class. Hydraulic systems are the major genetic pulse of many incorporative state formations and their management is deeply penetrated by government agents. They are charged with planning, building, and extending these works, managing the distribution of water, and overseeing the material wealth that governments derive from these works.

Compared to chiefly polities, incorporative governments are much better at curtailing the population's movements. Restricting migration keeps intact the political community and the workforce it provides. Some incorporative governments proclaim a territorial boundary to circumscribe the nation. Sometimes this is more symbolic than real. Most incorporative governments lack the power to enforce policy over the entire territory they claim. The effectiveness of government control may be restricted to populations close at hand. Populations on the frontiers of a nation are difficult to control, even for governments of modern industrial nations.

Incorporative governments ensure their power and survival largely by subverting local-level organizations of solidarity and allegiance that denote inchoateness because they provide sources of resistance to governments' vertical entrenchment. These might include secret societies, men's clubs, age sets, and the like. But in early incorporative formations, the lineage provides a major threat to centralizing governments because of the loyalty it commands from its members. In some incorporative formations the lineage may be an egalitarian association. In others it is part of the ramage structure of the chiefly polities from which the class structure of incorporative states evolves. The subversion of egalitarian lineages results in their demise. The subversion of ramages restructures their relationships. The highest-ranking lineages provide the line of inheritance to offices of head of state and other high officeholders. Ranks close to it may become the landed and privileged nobility. The lowest ranks become part of the lower-class structure of incorporative nations. The subversion of lineages can be accomplished by a variety of purposeful strategies.

Government revenue agents may impose taxes on each household instead of the lineage as a corporate unit, as is often the case in strong chiefdoms. This makes households independent of the lineage, for its members now have to seek their own fortunes. These practices may also undermine polygyny. Monogamy reduces the potential for the expansion of kinship relations, disenfranchises women, and relegates them to the status of their husbands' chattel. Husbands are likely to support governments that favor their male populations. Educators in state-run schools, usually priests, may make the attendance of children, especially boys, mandatory. The primary goal of universal education is to inculcate hegemonically the values that create a good, that is, productive, citizen. Recall that a major goal of hegemonic culturation is the inculcation of an ideology of work. Schools are a primary source for such hegemonic culturation. The inculcation of knowledge is a distant secondary goal of public education. Educated citizens can pose a threat to incorporative governments because they are more likely to resist government practices. When military leaders conscript young men into the armed forces, a large population of potential resisters is effectively transformed into an army that is trained and inculcated to fight for the state and nation, not the lineage. Furthermore, government police may seize the properties of lineages and individuals who resist and incorporate them into the government's political economy.

The degree of inchoateness of an incorporative state formation is also reflected in the organization of its pantheon and religious structure (Durkheim 1954 [1912]). Theoretically, polytheism, the condition in which many Gods are worshiped, correlates to an inchoate state. Monotheism, the worship of one God, reflects a state whose government has totally subverted all sources of local solidarity and shifted the allegiance of the political community to the government of the state and the nation it rules. Most incorporative nations are polytheistic with regard to the religion that government sponsors, as well as those that prevail at the local level. Some incorporative governments consciously try to engage people at the local level to participate in the worship of the gods of the state pantheon and in government-sponsored rituals and ceremonies. Some are more successful than others. But monotheism, the symbolic unity of one nation under one God, is almost impossible to attain. Even the most legitimate governments are unable to reduce religious heterogeneity below a condition of plural religions in which people worship variations of the same deity or deities, such as the Father, Son, and the Holy Ghost.

Incorporative governments may not invoke each of these strategies. Some governments may emphasize different strategies. Some strategies may not be applicable. For example, not all incorporative formations had schools.

Wittfogel makes much of the use of state terror in forcing compliance of the people to the despotic practices of government. Incorporative governments may institutionalize and either legalize or tolerate forms of human degradation, such as mass slaughter, human sacrifice, joint liability, incarcerations, torture, capital punishment, government surveillance, and so forth. The pursuit of human degradation also relies on agents and officeholders of government, such as trusted local headmen, police, military forces, judges, spies, torturers, priests who conduct human sacrifice, jailers, and executioners.

Early incorporative governments also enact laws or implement practices that regulate the sexual practices of their citizens, and regularly impose sentences of death, torture, or incarceration for incest, adultery, and premarital sex (Y. A. Cohen 1969). Control of a nation's affective practices symbolizes the ultimate power of incorporative governments over the behavior of their subjects. And an incorporative government that can effectively control the affective practices of its people has gone a long way toward effectively controlling the less emotional practices of their subjects.

Wittfogel and many anthropologists, especially some New World archaeologists, emphasize the role of government terror and coercion in the evolution of chiefdoms and early state formations (Sanders, Parsons, and Santley 1979; Sanders and Santley 1983; Earle 1991). But the existence of the means of terror does not necessarily prove their implementation. And there are peculiarities to the application of terror.

Governments do not usually resort to terror except under special conditions, such as when the government mentality perceives a threat. Even then the laws are rarely used indiscriminately against citizens in good standing with the government. Most often they are directed toward specific social categories of people that the government has identified as criminal, undesirable, or prisoners of war. If citizens are subject to terror, it is because they have fallen out of grace with the government, or the government mentality is extremely paranoid. Whatever the situation, those citizens that a government decides to terrorize are usually degraded in status or legally deprived of citizenship prior to or around the time that official terror begins. This may be terribly unjust and criminal, as the Holocaust proves. But the point is, governments of incorporative and other states are selective in their application of terror. It is simply not in their best interests to terrorize the people upon whom they rely for support and legitimacy. Some social anthropologists argue that political processes rarely involve the direct use of force and terror (Lowie 1927; Service 1975; Kertzer 1988; Kurtz and Nunley 1993; Kurtz 1996a), and Godelier suggests that "the consent of the dominated to their domination" (1978:676) is more powerful in accounting for the relationship of rulers to their subjects than is coercion.

The application and use of terror are dramatic and attention getting. The mere threat of terror is less dramatic, but more common. For example, if incorporative governments really prosecuted all those who were guilty under law of incest, adultery, and premarital sex, government executioners and incarcerators would be working overtime. If the hegemonic culturation of a government is successful, the use of terror is often unnecessary or minimal. In this case, many of the same practices that Wittfogel attributes to the terror of the Asiatic despotic state may operate as normative practices on behalf of the common good, such as road construction, corvée service to the community, and regulation of market exchange. Under these conditions, most people are not overly disturbed by the sybaritic lifestyle of the ruling class that sharply defines the real and symbolic social distance between rulers and ruled.

The vertical entrenchment of government is not restricted to early incorporative state formations. The idea of entrenchment reveals practices that are common to the governments of many contemporary state formations. Depending on the legitimacy of state governments and the inchoateness of states and nations, entrenchment practices can vary considerably. In any particular formation, if the government mentality feels threatened, it can quickly become as coercive as Wittfogel's model suggests.

Practice theory provides a good way to explore the role of political agents in the evolution of qualitatively different political formations and their role in securing the power and authority of government. Not everyone likes the role that government plays in their lives. But the better we understand the practices of political agents and their motivations, the more likely we will be able to do something about situations and conditions that induce government excesses. The attribution of all of these practices to an anthropomorphized state contributes nothing to our understanding of how the ongoing evolution of politics influences the day-to-day practices of the people and communities that constitute the nations of the world.

NOTES

1. Y. A. Cohen (1969) identified twelve incorporative state formations. These include the Albanians, the Puritans in seventeenth-century North America,

Amhara, Ashanti, Aztecs, Basuto, Egyptians (Dynastic), Ganda, Hebrews (Davidic), Inca, Japan (Tokugawa), and the Kazak (Sultanate). To follow the pattern established in Chapter 10, I will generalize the discussion on the evolution of the incorporative state and the vertical entrenchment of incorporative governments that follows. I will provide the ethnographic background to the latter process in another endnote at the appropriate place in the text.

2. The twelve societies that make up the analysis of the vertical entrenchment of the government of incorporative states were part of a larger analysis of the social and political organizations of 28 state formations that I did for Y. A. Cohen in 1966 and 1967. Dynastic Egypt was the earliest state in the study and Nazi Germany was the most recent. To account for the ethnographic reference for each characteristic of the process of entrenchment would consume too much space and result in too much clutter. Instead I will list below the references that provided the data on each state in the study and then relate information presented in the text to the appropriate incorporative state formation. The incorporative states include the Albanians (Coon 1950; Durham 1928; Hasluck 1954), Puritans of seventeenth-century North America (Perley 1924; Powell 1965), Amhara (Ethiopians) (Levine 1965), Ashanti (Busia 1951; Rattray 1923, 1929), Aztecs (Duran 1964 [1581]; Soustelle 1961; Thompson 1933; Zorita 1963 [1570s–1580s]), Basuto (Ashton 1952), Egyptians (Dynastic) (Petrie 1923; Mertz 1966; J. E. W. White 1963), Ganda (Richards 1959; J. Roscoe 1911), Hebrews (Davidic) (Pedersen 1926), Inca (Brundage 1963; Murra 1958; Rowe 1946), Japan (Tokugawa) (Bella 1957; Earl 1964; Matsumoto 1960; T. C. Smith 1959), and Kazak (Sultanate) (Hudson 1938).

Of these formations, the two that comply most completely with the model of vertical entrenchment of an incorporative government are the Aztecs and Tokugawa Japan. They are also the only ones to engage in a closed-door policy. Tokugawa Japan shut itself off between 1600 and 1854, at which time the United States, under Commander Perry, forced Japan to open its markets to international trade. Between 1300 and 1428, the Aztecs spent about 25 years building their capitol city, Tenochtitlan, following a crushing military defeat, and after about another 100 years of quietly conforming to cultural patterns in Central Mexico, they embarked on their binge of conquest and domination in 1428 (Berdan 1982). Other, more contemporary governments such as China (ancient and modern) and the Soviet Union have used closed-door policies. The United States refers to the closed-door policy it established in the early nineteenth century and invoked as recently as 1962 during the Cuban missile crisis as the Monroe Doctrine.

The governments of all twelve incorporative formations replaced local headmen with trusted supporters, engaged in varying degrees of human degradation to overcome real or perceived resistance, and imposed corvée service and/or collected taxes in kind. Only the Kazak failed to claim rights of eminent domain. All but the Ashanti, Ganda, and Hebrews established a central judiciary. All but the Puritans, Ashanti, Basuto, and Japan were polytheistic. All but the Kazak and Ashanti regulated and controlled markets. All but the Amhara, Ashanti, and Kazak developed a system of roads. In all but the Basuto, Ganda, Hebrews, and

Kazak either a centralized priesthood existed or the head of state served as the head priest. All but the Puritans, Amhara, Ashanti, Ganda, Hebrews, and Kazak developed irrigation works. The Ashanti, Basuto, Ganda, Hebrews, and Kazak lacked state schools. The Albanians, Amhara, Basuto, Egypt, and Inca conscripted young men into military service. The Aztecs, Basuto, and Inca purposefully undercut the lineage organization of their nations to help to produce a class-stratified society. Taken as a package, these data suggest a pattern to the entrenchment practices of the governments of early inchoate incorporative state formations.

12

THE POSTMODERN PARADIGM OF POLITICAL ANTHROPOLOGY

The Genre of Experimental Political Ethnography

Our Crusade was so horrible that only an idealist could
have thought it out.

—Squire to Knight Antimius Bloch,
Ingmar Bergman's *The Seventh Seal*

The idea of postmodernism as a paradigm does not comply with Kuhn's notion of a paradigm or the normal science with which it is associated. But a paradigm may also be defined in terms other than its scientific denotations. If we think of a paradigm as a pattern, example, or model around which a variety of complementary concepts and ideas revolve, then postmodernism may well represent a paradigm, or at least one in the making.

I will argue in this chapter that postmodern anthropologists have made considerable contributions to understanding and explaining political phenomena and that their writing on violence and terror, in particular, may provide the foundation for a paradigm of postmodern political anthropology. Topics on these phenomena appear in select journals, such as the *Political and Legal Anthropology Review (PoLAR)*, and as ethnographies (Feldman 1991; Mahmood 1996; Nordstrom 1997; Slyomovics 1998; Linke 1999; Sluka 2000; among others). The ethnographies demand attention because ethnographies, political or otherwise, represent the experimental forms of writing and representation that define the postmodern in anthropology. As with other anthropological paradigms, those ethnographies with political content provide the empirical foundation for theory. In postmodern political anthropology this theory is nascent, albeit emerging. The nature of this potential paradigm is best understood against the background of postmodernism and its anthropological manifestations.

THE ORIGINS AND CHARACTER OF POSTMODERNISM

The origins of postmodernism are ambiguous. Some attribute it to debates in architecture in the 1950s that culminated in the 1960s over how to represent the built environments of a changing world (Hutcheon 1989). Others attribute it to the failure in the late 1960s of Marxist traditions to prevail in French politics and disenchantment with the emerging dominance of capitalist media and consumerism (Lyotard 1993 [1979 in French]; Baudrillard 1983, 1985, 1998; Jameson 1984; Lilla 1998). Huyssen (1990) locates it in the United States in the 1950s among literary critics who were nostalgic for the richer literary past they believe prevailed before World War II (Oldani 1998). Jameson (1984) believes that it is a product of the late stages of capitalism. McGee and Warms (2000) suggest that it derived from hermeneutics and literary criticism in Europe after World War I. Tyler (1987) says the origins of postmodernism are unknown.

The definition of postmodernism is as elusive as its origin. It has been identified as a pastiche, collage, or fad, a bricolage of borrowed and cobbled fragments from an array of academic orientations, a problematic, a style, a cultural notion, and a discourse (Clifford 1988; Milner, Thomson, and Wirth 1990; Gellner 1992; Wikan 1996; among others). These notions of postmodernism derive in part from the language by which postmodernists, including many anthropologists, represent their subject matter. Postmodern scholars argue that they require a special vocabulary to represent the new and different manifestations of social and cultural phenomena that postmodernism engages. As a result postmodern writing is replete with an exclusive and arcane argot that, for critics of postmodernism, has become a topic for derision. Perhaps the best way to introduce the problem of this language is to use one of the characteristics of postmodern expression—parody—which, in the form of a joke, becomes the mimesis of the postmodern itself:

What do you get when you cross a postmodernist with a gangster?
An offer you can't understand. (Oldani 1998:83)

Other ideas regarding what postmodernism represents are more expansive. Lyotard (1993 [1979]), one of the founding fathers of postmodernism, defines it as an "incredulity toward metanarratives" (1993 [1979]: xxiv)—art, science, literature, capitalism, free enterprise, religion—that have defined the modern era. Hutcheon (1989) sympathetically refers to the postmodern as a problematic that is constituted of a set of complex and interrelated questions that have value for understanding the social and cultural world of the future. Tyler, who some think to be the father of postmodern anthropology, defines postmodernism "as the culmination of modernism's idea of representation" (1987:xi), and, elsewhere, as "the name of the congeries of negativities that end the modern epoch" (1987:3). Not all scholars are so sympathetic to the postmodern enterprise.

Habermas (1979) believes that postmodernism is an expression of a new social conservatism and is concerned about what a world dominated by postmodern ideas will be like. Gellner (1992) writes that postmodernism repudiates clarity and represents a hysteria of subjectivity, and equally apoplectic, Harris condemns postmodern research as "personalistic and idiosyncratic [and] carried out by untrained would-be novelists and ego-tripping narcissists afflicted with congenital logo-diarrhea" (1994:64). As we shall see, this simply is not always the case.

Postmodernism as construct and project may be clearer when it is contrasted with the idea of modernism, the character of which postmodernists reject. For some, modernism is identified with the study of literature and art from the 1920s to the 1970s (Manganaro 1990; McGee and Warms 2000). Rabinow (1986) suggests that modernist writing by anthropologists was characterized by literary, artistic, and modern scientific practices that resulted in the author's detachment from the subject of study, assumptions of scientific neutrality, objectivity, and rationalism. These ideas may have received expression in this period, but others trace the idea of modernism, especially its scientific aspects, to the eighteenth-century Enlightenment. Enlightenment thinkers argued that the power of reasoning and the perfectability of human nature provided the foundations upon which progress through science, objectivity, order, and the like would result in a better world (Gellner 1992; Meštrović 1992; Hastrup 1995). That which ensued represented the "modern."

Postmodernists perceive a failure of Enlightenment philosophy and science in the debaucheries and corruption of colonialism, internecine global wars, increased rates of suicide, social injustice, epidemic disease, violence, abuse of women, exploitation of minorities, and increased numbers of impoverished—the entire panoply of horrors that punctuate the modern era. Radical postmodernists attribute the nihilism, cynicism, and anarchism that they bring to their view of modern society to these failures. Their solution to this mess is to deconstruct utterly the meanings, values, institutions, ideas, and symbols that mark the remnants of modernity (Gellner 1992; Meštrović 1992). These views disturb many modern scholars, scientists, and humanists.

Still, even detractors of postmodernism can be sympathetic to some of these concerns when they consider the social, economic, political, and epidemiological plagues that afflict humanity and assault our sensibilities daily. But for many, the bankruptcy of postmodernism as project, ideology, and practice is the failure of its exemplars to suggest, much less formulate, an alternative postmodern vision to supplant the necrosis of modernity. The radical agenda of postmodernists derives from the nihilistic and anarchistic philosophies of some of its progenitors, such as Baudrillard (Kellner 1989; Gane 1991a, 1991b; Meštrović 1992), and they in turn draw sustenance from those cynical and nihilistic depictions of social life that are present in some of the philosophical speculation of Friedrich Nietzsche, Martin Heidegger, and Paul de Man, each of whom was complicit in the formulation or support of Nazi thought, policy, and practice (Meštrović 1992; Lilla 1998). These relations and their "negativities" fuel Habermas's concern with the political configuration of a postmodern world. For some radical postmodernists, such as Baudrillard, the deconstruction of contemporary society seems to be an end in itself. If there is an antidote to these concerns for detractors of postmodernism, it is the fact that postmodernism rests more on rhetoric than practice. The postmodern mantra of deconstruction that derives from the writings of Jacques Derrida, Paul de Man, and J. Hillis Miller (Bloom et al. 1990) has had the most impact on literature and art. In anthropology, the idea of deconstruction is expressed most emphatically in discourses related to the art of writing ethnography.

THE POSTMODERN CONDITION
IN ANTHROPOLOGY

The origins of postmodernism in anthropology are not as vague as those of postmodernism at large. Postmodern anthropology comes from several related sources. Ontologically the postmodernism current in anthropology flows from the rejection of the scientific agenda of the Enlightenment thinkers that emerged with the extreme cultural relativism of Franz Boas and his students. Although they were disenchanted with the nineteenth-century idea of evolutionary progress, anthropologists who were committed to the cultural concept did not deny that a better world might emerge. They even continued to gave lip service to the idea of a "Science of Culture." But early idealist alternatives to anthropology as science emerged in the literary writings of Ruth Benedict (1934), Oliver La Farge (1929 [1957]), Paul Radin (1926), and others. These continue today in the postmodern "ethnographies" of John Dorst (1989), Barbara Tedlock (1992), and Bruce Williams (1994), among others.

Dorst's (1989) work, *The Written Suburb*, is a "cultural discourse" on Chadds Ford, a Philadelphia suburb and tourist site because of the Wyeth art museum. It is replete with postmodern jargon. Tedlock's (1992) ethnography, *The Beautiful and the Dangerous* (Tedlock 1992), presents the ordinary everyday life of Zuni Indians as a humanistic novel in which the Tedlocks also have parts. *Bambo Jordan* (Williams 1994) is a fieldwork memoir that subordinates epistemology to dialogue to account for the complicated employer–employee (servant) relationship that Williams had with Bambo Jordan in Malawi in the 1960s as a Peace Corps volunteer and in the 1980s as an anthropologist. According to Tedlock, the goal of a postmodern ethnography is to produce a "seamless text" that depicts the "Other" through a methodology dedicated to the "observation of participation" instead of "participant observation" (1992:xiii). Critics claim that this methodology results in epistemological nihilism and narcissistic anthropologists who study themselves (Gellner 1992; Harris 1994). This criticism reflects the ongoing, acrimonious debate since Boas between materialist and idealist anthropologists (Harris 1968; Honigman 1976). Today this divide is expressed in the intellectual strife between postmodern and other anthropologists.

While the roots of postmodern ideology and practice in anthropology may be in the Enlightenment and cultural studies of the Boasians, the eventual challenge of postmodernism to normal anthropological practice emerged from complicated intersections in anthropology in the 1960s and 1970s. These currents involved the impact of structuralism and the rethinking of linguistic theory and the idea of the "sign" (Levi-Strauss 1963, 1969 [1949]; Saussure 1966 [1959]), the crystallizing and subsequent decline of cognitive anthropology (Tyler 1969, 1987), Geertz's personalized and symbolic interpretations of culture (1972, 1973, 1983), and the philosophical and antiscience speculations of Foucault (1965, 1973, and other works), Derrida (1978), Lyotard (1993 [1979]), and Baudrillard (1983, 1985, 1998). Other intellectual forces were the (post)structuralist semiotics of Barthes (1975, and other works), the literary theory of Bakhtin (1981, 1984), the growing interest of anthropologists in hermeneutics (McGee and Warms 2000), the widespread angst and guilt among the generation of post–Viet Nam anthropologists over anthropology's support of colonial enterprises, and a narcissistic confessional style of writing (James H. McDonald, personal communication, 2000). These trends were galvanized in the 1980s as a postmodern anthropology with the publication of *Writing Culture: The Poetics and Politics of Ethnography* (Clifford and Marcus 1986) and, especially, *Anthropology as Cultural Critique: An Experimental Moment in the Human Sciences* (Marcus and Fischer 1986).

Marcus, Fischer, Clifford, and other postmodern progenitors were not committed to normal scientific practice. They challenged the ethnographic foundation of scientific anthropology and strove to situate anthropology in the postmodern movement in cultural studies in the humanities. The strain between postmodern and positivist anthropologists in the 1980s forcefully expressed the tension between anthropology's status as the most humanistic of the sciences and the most scientific of the humanities (Wolf 1964). Postmodern anthropologists come down squarely on the side of the humanities in this divide.

Postmodern anthropologists derive intellectual nourishment from the culture concept and their methodology conforms to the epistemology and practice of the idealist tradition in anthropology. For most postmodern anthropologists, this means that they reject paradigmatic, "normal" science. They favor instead a humanistic methodology dedicated to the construction and writing of an ethnographic genre as the primary medium for presenting anthropological narratives and representing the subjects, the "Others," of ethnographic research (Geertz 1983; Clifford and Marcus 1986; Marcus and Fischer 1986; Behar and Gordon 1995; J. L. Lewis 1995). As a result, postmodern practice is driven more by the methodological assumptions of a genre than a paradigm (D. A. Gordon 1995; Kurtz n.d.).

The traditional concept of a genre, which is relevant to ethnography, refers to a literary type or class, a collective form of expression through a variety of writing styles that is sometimes classified by subject (Beckson and Ganz 1975; Holquist 1990; Hawthorne 1992), such as ethnography. In some ways a literary genre is similar to Kuhn's idea of a scientific paradigm. It represents the formation of a constellation of ideas, hypotheses, practices, and discursive properties—a methodology—that provide templates for creative writing (Todorov 1990). A literary genre emerges from existing genres and can shift, develop, and change over time. It may replace a previous genre whose practitioners have exhausted its creative potential (Todorov 1990; McLeish 1993). Yet it differs from a paradigm in one critical way. In mainstream science, researchers are required to make clear the methodological and epistemological assumptions of their projects. Individuals who work within a genre are under no such compulsion. Postmodern anthropologists have justifications for this.

The genre of ethnographic writing in experimental and novel styles is at the heart of the postmodern project in cultural anthropology. Postmodern anthropologists believe that their methods of ethnographic representation place them on the cusp of a new, experimental moment in "writing culture." Several critical issues underlie the genre of postmodern ethnography through which postmodern ethnographers assert their difference from "normal" anthropological practice. These relate to the act of writing ethnography, the problem of ethnographic authority, and the interpretation and representation of the ethnographic subject. In practice, writing, not fieldwork, is the postmodern methodology. But fieldwork provides the foundation for most postmodern projects that result in ethnography. The postmodern critique of anthropology begins with fieldwork and is epistemological in nature (McGee and Warms 2000).

Fieldwork is the first crucial step toward writing ethnography. Yet traditionally, most ethnography contains little information on the actual process of fieldwork. Postmodern anthropologists contend that since fieldwork is crucial to writing ethnography, the practices of fieldwork must be reflected in the ethnography, and that traditional ethnography is sorely wanting in this regard.

Postmodern ethnographers claim that traditional ethnographers hide behind a mask of scientific objectivity and neutrality and exert power over and remain detached from their ethnographic subjects. In paradigmatic research, ethnographers are the final authority of the interpretation of the data they collect, and the ethnographer's voice prevails over that of their subjects. Postmodernist ethnographers consider this to be poor practice. They assert that ethnographers can never be unbiased, objective observers and can never cover adequately all that they claim to observe. As a result, postmodern exemplars do not presume scientific objectivity and disclaim any power over the subject. Instead they acknowledge their subjective insights and biases and rely heavily on anecdotal information provided through the voices of their subjects.

Postmodern ethnographers believe that the traditional ethnographic representation of the subject, the ethnographic "Other," is incomplete, prejudiced, and wrong. To rectify these shortcomings, they insist on a reflexive dialogue and relationship with their subjects and respect the voice of the "Other" as the ethnographic authority instead of the anthropologist. They contend that truth is intrinsic to and revealed in the discourses, stories, and multiple voices through which the subjects of their research communicate. Postmodernist ethnographers rely on their intuition and the voices of their research subjects to decide what is important. Because of the more subjective style that postmodern ethnographers bring to their projects, they perceive the ethnographic product to be a text subject to evaluation by the standards of literary criticism instead of scientific verification (Geertz 1980; Clifford and Marcus 1986; Marcus and Fischer 1986; Clifford 1988). Postmodern ethnographic practices were responses to changes in the nature and context of anthropology's subjects.

Even before postmodernism provided a new style and writing format, ethnography as a genre was blurred (Geertz 1983). By the 1980s, anthropology's traditional subject matter—the "primitive Other"—was replaced by other "Others" and new problems reflected in more diverse, less "primitive" subjects and more complex contexts. Many younger as well as older anthropologists began to argue that styles of traditional ethnographic writing and discourse did not apply to these new circumstances, such as civil wars, terrorism, abuse of women, and others that will be discussed later. As anthropologists increasingly experimented with new ways of representing their subjects ethnographically, Marcus and Fischer (1986) argued that traditional ethnography represented the exhaustion of a paradigmatic style. Postmodernism provided them with an ideology, a movement, a haven, and compatriots equally disillusioned with "normal" anthropological science. They proclaimed ethnography as a scientific document and anthropology as a positivist science to be defunct.

In place of a scientific ethnography, postmodern anthropologists bring experimental styles of writing to the ethnographic genre. They reject the realist approach of traditional ethnography that tried to depict holistically self-contained populations in a presumed ethnographic present. Under the postmodernist lens, eclecticism and methodological chaos prevail. Postmodern exemplars rely on resources from literature, philosophy, and semiotics, among other fields, albeit with some pattern and rational end purpose in mind to construct their ethnographies. They may use their own words to describe, understand, and explain a situation, but they rely on stories, anecdotes, and commentaries told through the voices of their subjects to provide empirical verification of "reality" and to temper the voice and authority of the anthropologist. They allow rhetorical passion to hold sway in presenting information, and use revelation and imagination to establish authoritative statements in novel ways. Even the idea of "ethnography" has changed. Linke (1999), for example, has written an "ethnography" that explores the history of ideas regarding symbols of blood imagery and their relation to the power practices of European nations, in particular the Germans, on women and Jews from prehistory to the present!

Yet despite claims of postmodern ethnographers to the contrary, many who write experimental postmodern ethnographies on political matters do establish theoretical frameworks to direct their research. And, as with traditional scientific research, they often make claims to truth. But the major difference between postmodern and scientific research is that claims to truth by postmodern anthropologists are not subject to established forms of scientific validation. Instead, as in literary criticism, claims to truth are established in the elegance of their arguments and can be challenged only by the elegance of other arguments, not by the quality of a theory or the replication of its data. This kind of intellectual give and take represents a literary and not a scientific process. In general, postmodern ethnographers allow parody, satire, the sensational, and the disturbing to inseminate their imaginations and the representations of their subjects.

Postmodern ethnographers who write on political matters often complement their humanistic intent with scientific considerations that are not totally divorced from the traditional ethnography that postmodern ethnographers set out to deconstruct. Some ethnographers even suggest practical, applied solutions to the problems they confront (Mahmood 1996; Nordstrom 1997). Tyler (1987), a staunch defender of postmodernism, points out that the ideals of postmodern methodology also make it impossible to write a postmodern ethnography. Below I consider those ideas, topics, and practices that may begin to constitute a postmodern paradigm of political anthropology.

POSTMODERN POLITICAL ANTHROPOLOGY

In most anthropological research there is some disjunction between what people propose to do and what they actually do. Much of the postmodern scholarship that has political content is imbued with postmodern rhetoric and jargon. However, much of the practice and representation of postmodern research on political matters also has overt scientific and applied implications that contradict the rhetoric that distinguishes postmodern methodology and ideology.

Some postmodern anthropologists would resent the idea that they might be identified with a paradigm of postmodern political anthropology. These anthropologists do not commonly cite political anthropologists related to the previous paradigms. The interlocutors that mediate their political concerns are as likely to be anthropologists, such as Michael Taussig (1980, 1987) and Nancy Scheper-Hughes (1992, 1995), as others, such as Michel Foucault, Noam Chomsky, or the "Culture Czar" Homi Bhabha (1998; *India Today,* April 30, 1997, p. 45; Greenhouse 1997). And the topics on which they write often are less about politics and the political than they are charged with political content and implications. But if a postmodern political anthropology can be identified, it will be on the basis of what makes it political.

Many postmodern anthropologists would disagree that the experimental and new orientation they bring to politics has roots in a previous paradigm. But their political anthropology is heir to ideas of political analysis first propounded by exemplars of the processual paradigm. One idea is the concern with processes of conflict and its resolution. The second is with dynamic, diachronic analyses instead of static, synchronic analyses. A third is the rejection of formal political structures as the locus for politics and political analysis. The final and most important idea is the conceptualization of politics as "the processes involved in determining and implementing public goals and the differential achievement and use of power by the members of the group with those goals" (Swartz, Turner, and Tuden 1966:7). Those works that comprise a postmodern paradigm of political anthropology, especially the ethnographies, comply with the defining ideas, especially the fourth, that separated the processual from other political paradigms. Postmodern political anthropology brings only new subject matter and writing styles to these ideas.

Most of the contemporary topics that engage postmodern anthropologists with a bias for political matters have roots in other social sciences. These include persistent and recurrent issues related to citizenship, democracy, nationalism, minorities, and civil society. Other issues arose in the 1960s and 1970s and spread beyond the borders of the United States within which they were first addressed. These include the bigotry of the masculine and homophobic ideologies and practices that abuse gays and women and impede their success and self-expression. Other, newer problem areas include political terrorism and violence. Postmodern political anthropology has a curious relationship with issues related to the status of women in anthropology and the ethnography of political terror and violence.

The sexist attitude that some postmodernists, such as Baudrillard, expressed carried over into postmodern anthropology and contributed to the often socially uninformed and conservative image that many postmodernists projected. In anthropology, women anthropologists were excluded utterly from the postmodern project of "writing culture" in the new experimental style that was heralded by Clifford and Marcus (1986). Clifford accounted for this exclusion with the additional denigration that women who were "actively rewriting the male canon" had not "produced either unconventional forms of writing or a developed reflection on ethnographic textuality" (1986: 21–22). Behar sums up Clifford's argument tersely: Women "failed to fit the requirement of being feminist *and* textually innovative" (1995:5). This slight reinvigorated the rebellion by women anthropologists that began in the 1970s against the masculine culture that pervaded anthropology and the academy at large and demeaned their status and scholarship (Behar 1995; D. A. Gordon 1995). The result of this reaction was a proclamation in *Women Writing Culture* (Behar and Gordon 1995) not only to establish firmly a role for women writing culture but also to develop a genre of feminist ethnography (D. A. Gordon 1995).

The issues that *Women Writing Culture* raised regarding the scholarly status and expectation of women in the male-dominated academy are as political as issues can get. They sharpened the already forged and engendered political fields composed of male and female anthropologists and situated them in political arenas replete with material and ideational power that each gender uses strategically to try to maintain, change, or at least mediate contentious male–female relations. But this is more the stuff of the politics of anthropology of which Vincent (1990) has written about. A feminist ethnography is neither a feminist political anthropology nor a feminist approach to political problems, although it could become so.

Women have always made notable contributions to political anthropology. Several, such as Lucy Mair, Paula Brown, Audrey Richards, Christine Gailey, Eleanor Leacock, June Nash, and Sherry Ortner, among others, have been mentioned in this book. And the contributions to political and feminist issues by women such as Ruth Benedict and Margaret Mead have been reemphasized (Babcock 1995). But the politics of anthropology regarding the status of women in the field and the postmodern turn that anthropology took in the 1980s with the proclamation of new, experimental forms of ethnographic writing have, within a decade, engaged more women in writing political anthropology than was characteristic of the field's previous sixty years. A count of contributors to the journal *Political and Legal Anthropology Review (PoLAR)*, a major outlet for the political writings of anthropologists with postmodern proclivities, shows that of those issues dedicated to political anthropology (some are dedicated to legal anthropology and some are general), 35 of 63 articles (56%) are authored by women. And of the five ethnographies that consider problems of political violence and terror (Feldman 1991; Linke 1999; Nordstrom 1997; Slyomovics 1998; Mahmood 1996), all but Feldman's are authored by women. It is this body of work, especially the ethnographies, that establishes a postmodern paradigm of political anthropology. To the extent that women are deconstructing the "master narrative" of male hegemony and providing an alternative voice to theirs in anthropology, the idea that "feminism is a postmodernism" has some credibility (see the Sandra Harding interview in Hirsh and Olson 1995:24; and the Lyotard interview in Olson 1995:189).

It would be a daunting task to try to present the richness of ideas in the issues of *PoLAR* that reflect postmodern political interests since 1994. But *PoLAR* has been blessed with editors, such as professor Rebecca French, who adroitly introduce the substance of some of those issues that were dedicated to topics of political anthropology. For example, regarding the issue *Considering Violence*, French writes, "These articles present violence in terms of local understandings, personal internalizations, methods of resistance, folk narratives and social cosmologies in a combined attempt to increase the scope and theoretical basis of our own comprehension" (1994:vii). Regarding the issue *The New Europe: Nationality, Ethnicity and Memory*, French points out that "In the wake of the past decade's enormous upheavals in Europe, scholars are struggling to form new understandings and to have new conversations about the nature of 'the political'. . . . This issue reflects the . . . excitement of the formative stages of these investigations in Hungary, Sweden, Macedonia, Catalonia, Russia, England, Germany and Northern Ireland" (1995:v). In the issue *Forms of Civil Society in Postcolonial Contexts,* Rosemary J. Coombe, a guest editor, argues that "in a discipline [political anthropology] increasingly preoccupied with questions of identity and community, nation building and state formation, cultural specificities and universal human rights, colonial legal institutions and local interpretations, the question of civil society provides a provocative nexus of orientation" (1997:1).

Other issues of *PoLAR* focus on *Politics and Identity in the Americas* (1994), *Citizenship and Difference* (1996), *Statemaking at the Fringes of Development* (1998), *Subjects of Law, Objects of Politics* (1999), and symposia on *Citizenship and Its Alterities* (1999) and *City Spaces and Arts of Government* (2000). The articles in these issues are diverse and refer to problems related to "minoritization," gays, refugees, racism, society, nationhood, sites of resistance, genocide, spaces of contestation, and imagined communities, among others. The most recurrent theme addresses issues of citizenship and identity (Rosaldo 1994; Pi-Sunyer 1995; S. Smith 1996; Coutin 1999). Issues related to women are a close second (Hegland 1995; Chock 1996; Taylor 1999), and political terror and violence comes in third.

These works are notable for their differences from the political writings of other social scientists. Postmodern anthropologists address these issues from the point of view of the people and victims who are affected by these practices. The essence of postmodern ethnographic writing is the voice they give to the subjects of their studies—the tortured, the violated, the dislocated, the émigré, and the feminine "Other." True to the tradition of anthropology, these works are global in their representation. But unlike traditional modes of anthropological representation, they are written in a variety of styles and specialized language. They are occasionally confessional and epistolary, sometimes storied, commonly reflexive, rarely heavy on theory, and often interpretive. The material is presented thematically, not paradigmatically. Still, it is likely that instead of merely presenting and understanding these processes, the postmodern political paradigm will become more Kuhnian as anthropologists try to explain these phenomena in a cross-cultural context. This is beginning to happen in the theme dedicated to political violence and terror (*PoLAR* 1994).

Some of the anthropologists who address political violence and terror recognize that their work has practical implications for government and agency policy (Mahmood 1996; Nordstrom 1997; Sluka 2000). They also believe that the voices of terrorists themselves need to be heard. Modern governments silence the voices of terrorists, accord their demands little credence, and define them categorically as small groups of murderers who try to frighten larger groups of people into doing something they otherwise would not do. Postmodern political anthropologists reveal that the real terrorists often are the government agents who oppose terrorism. Some also believe that the demands of those individuals and groups that governments identify as terrorists can have credibility and that the voices of all terrorists, those of government and dissident alike, need to be listened to if practical solutions to the "congeries of negativities" and abominations of the modern era are to be resolved (Mahmood 1994, 1996; Aditjondro 2000; Sluka 2000; Warren 2000). Despite this, the ethnographies on state (read government) violence and terror overwhelmingly give voice to those who are identified as terrorists by modern governments and to the victims of government terror (Feldman 1991; Mahmood 1996; Nordstrom 1997; Slyomovics 1998; Sluka 2000).

This body of work makes it difficult to agree with those anthropologists who say that anthropology is ignoring all the critical issues of our time (Barth 1994; Godelier 1994; Keesing 1994; Salzman 1994). Postmodern political writings suggest the need for a solution to the problem of how to insert the disarticulated and dispossessed peoples of the modern world into the emerging postmodern world of postindustrial societies (Laclau and Mouffe 1985). If positivist methodologies do not respond to these problems, postmodern ethnographic methodologies may provide an alternative because of the visibility they provide these unheard voices.

Nonetheless, there are impediments to the practical application of postmodern writings. For example, the agents of terror that anthropologists think they are "writing against" may interpret that same writing as providing positive support for their actions (Starn 1994). Postmodern jargon can also be a detriment to understanding what an author is trying to say. Recall that exemplars of the processual paradigm introduced concepts into political anthropology, such as field, arena, support, and the like, that they claimed were new. While they were new to political anthropology, they were old hat in political science and political sociology. By comparison, postmodern writing on political themes is enlightening, informative, disturbing, engaging, and relevant. However, the language of representation can be frustrating to read, difficult to interpret, and, unless the reader is another postmodernist, mystifying of the authors' ideas. Most unfortunately, this language girds the circle of mutually admiring postmodernists who write largely for each other. The extent to which anthropologists ought to write only for other anthropologists (Kuper 1994) or for a larger audience (Taussig 1987; Scheper-Hughes 1992, 1995) is an old problem. But if postmodern political anthropologists want to better the conditions of the victims with whom they empathize, they cannot afford to alienate through opaque verbiage and occult semantics those who can help to rectify the problems they identify. If the powerful political content of postmodern writings is so obfuscated that no one except other postmodernists can read and understand it, then Gellner's (1992) assertion that postmodernist anthropologists are self-indulgent nihilists involved in a narcissistic hysteria of subjectivity will have merit (also see Murphy 1994).

Finally, perhaps because of the sheer number of women writing on politics and the threat they pose to male domination and hegemony in the academy, a persistent gender-phobia tends to confute the contribution of women to these political problems. Nordstrom tells of the offense she takes from those (read men in the academy) who question her research agenda on warfare and wonder if she engages in it for the "thrill . . . the adrenaline rush to studying violence . . . an addiction to the excitement of the frontlines . . . an inescapable perverse fascination in horror" (1997:19). And Mahmood points out that "just as women are asserting themselves as subjects . . . academia [read men] wants to do away with subjectivity" (1996: 251). Persistent male obdurateness to the contribution of women in anthropology threatens the willingness of women to accept men who are willing "to 'resee' reality in engendered terms" (Behar 1995:5), hardens the divide between the sexes in the academy, and incites the gender-based politics of anthropology instead of promoting collaboration on the pertinent issues of political anthropology.

THE ETHNOGRAPHY OF POLITICAL
VIOLENCE AND STATE TERROR

I will parse three of the ethnographies of terror and violence for their experimental qualities, methodology, authoritative voice, and representation of the subject. Each is different in topic, location, author's writing style, and method of representation. In *Formations of Violence*, Feldman (1991) uses the voices of victims to show how violence is inscribed historically on their bodies and those who perpetrate violence in the streets of Northern Ireland's cities and the cells of its prisons. *Fighting for Faith and Nation* (Mahmood 1996) evokes the many voices by which Sikh militants rationalized the formation of an autonomous homeland, Kalistan, and the consequences of their efforts. In *A Different Kind of War Story*, Nordstrom (1997) explores the devastation of the fifteen-year war in Mozambique from the voices and viewpoints of the warriors, profiteers, peacemakers, and victims. True to postmodern reflexive ethnographic concerns, the voices of ethnographic "Others" are loud and prevail in these works. But no work is devoid of copious commentary by its author as each, in varying degrees, interprets the voices of their subjects.

Feldman: Formations of Violence (1991)

Feldman's ethnography is powerful and disturbing. He refers to it as a "genetic history, a genealogical analysis," and states that his purpose is to trace the cultural construction of violence, body, and history in urban Northern Ireland between 1969 and 1986. His approach to political violence is in keeping with the general thrust of Northern Irish ethnography "to identify the underlying structural continuities and cultural reciprocities that mediate the ideological schisms between the Nationalist ('Catholic') and Loyalist ('Protestant') communities" (Feldman 1991:1). The book's back cover endorsements add other dimensions to his work. They assert that the work introduces "an astonishingly new discursive field of word and action . . . in its treatment of the body as text" and "contributes to . . . the embryonic task of building a truly performative theory of social life and social conflict."

The basis for Feldman's accomplishment is a statement of "theoretical preliminaries [that] enable the exploration of the material contexts within which the politicized body, violence, and oral history emerge as artifacts and instruments of agency" (Feldman 1991:2). These theoretical preliminaries occupy the book's opening pages. It is an understatement to say that the arcane postmodern argot of their presentation is turgid and challenges the reader's understanding (and patience). True to the skill of some postmodern writers to obfuscate reality, the "preliminaries" are better felt and sensed than read and understood. They initiate the strain between presentation and representation and the problem of how to present the polarity and tension between the evocative power of the book's subject matter and the suppressing force of its language of representation.

One way is to build on the idea that the work presents "a truly performative theory of . . . conflict." This requires taking postmodern license in a format that responds to the question, "How can we *story* violence in ways that is not itself violent?" (Cobb 1993:58, emphasis added). This may not be possible. But one way to try to "story" the violence meaningfully is to paraphrase and borrow from Hamlet the idea that "The plays the thing wherein to capture the conscience" of the reader and the tragedy that is *Formations of Violence*.

There is advantage to parsing this work as a play. The structure of the text lends itself to a script fit for Broadway or Soho. As a play, Feldman's postmodern commentary can be juxtaposed to the voices of the victims of terror, largely Catholic men in prison who have been identified as terrorists and subjected to the terrors of the prison. The political goals of those involved and the strategies and material power to attain them can be displayed sharply in the dialogue. Language harnesses the violence and mediates theatrically the presentation of violence to a larger audience than scholars. As tragedy the play dramatically presents the failed efforts of the prisoners to make a difference. This approach to Feldman's work is not meant to parody or detract from its power. Instead, in the context of this chapter, postmodern license is needed to present this difficult material in a clear manner.

The play begins with a chorus of postmodern anthropologists reciting the book's introductory theoretical preliminaries as a poetic prologue (recall that the preliminaries are better felt and sensed than read and understood).

Act 1 merges the subject matter of Feldman's Chapters 2 and 3, the urban setting (*spatial formations of violence*) and the *dramatis personae* (*Handmen, Gunmen, Butchers, Doctors, Stiffs, Ghosts, and Black Men*). Because of what happens later in *The Breakers Yard, The Blanket Phase,* and *The Dirty Protests,* the actors should be attired in ways that sartorially demonstrate the weight of the years of political domination, oppression, and counterinsurgency that birthed the reciprocal violence between Catholics and Protestants in Northern Ireland.

The spatial structure of the cities of Northern Ireland, which also structures the violence, is introduced in the dialogue of the people. Their voices can be juxtaposed to that of the chorus:[1]

> The origin [of the spatial structure of Northern Ireland's cities] guarantees the recursive characters of history through spatial metaphor. The mimesis of the origin in present events endows the latter with coherence. Linearity and repetition, metaphorized as history, are deployed in these tales to repress historicity—the anthropological capacity to generate dispersal, difference, and alterity in time and space. . . . And where this occurs, the recursive character of the history is often expressed and always legitimated by geographical metaphor. (Feldman 1991:18)

The *dramatis personae* act out and through their voices and dialogues tell who they are and why they engage in Northern Ireland's violence and what their political goals are. For each of these personae, such as that between *handman/gunman,* the chorus can provide a postmodern interpretation, such as:

> CHORUS: The handman/gunman polarity can be read as a techno-ethical opposition—the distinction between violence as a performative component of an individual agent and violence as a mechanical component of the gun, in which the human bodies at both ends of the instrument fulfill purely transitive functions. (Feldman 1991:52)

Act 2 interprets Chapter 4, *Being Done: Rites of Political Passage*. The violence that incorporates capture and arrest, resistance to arrest, interrogation, and incarceration can be expressed through the voices of those involved: police, suspect, prisoner. The chorus explains it this way:

CHORUS: Arrest and interrogation validate the sociological assumptions that animate terrorist ideologies and practice . . . arrest and interrogation contribute to the coercive collectivization of social life—a process that prepares the sociological and cognitive foundations for the collective ritualization of violence and the elevation of terror to the dominant symbolic logic of social life. Arrest and interrogation . . . transform social life and historical experience into encysted ritualized enclosures. (Feldman 1991:86)

Act 3 (three scenes), Chapter 5, *The Breaker's Yard*, is the climax of the play. The idea of the "breakers yard" is a strategy by prison officials to isolate prisoners from the political struggle outside and other prisoners inside and then break them so that no matter what, they will never do anything to risk being returned to prison. Prisoners decide that the solution to this strategy is to organize so that they do not break under prison torture. The prisoner's determination to organize and resist establishes the processes of confrontation, domination, resistance, escalation, and resolution of the conflict between the prisoners and the prison authorities.

Scene 1 portrays the prison regime and the expectations of the authorities regarding the prisoners' behavior and addresses the recognition by the prisoners of the need to organize to resist the regime. They refuse to wear the uniforms prescribed by the prison authorities. This requires them to enter into "compulsory visibility" (Foucault 1979). As a result of their resistance, the indignities the guards heap on them, beatings, body cavity searches followed by unsterilized inspections of their mouths, restrictions, and the like, the chorus becomes more strident:

CHORUS: Among the optics of domination practiced by the prison regime . . . the prison uniform occupies a pivotal place. . . . [It] is crucial to the visual serialization and training of the prisoner in the disciplinary regime. . . . [It] evokes the clothes of dead men; it is an artifact of used bodies. It belongs to both other bodies and bodies othered, and as such it transforms the body of the self into an alterity. As the apparatus through which the prison regime comes into direct physical contact with the inmate, the uniform is a stigmatic action upon the body. (Feldman 1991:156)

Scene 2 depicts the initiation of *The Blanket Phase* of incarceration. After the prisoners' clothes are taken away and they refuse to put on the prison uniforms, to cover their nakedness they wrap themselves in the blanket that each was provided, ergo the *Blanketmen*. As the tension between the prisoners and guards builds, the guards heap increasing indignities upon the prisoners, which the prisoners, through their organization, resist. This begins *The Dirty Protests*.

Scene 3 requires a discharge of scent to envelop the audience fully in its essence. To resist the progressive indignities of their persons, such as body cavity searches on the way to use the toilet, the prisoners decide not to shave, bathe, or go out of their cells to use the toilet. Slop bowls provided to them begin to run over after guards seal the windows through which prisoners disposed of the waste; the guards squeegee the overflow urine back into the cells. Ultimately, the only way to dispose of the waste is to spread the feces on the walls. This goes on for five years. It demonstrates "the failure of the prison regime to imprint the bodies of the Blanketmen with the discipline of the prison" (p. 173). Instead, a reversal takes place. The guards who attempted to dominate the prisoners are affected by *The Dirty Protests*. Each guard carries the stench home to his family and so becomes the "inadvertent emissary of the Blanketmen" (Feldman 1991:195).

> CHORUS: The body in the H-Blocks is "dirty" to the extent that it also bears the trace of the Other, that it is not purely proper to the self but is the place where self and Other come into contact and exchange affects. If the state practiced a forensics of the weapon, then the Blanketmen engaged in a forensics of the contested body. To the same extent that the penal regime left traces of itself on the outside and inside of the body, the Blanketmen left scatological traces of the body on the prison. (Feldman 1991:180)

Nevertheless, *The Dirty Protests* lead to the increasing isolation of the *Blanketmen*. Guards realize that their intimidation has failed. But the prisoners realize they also have failed to incite a political difference outside. The dirty protest ends, cells are cleaned, and the prisoners don clothes. But they are left to vegetate and become invisible in a different way. To gain influence again, especially over those outside the prison, the prisoners plan to perform a hunger strike.

Act 4 (Chapter 6, *Eschatology*) is the performance of the hunger strike by which the prisoners attempt through the decimation of their bodies to impel a widespread social and political movement outside. A new dynamic emerges: The silence and guilt of the living waiting for other men to die. The strategy was to send out dead prisoners on a regular basis. The prisoners miscalculated.

CHORUS: Hunger striking was posited as the last act because in its consumption of flesh it was the ultimate fragmentation technique that finally invoked the body whole in a shimmering moment of historical clarity. (Feldman 1991:204)

Despite the death of six prisoners, the hunger strike fails, as it must in a tragedy. Realities outside the prison have changed. The deaths do not incite the violent mass reaction the prisoners hoped for. The chorus chants an encomium to the tragedy of violence and postmodern political representation:

CHORUS: In Northern Ireland the ethnography of political violence is the ethnography of the historical surface, the somatics and erotics of historical alterity. There, political power first constructs itself by constructing surfaces and sites for the staging, display, and narration of power. These points of instantiation include the interrogation cell, the "interface," and the bodies of the tortured interrogatee, the sectarian stiff, the hunger striker. The performance of these sites and bodies aims at "making history appear." Whoever seeks power must first control the apparatuses for the production and mimesis of history as material spectacle. (Feldman 1991:234)

The politics of Feldman's work is related less to the dialectic of torture and resistance than to the process by which prisoners and prison authorities used material and ideational power at their disposal to attain their goals. Unfortunately, this work is most likely to appeal to a scholarly audience, especially those with postmodern predilections. But it could profitably provide a political lesson for prisoners, prison officials, guards, peacemakers, and laypeople. Yet these audiences and the communication of Feldman's political lessons are unlikely to develop because he relies so much on postmodern jargon and a complicated writing style.

Mahmood: Fighting for Faith and Nation (1996)

Mahmood's work (and Nordstrom's that follows) lacks Feldman's dramaturgical potential. But it is nonetheless a powerful contribution to the ethnography of political violence and a thoughtful challenge to the problems of representation in postmodern experimental ethnography. Mahmood's work is less about political violence per se than it is about Sikh militants and the consequences for them and others of their goal to establish an imagined homeland, Kalistan. Nonetheless, violence provides the main political strategy by which Sikh militants attempt to establish Kalistan and the Indian government attempts to thwart it through their military, police, and hit squads. The result of this dialectic has been a protracted slaughter of militants and Indians, but especially of innocent Sikhs since the 1970s. Mahmood reveals the complexity of the situation and the moral and ethical issues it raises for those who are involved in the violence and for those who write ethnographies on political violence.

Mahmood is of that generation of young anthropologists who were disillusioned with anthropology and her complaints resonate with their concerns. For her, the old anthropological paradigms seem empty, the anthropology that claimed to be science wanting, and that which was obligated to the colonial enterprise exploitative. This anthropology resulted in an ethnographic library of very ordinary, everyday circumstances of the human conditions and added almost nothing to those extraordinary conditions in which so many people find themselves. Because of these failures, Mahmood believes that anthropology suffers today from a lack of credibility and has been relegated to the margins of the public and political discourses of our times. She believes that the attention postmodern anthropologists give to issues, such as political violence and terror, can provide anthropologists with a meaningful voice. But she also admits that the new postmodern ethnography is as empty as that which they attempt to replace and provides a poor receptacle for anthropological writings on violence and other problems that plague contemporary humankind.

Mahmood has difficulty with the idea that it is sufficient to write a "good enough" ethnography (Scheper-Hughes 1995) and doubts the postmodern contention that anthropology is at an important experimental moment in its development. Despite the inability of anthropologists to deal meaningfully with the major problems of the world, such as political violence and terror, to her the alternative of "staying at home" is unacceptable. It is better, she believes, to "soldier on" and trust that our impulse to reach out to "alien" others and write about that experience is, somehow, of use and value.

Her goal is to give the voices of Sikh militants who seek to establish Kalistan, a "space" in which they can be heard. This is not because she sympathizes with the methods of Sikh terrorists. She makes clear that she abhors them. But she believes that it is important to know why Sikh and other political extremists think that it is important to die for what they believe. For Mahmood, ethnography provides a good vehicle for understanding the horrors of our time.

In her book, Mahmood introduces the history and doctrines of the Sikh faith to provide a feeling for what motivates the political terrorism of pious Sikhs and to consider the nature of their insurgency. Throughout the book she presents extended dialogues with Sikh militants and victims and their voices alone to depict the reciprocal violence and terror in the Punjab. The culmination of the cycle of violence was the attack in 1984 by military forces of the Indian government on the sacred sanctuary of the Sikh faith, the Golden Temple in Amritsar. Through these dialogues and Sikh voices, she accounts for the complicated political events that led up to the assault on the temple and the consequences of the assault. These involved more than the decimation of the militant Sikh leadership. They also resulted in the assassination of Prime Minister Indira Gandhi by her personal Sikh guards in 1986, a subsequent murderous rampage by Hindus against Sikh communities throughout India, and renewed Sikh insurgency.

Mahmood attempts to account for these events through interviews and dialogue with Sikh militants in the Punjab, India, the United States, and Canada. The problem of ethnographic authority that postmodern anthropology was supposed to rectify by giving voices to "Others" looms large here. As Feldman did with the Irish prisoners, Mahmood provides long explanations of the meanings she imputes to the voices of the militant Sikhs. But unlike Feldman, Mahmood relies on a language that is largely devoid of postmodern jargon. Instead, through her commentaries she tries to make sense out of the violence from the point of view of boys and girls, men and women, terrorists and victims by juxtaposing the voices of Sikhs and her own in a reflexive dialogue, as well as by elaborating the ideas she acquired as a result of interviews.

Mahmood concludes with a critical analysis of the new postmodern ethnography and its appropriateness for responding to problems of violence and terror. It is an exploration of her argument that the current replacements for the traditional paradigms of anthropology are not always much better. She explores this problem through a complicated format by which she intersects the dialogues between herself and the Sikhs with a dialogue between herself and other scholars. This represents an attempt to bring together the "complex point at which author, subjects, and academic audience are joined in somewhat dissonant conversation" (Mahmood 1996:236).

Here Mahmood considers how the writings of anthropologists and the voices of "Others" become involved in the problems and issues of representation. She points out how the availability of information and the literacy of "Others," such as the Sikh militants, result in tension when the "Others" possess up-to-date documentation of what researchers say about them. And despite contributing a new reflexive ethnography, Mahmood comes down hard on postmodern ideology and rhetoric. She points out the contradiction between the expressed desire of postmodernists to deconstruct political and social boundaries and identities for those who will inhabit their imagined postmodern world and the goals of many "Others," such as the Sikh militants, who are struggling to construct social, cultural, and ethnic boundaries around their newly established identities. As she says, "Academia . . . declared the end of modernism, the end of 'grand narratives' of emancipation before everyone has had the chance to reap their benefits" (Mahmood 1996:251).

Finally, she contradicts the denigration of applied anthropology by postmodern and other academic anthropologists. She makes a case for the responsibility that is incurred by researchers who conduct ethnographic fieldwork on violence. When she agreed to help agencies in Canada and the United States determine refugee status of Sikhs and other aliens, she was forced to question deeply how she felt about the violence in which her subject Sikhs were involved. Her experiences temper the claims of postmodern scholars to some special insight with the claims of those involved in the real political world.

Nordstrom: A Different Kind of War Story (1997)

Nordstrom's central concern is with the topic of war and the process of peace in Mozambique. But the title of her book is an enigma. What makes this a different war story? War is hell under any circumstances. It is grotesque, unspeakable, an abomination, a modern negativity. People, especially noncombatants, and especially women and children, suffer beyond comprehension but not description. Nordstrom graphically describes the grotesqueness of the fifteen-year war (1977–1992) in Mozambique, but with sensitivity and purpose.

Nordstrom's role as an anthropologist who is telling a story of the grotesqueness of war places her in a difficult position. How is one to justify presenting the simple poignancy of a mother's numb comment after a raid that "I did it, I did not know what else to do" as she tried to account for the horror of watching her son be cut up and cooked in a pot by bandits and then being forced "to eat some of this." And how can there be any redemption in the barbaric act of a bandit chief who slit open the vagina of a little girl, less than eight years old, with a pocketknife so that he could take her in blood? Do these horrors alone make this book a different kind of war story? Not really. But this story is different because the grotesque provided a basis for stopping the war.

Methodologically it is a different kind of war story because its horror is presented in the new ethnographic genre that complies with ideas of representation prescribed by the experimental postmodern ethnography. It is replete with anecdotes, poetry, dialogue, reflexive relationships, "Others'" voices (interpreted by the author), fragments, and the extraordinary. It is different because the subject matter is evoked imaginatively as a story and not as a traditional ethnography. In short, the genre sets the tone for the work.

Nordstrom's work is also a different kind of war story because it is told by those on the ground who suffer most. Compared to the approach of political scientists who tell war stories from the viewpoint of generals, politicians, and elite institutions, this story is told in the words of the people, even its children. Each chapter begins with a poem about the war written by a Mozambican teenager. Postmodern? Yes. Effective? Yes, as are other poems and remarkably lucid stories and explanations of war by even younger children. This is a different story in part also because Nordstrom justifies the idea that "poetry is politics" (1997:x) because poetry captures and relates the emotive, affective, and material consequences of the power the combatants bring to the processes by which they pursue their public and private goals.

Furthermore, her work is different because the poetry and stories that the people tell also were part of a goal-oriented process by which the noncombatants, men, women, children, and, in particular, healers worked against the legitimacy of this war, delegitimated it, and helped to bring it to an end. As Nordstrom points out, war leaders need warriors to fight. In Mozambique, the supply of warriors gradually dried up. With the help, direction, and wisdom of healers, who have a special respect among Mozambicans, the people gradually "unmade" the violence. The Rabelaisian, gargantuan grotesqueness of cannibalism, rape, depravity, and genital mutilation constituted at the same time not only acts of utter oppression but the rationale for resisting and undoing the violence. It is a different story because it is a story of hope. Community-generated solutions to the violence and horror were more important in stopping it than negotiations at a peace table. It is a different story because it tells of the constitutive power of violence; that from cannibalism and rape people can learn through resistance to create a culture of peace that overwhelms the violence. By focusing on the constitutive power of culture to create order and provide meaning in the midst of violence, Nordstrom explores the theory that the creativity by which average people construct cultures of peace as alternatives to cultures of violence can defeat violence altogether.

Nordstrom introduced the idea of *war-scapes* to demonstrate that anthropological subject matter is no longer isolated and self-contained. A war-scape is a concept, not a place, such as landscape, and has a slippery, nonlocal, fluid quality. A war-scape includes the local, national, and international connections among foreign strategists, arms suppliers, mercenaries, development and interest groups, international businesspeople, blackmarketeers, and others that today all too commonly constitute the dynamics of war settings. It identifies the transitory nature of these connections and their relationship to the cultural construction of violence across time and space.

Given the complexity of the war in Mozambique, Nordstrom uses different techniques to compile her "ethnography of a war zone." She points out the difficulty of inquiring into violence because what constitutes violence is hotly contested by the contending forces, resistance groups, the Mozambique government, mercenaries from South Africa, bandits, and other combatants. In this setting of contradictory practices and beliefs, the data-gathering techniques of traditional ethnography do not work. But neither does the inquisitive dialogic and reflexive strategy of postmodern ethnographic methodology. Instead, Nordstrom relies on a variety of novel data-gathering methods.

She introduces the idea of "The Anthropology of Listening" to get at the violence because "seeing the war is to listen" (1997:78). She merges reports of other scholars and the voices of victims to provide "An Introduction to the Ethnography of War" (1997:88). Trying to understand war and peace as process provides the justification for what she refers to as "Runway Research." To study war and its resolution as a process and not as a situated place, she decided to follow the threads of war and resistance across the country. Facilitated by a travel permit from the Ministry of Health, she flew in government planes to different places to see what it meant to live on the frontlines of a war. This strategy provided what she calls "fragments of war contes" (short stories or tales of extraordinary events, and one of her few postmodern tropes) of local people. The fragments accommodate what she identifies as an ethnography of a topic— war—and a process—peacemaking.

The fragments of war stories portrayed the related yet disjointed, incomplete, fluid, and contradictory aspects of life in a war zone. As Nordstrom points out, "People's lives are lived amid bits and pieces of information and misinformation, and their survival depends on trying to gather these into some pattern of meaning" (1997:109). But, like Feldman and Mahmood, the voice of the "Other" is interpreted by Nordstrom. There is no doubt that she is the ultimate ethnographic authority whose voice validates the theory that local cultural practices were responsible for resolving the conflict. The exception to her authoritative voice are the poems that introduce each chapter, and they are perhaps most powerful because they stand alone.

She compiles a dramatic picture of living on the frontlines of the war. Because of the chaotic distribution of fighting and mayhem, there were several frontlines. But living on the frontlines is more than another story of violence and resistance. It is on the frontlines where Nordstrom addresses the theoretical thrust of her work: "*Violence is culturally constitutive. Its enactment . . . forces new constructs of identity, new socio-cultural relationships, new threats and injustices that reconfigure people's life worlds, new patterns of survival and resistance*" (Nordstrom 1997:141).

In short, culture is transformative and creative. Through their creative cultural responses, Mozambicans delegitimatized (withdrew their support from) the violence and the politics of force and constructed a new political culture based on peace and reintegration. Demobilized soldiers who were complicit in the violence were reintegrated into their communities through rituals and ceremonies that took the violence out of them so they could function again in civil society.

Nordstrom's work is theoretically motivated, and it also has wider cross-cultural, ethnological import. On the one hand, she uses the idea of cross-cultural research to refer to the fragments of war that she pulled together from across the war zones of Mozambique. On the other, she believes that her work will contribute to a larger body of theory on violence and war derived from cross-cultural comparisons of different wars. Like Mahmood, she hopes that this will have practical implication for the abolishment of violence. She compares, for example, the war in Mozambique with that in Angola. The war in Mozambique was resolved largely by the actions of healers and local medical practitioners who served as interlocutors across the war zones. They were also central to the ritual and ceremony that reintegrated combatants into Mozambican society. In the war in Angola, all the creative responses that resolved the war in Mozambique also existed, but they did not coalesce into a cross-cultural set of linked practices nationwide. Nordstrom attributes this to the lack of interlocutors in Angola, a role that the healers of Mozambique provided. Nonetheless, she contends that the dynamics of contemporary culture theory, such as she developed, can provide a model for understanding how people can defeat oppressive violence.

Althusser (1990 [1965]; also Balibar 1994) suggested that paradigms and genres are subject to a natural history of development. New genres and paradigms emerge when there is a breach with traditional practices. They eventually culminate, and later are absorbed as a "positive trace" that has made some, but not usually a revolutionary, difference in their disciplinary context. Postmodernism as idea and practice in anthropology may be well on the way to becoming such a trace. But the ethnography of political violence and terror represents one context where the new, experimental postmodern ethnography may also form the nucleus for another durable paradigm of political anthropology.

NOTES

1. Quotes from *Formations of Violence: The Narrative of the Body and Political Terrorism in Northern Ireland* by Allen Feldman are used with permission of The University of Chicago Press, copyright 1991 by the University of Chicago.

REFERENCES

Abrams, Phillip. 1988. "Notes on the Difficulty of Studying the State." *Journal of Historical Sociology* 1(1):58–89.

Adams, Richard Newbold. 1975. *Energy and Structure: A Theory of Social Power.* Austin: University of Texas Press.

Adams, Robert Mc. 1966. *The Evolution of Urban Society: Early Mesopotamia and Prehispanic Mexico.* Chicago: Aldine.

Aditjondro, George J. 2000. "Ninjas, Nanggalas, Monuments, and Mossad Manuals: An Anthropology of Indonesian State Terror in East Timor." In Jeffrey A. Sluka, ed., *Death Squad: The Anthropology of State Terror,* pp. 158–188. Philadelphia: University of Pennsylvania Press.

Allen, Michael. 1984. "Elders, Chiefs, and Big Men: Authority Legitimation and Political Evolution in Melanesia." *American Anthropologist* 11:20–41.

Althusser, Louis. 1990 [1965]. *For Marx.* London: Verso.

Applebaum, Herbert. 1987. "The Universal Aspects of Work." In Herbert Applebaum, ed., *Perspectives in Cultural Anthropology,* pp. 386–399. Albany: State University of New York Press.

Aristotle. 1943. *Aristotle's Politics.* New York: The Modern Library.

Ashton, Hugh. 1952. *The Basuto.* London: Oxford University Press.

Babcock, Barbara. 1995. "'Not in the Absolute Singular': Rereading Ruth Benedict." In Ruth Behar and Deborah A. Gordon, eds., *Women Writing Culture,* pp. 104–130. Berkeley: University of California Press.

Bachofen, J. J. 1967 [1861]. "Myth, Religion, and Mother Right." In *Selected Writings of J. J. Bachofen* (translated by M. Manheim), Bollinger Series LXXXIV. Princeton: Princeton University Press.

Bailey, F. G. 1960. *Tribe, Caste and Nation.* Manchester, England: Manchester University Press.

_____. 1963. *Politics and Social Change in Orissa in 1959.* Berkeley: University of California Press.

_____. 1968. "Parapolitical Systems." In Marc Swartz, ed., *Local Level Politics,* pp. 281–294. Chicago: Aldine.

_____. 1969. *Stratagems and Spoils.* New York: Schocken Books.

_____. 1977. *Morality and Expediency: The Folklore of Academic Politics.* Oxford: Basil Blackwell.

_____. 1983. *Tactical Uses of Passion: An Essay on Power, Reason, and Reality*. Ithaca: Cornell University Press.

_____. 1988. *Humbuggery and Manipulation: The Art of Leadership*. Ithaca: Cornell University Press.

_____. 1991. *The Prevalence of Deceit*. Ithaca: Cornell University Press.

_____. 1994. *The Witch Hunt*. Ithaca: Cornell University Press.

Bakhtin, Michail M. 1981. *The Dialogic Imagination* (edited by Michael Holquist). Austin: University of Texas Press.

_____. 1984. *Problems of Dostoevsky's Poetics* (edited and translated by Carol Emerson). Minneapolis: University of Minnesota Press.

Balandier, Georges. 1970. *Political Anthropology* (translated by A. M. Sheridan Smith). New York: Pantheon Books.

Balibar, Etienne. 1994. "Althusser's Object." *Social Text* 39 (summer):157–188.

Barker, Alex W., and Timothy R. Pauketat. 1992. "Introduction: Social Inequality and the Native Elites of Southeastern North America." In Alex W. Barker and Timothy R. Pauketat, eds., *Lords of the Southeast*. Archaeological Papers No. 3, pp. 1–10. Washington, D.C.: American Anthropological Association.

Barth, Fredrick. 1959. *Political Leadership among Swat Pathans*. London: University of London/The Athlone Press.

_____. 1994. "A Personal View of Present Tasks and Priorities in Cultural and Social Anthropology." In Robert Borofsky, ed., *Assessing Cultural Anthropology*, pp. 349–361. New York: McGraw-Hill.

Barthes, Roland. 1975. *The Pleasure of the Text*. New York: Hill and Wang.

Basso, Ellen B. 1973. *The Kalapalo Indians of Central Brazil*. New York: Holt, Rinehart, and Winston.

Baudrillard, Jean. 1983. *In the Shadow of the Silent Majority*. New York: Semiotext(e) Inc.

_____. 1985. *Simulations*. New York: Semiotext(e) Inc.

_____. 1998. *The Consumer Society: Myths and Structures*. London: Sage.

Beard, William. 1957. *The Economic Basis of Politics*. New York: Vintage Books.

Beattie, John. 1964. *Other Cultures*. London: Cohen & West.

Beckson, Karl, and Arthur Ganz. 1975. *Literary Terms: A Dictionary*. New York: Farrar, Straus, and Giroux.

Befu, Harumi, and Leonard Plotnicov. 1962. "Types of Unilineal Descent Groups." *American Anthropologist* 64:313–318.

Behar, Ruth. 1995. "Introduction: Out of Exile." In Ruth Behar and Deborah A. Gordon, eds., *Women Writing Culture*, pp. 1–32. Berkeley: University of California Press.

Behar, Ruth, and Deborah A. Gordon, eds. 1995. *Women Writing Culture*. Berkeley: University of California Press.

Bella, Robert N. 1957. *Tokugawa Religion: The Values of Pre-Industrial Japan*. Glencoe, Ill.: The Free Press.

Benedict, Ruth. 1934. *Patterns of Culture*. Boston: Houghton Mifflin.

Berdan, Frances F. 1982. *The Aztecs of Central Mexico: An Imperial Society*. New York: Holt, Rinehart and Winston.

Bernaldi, Bernard. 1952. "The Age-System of the Nilo-Hamitic Peoples: A Critical Evaluation." *Africa* 22:316–332.

Berndt, R. U., and P. Lawrence, eds. 1973. *Politics in New Guinea.* Seattle: University of Washington Press.

Bhabha, Homi K. 1998. "Anxiety in the Midst of Difference." *Political and Legal Anthropology Review* 21(1):123–137.

Birmingham, Stephen. 1990. *America's Secret Aristocracy.* New York: Berkeley Books.

Bloch, Marc. 1964. *Feudal Society* (translated by L. A. Manyon). Chicago: University of Chicago Press.

Bloch, Maurice. 1975. "Introduction." In Maurice Bloch, ed., *Political Language and Oratory in Traditional Society,* pp. 1–28. New York: Academic Press.

———. 1978. "Ritual." In J. Friedman and M. J. Rowlands, eds., *The Evolution of Social Systems,* pp. 303–340. Pittsburgh: University of Pittsburgh Press.

———. 1983. *Marxism and Anthropology: The History of a Relationship.* Oxford: Clarendon Press.

———. 1985. "From Cognition to Ideology." In R. Fardon, ed., *Power and Knowledge,* pp. 21–48. Edinburgh: Scottish Academic Press.

Bloom, H., P. de Man, J. Derrida, G. Hartman, and J. H. Miller. 1990. *Deconstruction and Criticism.* New York: Continuum.

Bodley, John H. 1982. *Victims of Progress.* Mountain View, Calif.: Mayfield Publishing Company.

———. 1983. *Anthropology and Contemporary Human Problems.* Palo Alto, Calif.: Mayfield Publishing Company.

Bohannon, Paul, and Laura Bohannon. 1953. *The Tiv of Central Nigeria,* Ethnographic Survey of Africa, Vol. 3, Pt. 8. London: International African Institute.

Bott, Elizabeth. 1955. "Urban Families: Conjugal Roles and Social Networks." *Human Relations* 8:345–384.

———. 1957. *Family and Social Networks: Roles, Norms, and External Relations in Ordinary Urban Families.* London: Tavistock Publications.

Bourdieu, Pierre. 1977. *Outline of a Theory of Practice.* Cambridge, England: Cambridge University Press.

———. 1978. *Highland Peoples of New Guinea.* Cambridge, England: Cambridge University Press.

———. 1990. *The Logic of Practice.* Stanford: Stanford University Press.

Brown, Paula. 1972. *The Chimbu.* Cambridge, Mass.: Schenkman.

Brumfiel, Elizabeth M., and John W. Fox. eds. 1996. *Factional Competition and Political Development in the New World.* Cambridge, England: Cambridge University Press.

Brundage, Burr C. 1963. *Empire of the Inca.* Norman: University of Oklahoma Press.

Bujra, Janet M. 1973. "The Dynamics of Political Action: A New Look at Factionalism." *American Anthropologist* 75:132–152.

Burkhart, Louise M., and Janine Gasco. 1996. "The Colonial Period in Mesoamerica." In Robert M. Carmack, Janine Gasco, and Gary H. Gossen, eds.,

The Legacy of Mesoamerica: History and Culture of a Native American Civilization, pp. 154–195. Upper Saddle River, N.J.: Prentice-Hall.

Busia, K. J. A. 1951. *The Position of the Chief in the Modern Political System of Ashanti.* London: Oxford University Press.

Callinicos, Alex. 1988. *Making History*. Ithaca: Cornell University Press.

Carlsnaes, Walter. 1981. *The Concept of Ideology and Political Analysis.* Westport, Conn.: Greenwood Press.

Carmack, Robert, Janine Gasco, and Garry Gossen. 1996. *The Legacy of Mesoamerica: History and Culture of a Native American Civilization.* Upper Saddle River, N.J.: Prentice-Hall.

Carneiro, Robert L. 1970. "A Theory of the Origin of the State." *Science* 169(3947):733–738.

———. 1981. "The Chiefdom: Precursor of the State." In Grant D. Jones and Robert R. Krautz, eds., *The Transition to Statehood in the New World*, pp. 37–79. Cambridge, England: Cambridge University Press.

———. 1987. "Further Reflection on Resource Concentration and Its Role in the Rise of the State." In Linda Manzanilla, ed., *Studies in the Neolithic and Urban Revolutions. The V. Gordon Childe Colloquium, Mexico, 1986.* BAR International Series 349, pp. 245–260.

Carstens, Peter. 1991. *The Queen's People: A Study of Hegemony, Coercion, and Accommodation among the Okanagan of Canada.* Toronto: University of Toronto Press.

Cavalcanti, Pedro, and Paul Piccone, eds. 1975. *History, Philosophy, and Culture in the Young Gramsci.* St. Louis: Telos Press.

Chagnon, Napoleon A. 1992. *Yanomamö.* New York: Holt, Rinehart and Winston.

Childe, V. Gordon. 1946. *What Happened in History.* New York: Pelican.

———. 1951a. *Social Evolution.* New York: Henry Schuman.

———. 1951b. *Man Makes Himself.* New York: New American Library/Mentor.

Chock, Phyllis Pease. 1996. "No New Women: Gender, 'Alien,' and 'Citizen' in the Congressional Debates on Immigration." *Political and Legal Anthropology Review* 19(1):1–10.

Claessen, Henri J. M. 1978. "The Early State: A Structural Approach." In Henri J. M. Claessen and Peter Skalník, eds., *The Early State*, pp. 533–596. The Hague: Mouton Publishers.

———. 1988. "Changing Legitimacy." In Ronald Cohen and Judith D. Toland, eds., *State Formations and Political Legitimacy*, pp. 21–44. New Brunswick, N.J.: Transaction Books.

———. 2000. *Structural Change: Evolution and Evolutionism in Cultural Anthropology.* Leiden, The Netherlands: Research School CNWS, Leiden University.

Claessen, Henri J. M., and Jarich G. Oosten, eds. 1996. *Ideology and the Formation of Early States.* Leiden, The Netherlands: E. J. Brill.

Claessen, Henri J. M., and Peter Skalník, eds. 1978. *The Early State.* The Hague: Mouton Publishers.

———. 1981. *The Study of the State.* The Hague: Mouton Publishers.

Claessen, Henri J. M., and Pieter van de Velde, eds. 1987. *Early State Dynamics.* Leiden, The Netherlands: E. J. Brill.

_____. 1991. *Early State Economics*. New Brunswick, N.J.: Transaction Books.

Claessen, Henri J. M., Pieter van de Velde, and M. Estellie Smith, eds. 1985. *Development and Decline: The Evolution of Sociopolitical Organization*. South Hadley, Mass.: Bergin and Garvey.

Clastres, Pierre. 1977. *Society against the State: The Leader as Servant and the Humane Use of Power among the Indians of the Americas* (translated by Robert Hurley in collaboration with Abe Stein). New York: Mole Editions, Urizen Books.

Clifford, James, 1986. "Introduction: Partial Truths." In James Clifford and George Marcus, eds., *Writing Culture: The Poetics and Politics of Ethnography*, pp. 1–26. Berkeley: University of California Press.

_____. 1988. *The Predicament of Culture: Twentieth-Century Ethnography, Literature, and Art*. Cambridge, Mass.: Harvard University Press.

Clifford, James, and George Marcus, eds. 1986. *Writing Culture: The Poetics and Politics of Ethnography*. Berkeley: University of California Press.

Cobb, Sara. 1993. "Toward an Aesthetics of Violence: A Comment on Feldman's 'The Formations of Violence.' *Political and Legal Anthropology Review* 16(3): 57–60.

Codere, Helen. 1950. *Fighting with Property: A Study of Kwakiutl Potlatching and Warfare*. New York: J. J. Augustin.

Cohen, Abner. 1969. "Political Anthropology: The Analysis of The Symbolism of Power Relations." *Man* 4:215–235.

_____. 1974. *Two-Dimensional Man: An Essay on the Anthropology of Power and Symbolism in Complex Society*. Berkeley: University of California Press.

_____. 1979. "Political Symbolism." *Annual Review of Anthropology* 8:87–113.

Cohen, Ronald. 1965. "Political Anthropology: The Future of a Pioneer." *Anthropological Antiquity* 38:117–131.

_____. 1970a. "The Political System." In Raoul Naroll and Ronald Cohen, eds., *A Handbook of Method in Cultural Anthropology*, pp. 484–499. New York: Columbia University Press.

_____. 1970b. "Review of *Local Level Politics*, Marc Swartz, ed." *American Anthropologist* 72:112–115.

_____. 1978. "State Origins: A Reappraisal." In Henri J. M. Claessen and Peter Skalník, eds, *The Early State*, pp. 31–70. The Hague: Mouton Publishers.

_____. 1979. "Introduction." In R. Cohen and E. R. Service, eds., *The Anthropology of Political Evolution*, pp. 1–20. Philadelphia: Institute for the Study of Human Issues.

Cohen, Y. A. 1968. *Man in Adaptation: The Cultural Present*. Chicago: Aldine.

_____. 1969. "Ends and Means in Political Control: State Organization and the Punishment of Adultery, Incest, and Violation of Celibacy." *American Anthropologist* 71:658–687.

Comaroff, Jean. 1985. *Body of Power, Spirit of Resistance: The Culture and History of a South African People*. Chicago: University of Chicago Press.

Comaroff, Jean, and John Comaroff. 1991. *Of Revelation and Revolution: Christianity, Colonialism, and Consciousness in South Africa*. Chicago: University of Chicago Press.

Cook, Scott. 1966. "The Obsolete 'Anti-Market' Mentality: A Critique of the Substantive Approach to Economic Anthropology." *American Anthropologist* 68:323–345.

Coombe, Rosemary J. 1997, "Identifying and Engendering the Forms of Emergent Civil Societies: New Direction in Political Anthropology." *Political and Legal Anthropology Review* 20(1):1–12.

Coon, C. S. 1950. "The Mountains of Giants." *Papers of the Peabody Museum of American Archaeology and Ethnology* 23(3):1–105.

Coult, Alan D. 1962. "The Determinants of Differential Cross-Cousin Marriage." *Man* 62:34–37.

Coutin, Susan. 1999. "Citizenship and Clandestinity among Salvadorian Immigrants." *Political and Legal Anthropology Review* 22(2):53–63.

Dahl, Robert A. 1961. *Who Governs?* New Haven: Yale University Press.

Dalton, George. 1961. "Economic Theory and Primitive Economy." *American Anthropologist* 63:1–25.

Damas, David. 1968. "The Diversity of Eskimo Societies." In Richard B. Lee and Irven DeVore, eds., *Man the Hunter*, pp. 111–117. Chicago: Aldine-Atherton.

De Certeau, Michel. 1984. *The Practice of Everyday Life* (translated by Steven F. Rendall). Berkeley: University of California Press.

Derrida, Jacques. 1978. *Writing and Difference.* Chicago: University of Chicago Press.

Dolgin, Janet L., David S. Kemnitzer, and David M. Schneider, eds. 1977. *Symbolic Anthropology: A Reader in the Study of Symbols and Meaning.* New York: Columbia University Press.

Donham, Donald. 1999. *History, Power, Ideology: Central Issues in Marxism and Anthropology.* Berkeley: University of California Press.

Dorst, John D. 1989. *The Written Suburb: An American Site, an American Dilemma.* Philadelphia: University of Pennsylvania Press.

Downs, James F. 1966. *The Two Worlds of the Washo: An Indian Tribe of California and Nevada.* New York: Holt, Rinehart and Winston.

Durán, Fray Diego. 1964 [1581]. *The Aztecs: The History of the Indies of New Spain* (translated and edited by F. Horcasitas and D. Heyden). Norman: University of Oklahoma Press.

Durham, M. E. 1928. *Some Tribal Origins and Customs of the Balkans.* London: Allen & Unwin.

Durkheim, Émile. 1954 [1912]. *The Elementary Forms of Religious Life* (translated by J. W. Swain). Glencoe, Ill.: The Free Press.

Earl, D. M. 1964. *Emperor and Nation in Japan: Political Thinking of the Tokugawa Period.* Seattle: University of Washington Press.

Earle, Timothy, ed. 1991. *Chiefdoms: Power, Economy, and Ideology.* Cambridge, England: Cambridge University Press.

Easton, David. 1959. "Political Anthropology." In B. J. Siegal, ed., *Biennial Reviews of Anthropology*, pp. 210–262. Stanford: Stanford University Press.

Engels, Frederick. 1942 [1884]. *The Origin of the Family, Private Property, and the State.* New York: International Publishers.

Evans-Pritchard, E. E. 1940. *The Nuer.* Oxford: Clarendon Press.

———. 1951. *Kinship and Marriage among the Nuer.* Oxford: Clarendon Press.

Even, T. S. 1985. "The Paradox of the Nuer Feud and the Leopard Skin Chief: A 'Creative' Solution to the Prisoner's Dilemma." *American Ethnologist* 12:84–102.

Fallers, Lloyd. 1955. "Predicament of the Modern African Chief: An Instance from Uganda." *American Anthropologist* 57:290–305.

_____. 1965. *Bantu Bureaucracy: A Century of Political Evolution among the Basoga of Uganda*. Chicago: University of Chicago Press.

Feinman, Gary. 1996. *PreColumbian World Systems*. Madison: University of Wisconsin Press

Feldman, Allen. 1991. *Formations of Violence: The Narrative of the Body and Political Terror in Northern Ireland*. Chicago: University of Chicago Press.

Firth, Raymond. 1957 [1936]. *We, the Tikopia*. London: Allen & Unwin.

Fleming, Patricia H. 1973. "The Politics of Marriage among Non-Catholic European Royalty." *Current Anthropology* 14:231–250.

Fogelson, Raymond, and Richard N. Adams, eds. 1977. *The Anthropology of Power: Ethnographic Studies from Asia, Oceania, and the New World*. New York: Academic Press.

Fortes, Meyer. 1945. *The Dynamics of Clanship among the Tallensi*. London: Oxford University Press.

_____. 1959. "Descent, Filiation, and Affinity: A Rejoinder to Dr. Leach." *Man* 41(pt.1):193–197; 41(pt.2):206–212.

_____. 1969. *Kinship and the Social Order: The Legacy of Lewis Henry Morgan*. Chicago: Aldine.

Fortes, Meyer, and E. E. Evans-Pritchard, eds. 1940. *African Political Systems*. London: Oxford University Press.

Foucault, Michel. 1965. *Madness and Civilization*. New York: Random House.

_____. 1972. *Power and Knowledge: Selected Interviews and Other Writings* (Colin Gordon, ed.). New York: Pantheon Books.

_____. 1973. *The Birth of the Clinic*. New York: Pantheon Books.

_____. 1979. *Discipline and Punish: The Birth of the Prison* (translated by Alan Sheridan). New York: Vintage Books.

_____. 1980. *The History of Sexuality* (translated by Robert Hurley), Vol. 1. New York: Vintage Books.

_____. 1984. "The Subject and Power." In Brian Wallis, ed., *Art after Modernism: Rethinking Representation*, pp. 417–432. Boston/New York: New Museum of Contemporary Art.

_____. 1991. "Governmentality." In Graham Burchell, Colin Gordon, and Peter Miller, eds., *The Foucault Effect: Studies in Governmentality*, pp. 87–104. Chicago: University of Chicago Press.

Fox, Robin. 1967. *Kinship and Marriage: An Anthropological Perspective*. Baltimore: Penguin Books.

Frank, A. G. 1967. *Capitalism and Underdevelopment in Latin America*. New York: Monthly Review Press.

_____. 1969. *Latin America: Underdevelopment or Revolution*. New York: Monthly Review Press.

Freedman, Maurice. 1958. *Lineage Organization in Southeast China*. London: Athlone Press.

French, Rebecca. 1994. "From the Editor." *Political and Legal Anthropology Review* 17(1):vii–xii.

_____. 1995. "From the Editor." *Political and Legal Anthropology Review* 18(1):v–xii.

Fried, Morton. 1960. "On the Evolution of Social Stratification and the State." In Stanley Diamond, ed., *Culture and History: Essays in Honor of Paul Radin*, pp. 713–731. New York: Columbia University Press.

———. 1964. "Anthropology and the Study of Politics." In Sol Tax, ed., *Horizons of Anthropology*, pp. 181–190. Chicago: University of Chicago Press.

———. 1967. *The Evolution of Political Society: An Essay in Political Anthropology*. New York: Random House.

Gailey, Christine Ward. 1987. *Kinship to Kingship: Gender Hierarchy and State Formation in the Tongan Islands*. Austin: University of Texas Press.

Gane, Mike. 1991a. *Baudrillard: Critical and Fatal Theory*. London/New York: Routledge.

———. 1991b. *Baudrillard's Bestiary: Baudrillard and Culture*. London/New York: Routledge.

Ganshof, F. L. 1961. *Feudalism*. New York: Harper Torchbooks.

Garland, David. 1990. *Punishment and Modern Society: A Study in Social Theory*. Chicago: University of Chicago Press.

Geertz, Clifford, ed. 1963. *Old Societies and New States: The Quest for Modernity in Asia and Africa*. New York: The Free Press.

Geertz, Clifford. 1972. "Deep Play: Notes on the Balinese Cockfight." *Daedalus* 101:1–37.

———. 1973. *The Interpretation of Cultures*. New York: Basic Books.

———. 1980. *NEGARA: The Theatre State in Nineteenth-Century Bali*. Princeton: Princeton University Press.

———. 1983. *Local Knowledge: Further Essays in Interpretive Anthropology*. New York: Basic Books.

Gellner, Ernest. 1992. *Postmodernism, Reason, and Religion*. New York: Routledge.

Gibb, Cecil A., ed. 1969. *Leadership: Selected Readings*. Harmondsworth, England: Penguin Books.

Gibbon, Edward. 1897. *The History of the Decline and Fall of the Roman Empire*. London: Methuen & Co.

Gibson, Charles. 1966. *Spain in America*. New York: Harper & Row.

Giddens, Anthony. 1979. *Central Problems in Social Theory: Action, Structure and Contradiction in Social Analysis*. Berkeley: University of California Press.

Giesbrecht, Martin Gerhard. 1972. *The Evolution of Economic Society*. San Francisco: W.H. Freeman.

Gleick, J. 1987. *Chaos: Making a New Science*. London: Cardinal.

Gluckman, Max. 1956. *Custom and Conflict in Africa*. London: Basil Blackwell.

———. 1963. *Order and Rebellion in Tribal Africa*. London: Cohen & West.

———. 1965. *Politics, Law, and Ritual in Tribal Society*. Chicago: Aldine.

Godelier, Maurice. 1978. "Infrastructures, Societies, and History." *Current Anthropology* 19:763–771.

———. 1986. *The Making of Great Men: Male Domination and Power among the New Guinea Baruya* (translated by Rupert Sawyer). Cambridge, England: Cambridge University Press.

———. 1988. *The Mental and the Material: Thought, Economy and Society*. London: Verso.

_____. 1994. "Mirror, Mirror on the Wall . . . The Once and Future Role of Anthropology: A Tentative Assessment." In Robert Borofsky, ed., *Assessing Cultural Anthropology*, pp. 97–113. New York: McGraw-Hill.

Godelier, Maurice, and Marilyn Strathern, eds. 1991. *Big Men and Great Men: Personifications of Power in Melanesia*. Cambridge, England: Cambridge University Press.

Goldschmidt, Walter. 1959. *Man's Way: A Preface to the Understanding of Human Society*. New York: Holt, Rinehart and Winston.

_____. 1965. "Theory and Strategy in the Study of Cultural Adaptability." *American Anthropologist* 67:402–407.

Goode, William J. 1959. "The Theoretical Importance of Love." *American Sociological Review* 24:38–47.

Goody, Jack. 1961. "The Classification of Double Descent Systems." *Current Anthropology* 2:3–25.

_____. 1966. *Succession to High Office*. Cambridge, England: Cambridge University Press.

Gordon, Deborah A. 1995. "Conclusion: Culture Writing Women: Inscribing Feminist Anthropology." In Ruth Behar and Deborah A. Gordon, eds., *Women Writing Culture*, pp. 429–441. Berkeley: University of California Press.

Gough, Kathleen. 1971. "Nuer Kinship: A Re-examination." In T. O. Beidelman, ed., *The Translation of Culture: Essays to E. E. Evans-Pritchard*, pp. 79–121. London: Tavistock.

Gouldner, Alvin W., ed. 1950. *Studies in Leadership: Leadership and Democratic Action*. New York: Harper & Brothers, Publishers.

Gramsci, Antonio. 1917. "Philanthropy, Goodwill, and Organization." *Avanti* 24(December). In Pedro Cavalcanti and Paul Piccone, eds. 1975. *History, Philosophy and Culture in the Young Gramsci*. St. Louis: Telos Press.

_____. 1971. *Selections from the Prison Notebooks*. New York: International Publishers.

Greenhouse, Carol J. 1997. "Commentary on the Annual Meeting." *Anthropology News*, April 1997.

Gruel, Peter J. 1971. "The Leopard-Skin Chief: An Example of Political Power among the Nuer." *American Anthropologist* 73:1115–1120.

Habermas, Jurgen. 1979. *Communication and the Evolution of Society*. Boston: Beacon Press.

Hanson, Jerry. 1990. "Economy, Success, and Ideology among Midwestern Farmers." *Human Mosaic* 24(1&2):50–69.

Harris, Marvin. 1959. "The Economy Has No Surplus." *American Anthropologist* 61:185–199.

_____. 1968. *The Rise of Anthropological Theory*. New York: Thomas Y. Crowell.

_____. 1977. *Cannibals and Kings: The Origins of Cultures*. New York: Vintage Books.

_____. 1979. *Cultural Materialism: The Struggle for a Science of Culture*. New York: Vintage Books.

_____. 1994. "Cultural Materialism Is Alive and Well and Won't Go Away until Something Better Comes Along." In Robert Borofsky, ed., *Assessing Cultural Anthropology*, pp. 62–76. New York: McGraw-Hill.

_____. 1998. *Theories of Culture in Postmodern Times*. Walnut Creek, Calif.: Altamira Press.

Hart, C. W. M., and Arnold R. Pilling. 1960. *The Tiwi of North Australia*. New York: Holt, Rinehart and Winston.

Hasluck, Margaret. 1954. *The Unwritten Law in Albania*. Cambridge, England: Cambridge University Press.

Hastrup, Kirsten. 1995. *A Passage to Anthropology: Between Experience and Theory*. London/New York: Routledge.

Hawthorne, Jeremy. 1992. *A Glossary of Contemporary Literary Theory*. London: Edward Arnold.

Hegland, Mary Elaine. 1995. "Shi'a Women of Northwest Pakistan and Agency through Practice, Resistance, Resilience." *Political and Legal Anthropology Review* 1995, 18(2):65–80.

Heider, Karl G. 1970. *The Dugum Dani: A Papuan Culture in the Highlands of West New Guinea*. Viking Fund Publication in Anthropology, No. 49. New York: Wenner-Gren Foundation for Anthropological Research, Incorporated.

_____. 1979. *The Grand Valley Dani: Peaceful Warriors*. New York: Holt, Rinehart and Winston.

Helm, June, ed. 1967. "Essays and Problems of the Tribe." *Proceedings of the Annual Spring Meeting of the American Ethnological Society*. Seattle: University of Washington Press.

Helms, Mary W. 1979. *Ancient Panama: Chiefs in Search of Power*. Austin: University of Texas Press.

Herdt, Gilbert H. 1981. *Guardians of the Flutes: Idioms of Masculinity*. New York: McGraw-Hill.

Herdt, Gilbert, ed. 1984. *Ritualized Homosexuality in Melanesia*. Berkeley: University of California Press.

Hertzberg, Hendrik. 1999. "Someday, All This Will Be Yours." *The New Yorker*, June 14, pp. 27–28.

Hindess, Barry, and Paul Q. Hirst. 1975. *Pre-capitalist Modes of Production*. London: Routledge/Kegan Paul.

Hirsh, Elizabeth, and Gary A. Olson. 1995. "Starting from Marginalized Lives: A Conversation with Sandra Harding." In Ruth Behar and Deborah A. Gordon, eds., *Women Writing Culture*, pp. 3–44. Berkeley: University of California Press.

Hoebel, E. Adamson. 1949a. *The Political Organization and Law Ways of the Comanche Indians*. American Anthropological Association Memoir 54, Contributions from the Santa Fe Laboratory of Anthropology, No. 4. Washington, D.C.: American Anthropological Association.

_____. 1949b. *Man in the Primitive World*. New York: McGraw-Hill.

_____. 1954. *The Law of Primitive Man: A Study in Comparative Legal Dynamics*. Cambridge, Mass.: Harvard University Press.

Hogbin, Ian. 1964. *A Guadalcanal Society: The Kaoka Speakers*. New York: Holt, Rinehart, and Winston.

Holquist, Michael. 1990. *Dialogism: Bakhtin and His World*. London: Routledge.

Holy, Ladislav, ed. 1979. *Segmentary Lineage Systems Reconsidered*. Queens University Papers on Social Anthropology No. 4. Belfast: Queens University.

Homans, George C., and David M. Schneider. 1955. *Marriage, Authority and Final Causes. A Study of Unilateral Cross-Cousin Marriage.* New York: The Free Press.

Honigman, John. 1976. *The Development of Anthropological Ideas.* Homewood, Ill.: Dorsey Press.

Hudson, A. E. 1938. *Kazak Social Structure.* Yale University Publications in Anthropology, No. 20. New Haven: Yale University.

Hutcheon, Linda. 1989. *The Politics of Postmodernism.* London/New York: Routledge.

Huyssen, Andreas. 1990. "Mapping the Postmodern." In Jeffrey C. Alexander and Steven Seidman, eds. *Culture and Society: Contemporary Debates*, pp.353–375. Cambridge, England: Cambridge University Press.

Ibn Khaldun. 1967 [1377]. *The Maquaddimah: An Introduction to History* (translated from Arabic by F. Rosenthat; abridged and edited by N. J. Dawood). London: Routledge/Kegan Paul.

James, William. 1956 [1897]. *The Will to Believe and Other Essays in Popular Philosophy.* New York: Dover.

Jameson, Fredric. 1984. "Postmodernism, or the Cultural Logic of Late Capitalism." *New Left Review* 146:53–93.

Kang, Gay Elizabeth. 1979. "Exogamy and Peace: Relations of Social Units: A Cross-Cultural Test." *Ethnology* 18:85–99.

Kaplan, Martha, and John D. Kelly. 1994. "Rethinking Resistance: Dialogues of 'Disaffection' in Colonial Fiji." *American Ethnologist* 21:123–151.

Keesing, Roger H. 1994. "Theories of Culture Revisited." In Robert Borofsky, ed., *Assessing Cultural Anthropology*, pp. 301–319. New York: McGraw-Hill.

Kehoe, Alice. 1992. Cahokia as a Mesoamerican City. Paper presented at the Dumbarton Oaks, Washington, D.C., October 14, 1992.

Kellner, Douglas. 1989. *Jean Baudrillard: From Marxism to Postmodernism and Beyond.* Stanford: Stanford University Press.

Kertzer, David L. 1988. *Ritual, Politics, and Power.* New Haven: Yale University Press.

Kirchhoff, Paul. 1959 [1955]. "The Principles of Clanship in Human Society." In Morton H. Fried, ed., *Readings in Anthropology. Volume II: Cultural Anthropology*, pp. 259–270. (Written in 1935, appeared first in the *Davidson Journal of Anthropology*, 1955, 1:1–10.) New York: Thomas Y. Crowell Company.

Klima, George J. 1970. *The Barabaig: East African Cattle-Herders.* New York: Holt, Rinehart and Winston.

Koch, Klaus-Friedrich. 1974. *War and Peace in Jalémó: The Management of Conflict in Highland New Guinea.* Cambridge, Mass.: Harvard University Press.

Kracke, Waud H. 1978. *Force and Persuasion: Leadership in an Amazonian Society.* Chicago: University of Chicago Press.

Krader, Lawrence. 1968. *The Formation of the State.* Engelwood Cliffs, N.J.: Prentice-Hall.

_____. 1975. *The Asiatic Mode of Production.* Assen, The Netherlands: Van Gorcum.

Kroeber, Alfred. 1948 [1923]. *Anthropology.* New York: Harcourt, Brace and Company.

Kuhn, Thomas. 1970. *The Structure of Scientific Revolutions.* Chicago: University of Chicago Press.

Kuper, Adam. 1994. "Culture, Identity, and the Project of a Cosmopolitan Anthropology." *Man* 29:537–554.

Kurtz, Donald V. 1973. *The Politics of a Poverty Habitat*. Cambridge, Mass.: Ballinger.

_____. 1974. "Peripheral and Transitional Markets: The Aztec Case." *American Ethnologist* 1:685–705.

_____. 1978."The Legitimation of the Aztec State." In Henri J. M. Claessen and Peter Skalník, eds., *The Early State*, pp. 169–190. The Hague: Mouton Publishers.

_____. 1979. "Political Anthropology: Issues and Trends on the Frontier." In S. Lee Seaton and Henri J. M. Claessen, eds., *Political Anthropology*, pp. 31–62. The Hague: Mouton Publishers.

_____. 1981. "A Model for the Legitimation of Early Incorporative States." In Henri J. M. Claessen and Peter Skalník, eds., *The Study of the State*, pp. 177–200. The Hague: Mouton Publishers.

_____. 1984. "Strategies of Legitimation and the Aztec State." *Ethnology* 22:301–314.

_____. 1993. "A Reconceptualization of the Anthropomorphized State and the Centrality of Political Agency in State Formations." *Political and Legal Anthropology Review* 16(1):16–30.

_____. 1994a. *Contradictions and Conflict: A Dialectical Political Anthropology of a University in Western India*. Leiden, The Netherlands: E. J. Brill.

_____. 1994b. "Winnowing the 'The Great Kalahari Debate': Its Impact on Hunter-Gatherer Studies." *Political and Legal Anthropology Review* 17(1):67–80.

_____. 1996a. "Hegemonic Culturation and Work in State Formations." In Henri J. M. Claessen and Jarich G. Oosten, eds., *Ideology and the Formation of Early States*, pp. 278–297. Leiden, The Netherlands: E. J. Brill.

_____. 1996b. "Hegemony and Anthropology: Gramsci, Exegetes, Transformations." *Critique of Anthropology* 15:103–135.

_____. n.d. The Paradigmatic and Epistemological Break in Cultural Anthropology. Unpublished paper, available upon request.

Kurtz, Donald V., and Mary Christopher Nunley. 1993. "Ideology and Work at Teotihuacan: A Hermeneutic Interpretation." *Man* 28:1–18.

Laclau, Ernesto. 1979. *Politics and Ideology in Marxist Theory*. London: NLB.

Laclau, Ernesto, and Chantal Mouffe. 1985. *Hegemony and Socialist Strategy: Toward a Radical Democratic Politics* (translated by W. Moore and P. Carmack). London: Verso.

La Farge, Oliver. 1929 [1957]. *Laughing Boy*. Boston: Signet Classic.

Lambert, H. E. 1956. *Kikuyu Social and Political Institutions*. London: Oxford University Press.

Lane, R. S. 1962. "Patrilateral Cross Cousin Marriage." *Ethnology* 14:467–501.

Lasswell, H., and A. Kaplan. 1950. *Power and Society: A Framework for Political Inquiry*. New Haven: Yale University Press.

Leach, Edmund R. 1954. *Political Systems of Highland Burma*. Boston: Beacon Press.

_____. 1961. *Rethinking Anthropology*. Monographs on Social Anthropology, No.22. London: London School of Economics.

Leacock, Eleanor B. 1954. *The Montagnais "Hunting Territory" and the Fur Trade*. American Anthropological Association Memoir 78. Washington, D.C.: American Anthropological Association.

Leclair, Edward R., Jr., and Harold K. Schneider, eds. 1968. *Economic Anthropology: Readings in Theory and Analysis*. New York: Holt, Rinehart and Winston.

Lee, Richard. 1982. *The Dobe !Kung*. New York: Holt, Rinehart and Winston.

Lemay, J. A. Leo. 1991. *The American Dream of Captain John Smith*. Charlottesville: University of Virginia Press.

Lenski, Gerhard E. 1966. *Power and Privilege: A Theory of Social Stratification*. New York: McGraw-Hill.

Lett, James. 1987. *The Human Enterprise: A Critical Introduction to Anthropological Theory*. Boulder: Westview Press.

Levine, Donald. 1965. *The Wax and the Gold*. Chicago: University of Chicago Press.

Levi-Strauss. 1961 [1955]. *Tristes Tropiques* (translated by J. Russel). New York: Criterion Books.

_____. 1963. *Structural Anthropology*. New York: Basic Books.

_____. 1969 [1949 in French]. *The Elementary Structure of Kinship*. Boston: Beacon Press.

Lewis, Herbert S. 1974. *Leaders and Followers: Some Anthropological Perspectives*. An Addison-Wesley Module in Anthropology, No. 50. Reading, Mass.: Addison-Wesley Publishing Company.

_____. 1993. "Comment on Roscoe, Paul B., 'Politics and Political Centralization: A New Approach to Political Evolution.'" *Current Anthropology* 34:128–129.

Lewis, Herbert S., and Sidney M. Greenfield. 1983. "Anthropology and the Evolution of the State: A Critical Review and an Alternative Formulation." *Anthropology* 7(1):1–16.

Lewis, I. M. 1961. *A Pastoral Democracy: A Study of Pastoralism and Politics among the Northern Somali of the Horn of Africa*. New York: Oxford University Press.

Lewis, J. Lowell. 1995. "Genre and Embodiment: From Brazilian 'Capoeira' to the Ethnology of Human Movement." *Cultural Anthropology* 10:221–243.

Lilla, Mark. 1998. "The Politics of Jacques Derrida." *The New York Review of Books*, June 25, 45(11):36–41.

Linger, Daniel T. 1993. "The Hegemony of Discontent." *American Ethnologist* 20:3–24.

Linke, Uli. 1999. *Blood and Nation: The European Aesthetics of Race*. Philadelphia: University of Pennsylvania Press.

Linton, Ralph. 1936. *The Study of Man: An Introduction*. New York: Appleton-Century-Crofts.

Livingston, Frank B. 1964. "Prescriptive Patrilateral Cross Cousin Marriage." *Man* 64:56–57.

Lloyd, Peter. 1965. "The Structure of African Kingdoms: An Exploratory Model." In Michael Banton, ed., *Political Systems and the Distribution of Power*, pp. 63–112. London: Tavistock.

Lowie, Robert. 1927. *The Origin of the State*. New York: Harcourt Brace.

Lyotard, Jean-François. 1993 [1979 in French]. *The Postmodern Condition: A Report on Knowledge* (translated by Geoff Bennington and Brian Massumi). Minneapolis: University of Minnesota Press.

MacLeod, W. C. 1931. *The Origin and History of Politics*. New York: John Wiley & Sons.

MacNeish, Richard S. 1964. "Ancient Mesoamerican Civilization." *Science* 143(3606):531–537.

MacNeish, Richard S., ed. 1967. *The Prehistory of the Tehuacan Valley*. Austin: University of Texas Press.

Mahmood, Cynthia Keppley. 1994. "Violence and the Culture of Sikh Separatism." *Political and Legal Anthropology Review* 17(1):11–22.

_____. 1996. *Fighting for Faith and Nation: Dialogues with Sikh Militants*. Philadelphia: University of Pennsylvania Press.

_____. 2000. "Trials by Fire: Dynamics of Terror in Punjab and Kashmir." In Jeffrey A. Sluka, ed., *Death Squad: The Anthropology of State Terror*, pp. 70–90. Philadelphia: University of Pennsylvania Press.

Maine, Henry Summer. 1963 [1861]. *Ancient Law: Its Connection with the Early History of Society and Its Relation to Modern Ideas*. Boston: Beacon Press.

Mair, Lucy. 1962. *Primitive Government*. Baltimore: Penguin Books.

Malinowski, Bronislaw. 1961 [1922]. *Argonauts of the Western Pacific*. London: Routledge.

Manganaro, Marc, ed. 1990. *Modernist Anthropology: From Fieldwork to Text*. Princeton: Princeton University Press.

Marcus, George E., and Michael M. J. Fischer. 1986. *Anthropology as Cultural Critique: An Experimental Moment in the Human Sciences*. Chicago: University of Chicago Press.

Marquit, Erwin, Philip Moran, and Willis H. Truit, eds. 1982. *Dialectical Contradictions: Contemporary Marxist Discussions*. Studies in Marxism, Vol. 10. Minneapolis: Marxist Educational Press.

Martin, M. Kay. 1969. "South American Foragers: A Case Study in Cultural Devolution." *American Anthropologist* 71:243–260.

Marx, Karl. 1888 [1848]. *The Communist Manifesto*. London: W. Reeves.

_____. 1964 [1858]. *Pre-Capitalist Economic Formations* (E. Hobsbawn, ed.). London: Lawrence and Wishart.

_____. 1970 [1859]. *A Contribution to the Critique of Political Economy* (translated by S.W. Ryazanskaya and edited by Maurice Dobb). Moscow: Progress Publishers.

Marx, Karl, and Frederick Engels. 1970 [1932, written in 1845–1846]. *The German Ideology* (C. J. Arthus, ed.). London: Lawrence and Wishart.

Matsumoto, Yoshiharu Scott. 1960. "Contemporary Japan: The Individual and the Group." *Transactions of the American Philosophical Society, New Series* 50(1):3–75.

Mayberry-Lewis, D. H. 1965. "Prescriptive Marriage Systems." *Southwestern Journal of Anthropology* 21:207–230.

Mayer, Adrian. 1966. "The Significance of Quasi-Groups in the Study of Complex Societies." In Michael Blanton, ed., *The Social Anthropology of Complex Societies*, pp. 97–122. London: Tavistock.

McDonald, James H. 1993a. "Whose History? Whose Voice?: Myth and Resistance in the Rise of the New Left in Mexico." *Cultural Anthropology* 8:96–116.

_____. 1993b. "Corporate Capitalism and the Family Farm in the U.S. and Mexico." *Culture and Agriculture* 45/46:25–28.

_____. 1994. "NAFTA and Basic Food Production: Dependency and Marginalization on Both Sides of the US–Mexico Border." *Research in Economic Anthropology* 15:129–143.

_____. 1995. "NAFTA and the Milking of Dairy Farmers in Central Mexico." *Culture and Agriculture* 51/52:13–18.

_____. 1996. "The Milk War: The Effects of NAFTA on Dairy Farmers in the United States and Mexico." In Karen Roberts and Mark I. Wilson, eds., *Policy Choices: Free Trade among NAFTA Nations*, pp. 75–105. East Lansing: Michigan State University Press.

_____. 1997a. "A Fading Aztec Sun: The Mexican Opposition and Politics of Everyday Fear in 1994." *Critique of Anthropology* 17:263–292.

_____. 1997b. "Privatizing the Private Family Farmer: NAFTA and the Transformation of the Mexican Dairy Sector." *Human Organization* 56:321–332.

_____. 1999. "The Neoliberal Project and Governmentality in Rural Mexico: Emergent Farmer Organization in the Michoacan Highlands." *Human Organization* 58:274–284.

McGee, R. Jon, and Richard L. Warms, eds. 2000. *Anthropological Theory: An Introductory History*. Mountain View, Calif.: Mayfield Publishing Company.

McGlynn, Frank, and Arthur Tuden. 1991. "Introduction." In F. McGlynn and A. Tuden, eds., *Approaches to Political Behavior*, pp. 3–44. Pittsburgh: University of Pittsburgh Press.

McLeish, Kenneth. 1993. *Key Ideas in Human Thought*. New York: Facts on File.

McLennan, J. F. 1865. *Primitive Marriage*. Edinburgh: Adam and Charles Black.

Meggitt, Mervyn. 1958. "The Enga of the New Guinea Highlands: Some Preliminary Observations." *Oceania* 28:253–330.

_____. 1977. *Blood Is Their Argument: Warfare among the Mae Enga Tribesmen of the New Guinea Highlands*. Palo Alto, Calif.: Mayfield Publishing Company.

Meillasoux, Claude. 1981. *Maidens, Meal and Money: Capitalism and the Domestic Community*. Cambridge, England: Cambridge University Press.

Mertz, Barbara. 1966. *Red Land, Black Land: The World of the Ancient Egyptians*. New York: Coward-McCann.

Meštrović, Stjepan G. 1992. *Durkheim and Post Modern Culture*. New York: Aldine/de Gruyter.

Middleton, John, and D. Tate, eds. 1958. *Tribes without Rulers: Studies in West African Segmentary Systems*. London: Routledge/Kegan Paul.

Mill, James. 1844. *Elements of Political Economy*. London: Henry G. Bohn.

Mill, John Stuart. 1848. *Essays on Some Unsettled Questions of Political Economy*. London: John W. Parker.

Milner, Andrew, P. Thomson, and C. Wirth, eds. 1990. *The Postmodern Condition*. New York: Berg.

Mintz, Sidney W. 1985. *Sweetness and Power: The Place of Sugar in Modern History*. New York: Viking.

Mitchell, J. Clyde. 1969. *Social Networks in Urban Situations. Analysis of Personal Relationships in Central African Towns*. Manchester, England: Manchester University Press.

Morgan, Lewis Henry. 1870. "Systems of Consanguinity and Affinity of the Human Family." *Smithsonian Contributions to Knowledge* 17:4–602.

_____. 1901 [1851]. *League of the Ho-De-No-Sau-Nee*. New York: Dodd Mead.

_____. 1963 [1877]. *Ancient Society* (edited with an introduction and annotations by Eleanor Burke Leacock). Cleveland/New York: The World Publishing Company.

Mueller, Claus. 1973. *Politics of Communication*. New York: Oxford University Press.

Murdock, George P. 1949. *Social Structure*. New York: Macmillan.

_____. 1957. "World Ethnographic Sample." *American Anthropologist* 59:664–687.

_____. 1960. "Cognatic Forms of Social Organization." In G. P. Murdock, ed., *Social Structure in Southeast Asia*, pp. 1–14. Chicago: Quadrangle Books.

Murphy, Robert. 1957. "Intergroup Hostility and Social Cohesion." *American Anthropologist* 59(6):1018–1035.

_____. 1960. *Headhunter's Heritage*. Berkeley: University of California Press.

_____. 1971. *Dialectics of Social Life: Alarms and Excursions in Anthropological Theory*. New York: Basic Books.

_____. 1994. "The Dialectics of Deeds and Words." In Robert Borofsky, ed., *Assessing Cultural Anthropology*, pp. 55–61. New York: McGraw-Hill.

Murphy, Robert F., and L. Kasdan. 1959. "The Structure of Parallel Cousin Marriage." *American Anthropologist* 61:17–29.

Murra, John V. 1958. "On Inca Political Structure." In Verne F. Ray, ed., *Systems of Political Control and Bureaucracy in Human Societies*, pp. 30–41. Proceeding of the 1958 Annual Meeting of the American Ethnological Society. Seattle: University of Washington Press.

Nader, Laura. 1969. *Law in Culture and Society*. Chicago: Aldine.

Nash, June. 1979. *We Eat the Mines and the Mines Eat Us: Dependency and Exploitation in Bolivian Tin Mines*. New York: Columbia University Press.

Needham, Rodney. 1958. "Structural Analysis of Purum Society." *American Anthropologist* 60:75–100.

Needham, Rodney, ed. 1962. *Structure and Sentiment: A Test Case in Social Anthropology*. Chicago: University of Chicago Press.

Newman, Philip L. 1965. *Knowing the Gururumba*. New York: Holt, Rinehart and Winston.

Nicholas, Ralph W. 1965. "Factions: A Comparative Analysis." In Michael Banton, ed., *Political Systems and the Distribution of Power*, pp. 21–61. London: Tavistock Publications.

_____. 1966. "Segmentary Factional Political Systems." In Marc J. Swartz, Victor W. Turner, and Arthur Tuden, eds., *Political Anthropology*, pp. 49–60. Chicago: Aldine.

_____. 1968. "Rules, Resources, and Political Activity." In Mark J. Swartz, ed., *Local Level Politics*, pp. 295–322. Chicago: Aldine.

Nordstrom, Carolyn. 1997. *A Different Kind of War Story*. Philadelphia: University of Pennsylvania Press.

Oberg, Kalvero. 1955. "Types of Social Structure among the Lowland Tribes of South and Central America." *American Anthropologist* 57:472–487.

Oldani, Michael. 1998. "Postmodernism and Anthropology: Conflict or Cooperation." *Kroeber Anthropological Papers* 83: 87–105.

Oliver, Douglas. 1955. *A Solomon Island Society: Kinship and Leadership among the Siuai of Bouganville*. Cambridge, Mass.: Harvard University Press.

———. 1958. *The Pacific Islands*. Cambridge, Mass.: Harvard University Press.

Olson, Gary A. 1995. "Resisting a Discourse of Mastery: A Conversation with Jean-François Lyotard." In Ruth Behar and Deborah A. Gordon, eds., *Women Writing Culture*, pp. 169–194. Berkeley: University of California Press.

Oppenheimer, Franz. 1975 [1914]. *The State*. New York: Free Life Editions.

Orans, Martin. 1966. "Surplus." *Human Organization* 25:24–32.

Orenstein, Henry. 1980. "Asymmetrical Reciprocity: A Contribution to the Theory of Political Legitimacy." *Current Anthropology* 21:69–91.

Ortner, Sherry B. 1984. "Theory in Anthropology Since the Sixties." *Comparative Studies in Society and History* 26:126–166.

Ottenberg, Simon. 1971. *Leadership and Authority in an African Society: The Afikpo Village-Group*. Seattle: University of Washington Press.

Otterbein, Keith F. 2000. "Five Feuds: An Analysis of Homicides in Eastern Kentucky in the Late Nineteenth Century." *American Anthropologist* 102:231–243.

Otterbein, Keith F., and Charlotte Swanson Otterbein. 1965. "An Eye for an Eye, a Tooth for a Tooth: A Cross-Cultural Study of Feuding." *American Anthropologist* 67:1470–1482.

Paine, Robert. 1981. "Introduction." In Robert Paine, ed., *Politically Speaking: Cross-Cultural Studies in Rhetoric*. Social and Economic Papers, No. 10, pp. 1–6. Institute of Social and Economic Research, Memorial University of Newfoundland. Philadelphia: ISHI.

Parsons, Talcott. 1964. "Introduction; The Author and His Career." In Talcott Parsons, ed., *Max Weber: The Theory of Social and Economic Organization*, pp. 3–86. New York: The Free Press.

Pastner, Carroll McC. 1979. "Cousin Marriage among the Zikri Baluch of Coastal Pakistan." *Ethnology* 18:31–49.

Patterson, Thomas C., and Christine W. Gailey, eds. 1987. *Power Relations and State Formation*. Washington, D.C.: Archaeology Section, American Anthropological Association.

Peacock, James L., and A. Thomas Kirsch. 1973. *The Human Direction: An Evolutionary Approach to Social and Cultural Anthropology*. New York: Appleton-Century-Crofts.

Pedersen, Johannes. 1926. *Israel, Its Life and Culture*, Vols. I–II. London: Geoffrey Cumberledge, Oxford University Press/Copenhagen: Branner Og Korch.

Perley, Sidney. 1924. *The History of Salem, Massachusetts. Vol. 1, 1626–1637*. Salem, Mass.: Sidney Perley.

Peters, E. L. 1967. "Some Structural Aspects of the Feud among the Camel-Herding Bedouin of Cyrenaica." *Africa* 37:261–282.

Petrie, W. M. Flinders. 1923. *Social Life in Ancient Egypt*. London: Constable & Company.

Pi-Sunyer, Oriol. 1995. "Under Four Flags: The Politics of National Identity in the Barcelona Olympics." *Political and Legal Anthropology Review* 18(1):35–56.

Podolefsky, Aaron. 1984. "Changing Warfare in the New Guinea Highlands." *Ethnology* 23:73–88.

Polanyi, Karl. 1944. *The Great Transformation.* New York: Rinehart.

_____. 1947. "Our Obsolete Market Mentality." *Commentary* 13:109–117.

_____. 1957. "The Economy as Instituted Process." In Karl Polanyi, Conrad W. Arensberg, and Harry W. Pearson, eds., *Trade and Market in the Early Empires*, pp. 243–270. New York: The Free Press.

_____. 1966. *Dahomey and the Slave Trade: An Analysis of an Archaic Economy.* Seattle: University of Washington Press.

Polanyi, Karl, Conrad W. Arensberg, and Harry W. Pearson, eds. 1957. *Trade and Market in the Early Empires.* New York: The Free Press.

Pospisil, Leopold. 1958. "Kapauka Papuan Political Structure." In Verne F. Ray, ed., *Systems of Political Control and Bureaucracy in Human Societies*, pp. 9–22. Proceedings of the Annual Spring Meeting of the American Ethnological Society. Seattle: University of Washington Press.

_____. 1963. *The Kapauku Papuans of West New Guinea.* New York: Holt, Rinehart and Winston.

_____. 1971. *Anthropology of Law.* New York: Harper and Row.

Powell, Sumner Chilton. 1965. *Puritan Village: The Formation of a New England Town.* Garden City, N.Y.: Doubleday Anchor.

Rabinow, Paul. 1986. "Representations Are Social Facts: Modernity and Post-modernity in Anthropology." In James Clifford and George Marcus, eds., *Writing Culture: The Poetics and Politics of Ethnography*, pp. 234–261. Berkeley: University of California Press.

Radcliffe-Brown, A.R. 1922. *The Andaman Islanders.* London: Cambridge University Press.

_____. 1940. "Preface." In M. Fortes and E. E. Evans-Pritchard, eds., *African Political Systems*, pp. xi–xxiii. London: Oxford University Press.

_____. 1965 [1952]. *Structure and Function in Primitive Society.* New York: The Free Press.

Radin, Paul. 1926. *Crashing Thunder: The Autobiography of an American Indian.* New York: Appleton.

Rappaport, Roy A. 1968. *Pigs for the Ancestors: Ritual in the Ecology of a New Guinea People.* New Haven: Yale University Press.

Rattray, R. S. 1923. *Ashanti.* London: Oxford University Press.

_____. 1929. *Ashanti Law and Constitution.* London: Oxford University Press.

Read, Kenneth E. 1959. "Leadership and Consensus in New Guinea Society." *American Anthropologist* 61:425–436.

_____. 1965. *The High Valley.* New York: Charles Scribner's Sons.

Redfield, Robert. 1956. *Peasant Society and Culture.* Chicago: University of Chicago Press.

Richards, A. I. 1959. "The Ganda." In A. I. Richards, ed., *East African Chiefs*, pp. 41–77. London: Faber & Faber.

Roberts, Simon. 1979. *Order and Dispute: An Introduction to Legal Anthropology.* New York: St. Martin's Press.

Roberts, Wess. 1989. *Leadership Secrets of Attila the Hun.* New York: Warner Books.

Rogers, E. S. 1970. *New Guinea: Big Man Island.* Toronto: Royal Ontario Museum.

Rosaldo, Renato. 1994. "Cultural Citizenship in San Jose, California." *Political and Legal Anthropology Review* 17(2):57–64.

Roseberry, William. 1988. "Political Economy." *Annual Review of Anthropology* 17:161–185.

Roscoe, John. 1911. *The Baganda*. London: Macmillan.

Roscoe, Paul B. 1993. "Politics and Political Centralization: A New Approach to Political Evolution." *Current Anthropology* 34:111–140.

Rowe, John H. 1946. "Inca Culture at the Time of the Spanish Conquest." In J. H. Steward, ed., *Handbook of South American Indians*. Bureau of American Ethnology, Bulletin 143, Vol. 2, pp. 183–330. Washington, D.C.: Smithsonian Institution.

Ruyle, Eugene E. 1973. "Slavery, Surplus, and Stratification on the Northwest Coast: The Energetic of an Incipient Stratification System." *Current Anthropology* 14:603–631.

Sahlins, Marshall. 1958. *Social Stratification in Polynesia*. Seattle: University of Washington Press.

_____. 1960. "Political Power and the Economy in Primitive Society." In Gertrude Dole and Robert L. Carneiro, eds., *Essays in the Science of Culture in Honor of Leslie White*, pp. 390–415. New York: Thomas Crowell Co.

_____. 1961. "The Segmentary Lineage: An Organization of Predatory Expansion." *American Anthropologist* 63:322–345.

_____. 1963. "Poor Man, Rich Man, Big Man, Chief: Political Types in Melanesia and Polynesia." *Comparative Studies in Society and History* 5:285–303.

_____. 1968. *Tribesmen*. Englewood Cliffs, N.J.: Prentice-Hall.

_____. 1972. *Stone Age Economics*. Chicago: Aldine.

Sahlins, Marshall, and Elman Service, eds. 1960. *Evolution and Culture*. Ann Arbor: University of Michigan Press.

Salisbury, Richard F. 1956. "Asymmetrical Marriage Systems." *American Anthropologist* 58:639–655.

Salzman, Philip Carl. 1994. "The Lone Stranger in the Heart of Darkness." In Robert Borofsky, ed., *Assessing Cultural Anthropology*, pp. 29–39. McGraw-Hill.

Sanders, William T., and Barbara J. Price. 1968. *Mesoamerica: The Evolution of a Civilization*. New York: Random House.

Sanders, William T., and Robert S. Santley. 1983. "A Tale of Three Cities: Energetics and Urbanization in Pre-Hispanic Central Mexico." In Evon Z. Vogt and Richard M. Levanthal, eds., *Prehistoric Settlement Patterns: Essays in Honor of Gordon Wiley*, pp. 243–291. Cambridge, Mass.: Peabody Museum of Archaeology and Ethnology/Albuquerque: University of New Mexico Press.

Sanders, William T., J. R. Parsons, and Robert S. Santley. 1979. *The Basin of Mexico: Ecological Processes in the Evolution of Civilization*. New York: Academic Press.

Saussure, Ferdinand de. 1966 [1959]. *Course in General Linguistics*. New York: McGraw-Hill.

Schapera, I. 1956. *Government and Politics in Tribal Societies*. New York: Schocken Books.

Scheper-Hughes, Nancy. 1992. *Death without Weeping: The Violence of Everyday Life in Brazil*. Berkeley: University of California Press.

_____. 1995. "The Primacy of the Ethnical: Propositions for a Militant Anthropology." *Current Anthropology* 36:409–440.

Schneider, H. 1957. "The Subsistence Role of Cattle among the Pokot and in East Africa." *American Anthropologist* 59:278–300.

Schneider, Jane, and Peter Schneider. 1976. *Culture and Political Economy in Western Sicily.* New York: Academic Press.

Service, Elman. 1962. *Primitive Social Organization: An Evolutionary Perspective.* New York: Random House.

———. 1971. *Cultural Evolution: Theory in Practice.* New York: Holt, Rinehart and Winston.

———. 1975. *Origin of the State and Civilization.* New York: Harper and Row.

———. 1979. *The Hunters.* Englewood Cliffs, N.J.: Prentice-Hall.

Sharp, Lauriston I. 1958. "People without Politics: Australian Yir Yoront." In Verne F. Ray, ed., *Systems of Political Control and Bureaucracy in Human Society,* pp. 1–8. Proceedings of the Annual Spring Meeting of the American Ethnological Society. Seattle: University of Washington Press.

Shelly, Mrs. [Mary]. n.d. *Frankenstein or The Modern Prometheus.* Chicago: Donahue, Henneberry & Co.

Skinner, Elliot. 1964. *The Mossi of the Upper Volta: The Political Development of a Sudanese People.* Stanford: Stanford University Press.

Sluka, Jeffrey, ed. 2000. *Death Squad: The Anthropology of State Terror.* Philadelphia: University of Pennsylvania Press.

Slyomovics, Susan. 1998. *The Object of Memory: Arab and Jew Narrate the Palestinian Village.* Philadelphia: University of Pennsylvania Press.

Smith, Adam. 1804 [1759]. *The Theory of Moral Sentiment.* Edinburgh: Creech, Bell, & Bradfute.

———. 1904 [1776]. *An Inquiry into the Nature and Cause of the Wealth of Nations,* Cannan's edition. London: Methuen and Co.

Smith, M. G. 1956. "On Segmentary Lineage Systems." *Journal of the Royal Anthropological Institute* 82:39–80.

———. 1960. *Government in Zazzau: 1890–1950.* London: Oxford University Press.

———. 1968. "Political Anthropology: Political Organization." In David Sills, ed., *International Encyclopedia of the Social Sciences,* pp. 192–202. New York: Macmillan/The Free Press.

Smith, Susan. 1996. "Citizenship is the Colony: Naturalization Law and Legal Assimilation in 19th Century Algeria." *Political and Legal Anthropology Review* 19(1):33–50.

Smith, Thomas C. 1959. *The Agrarian Origins of Modern Japan.* Stanford: Stanford University Press.

Soustelle, Jacques. 1961. *Daily Life of the Aztecs on the Eve of the Spanish Conquest.* Stanford: Stanford University Press.

Southall, Aiden. 1956. *Alur Society.* Cambridge, England: Cambridge University Press.

———. 1965. "A Critique of the Typology of States and Political Systems." In Michael Banton, ed., *Political Systems and the Distribution of Power,* pp. 113–140. London: Tavistock Publications.

Spiro, M. E. 1964. "Causes, Functions and Cross Cousin Marriage: An Essay in Anthropological Explanation." *Journal of the Royal Anthropological Institute* 93:30–45.

Starn, Orin. 1994. "Rethinking the Politics of Anthropology: The Case of the Andes." *Current Anthropology* 35:13–38.

Stevenson, R. F. 1965. *Population Density and State Formation in Sub-Saharan Africa.* Unpublished doctoral dissertation, Columbia University, New York. [Cited in Marvin Harris. 1968. *The Rise of Anthropological Theory.* New York: Thomas Y. Crowell Company.]

Steward, Julian H. 1938. *Basin–Plateau Aboriginal Sociopolitical Groups.* Bureau of American Ethnology, Bulletin 120. Washington, D.C.: Smithsonian Institution.

_____. 1943. "Culture Element Distributions: xxiii, Northern and Gosciute Shoshoni." *Anthropological Records, University of California* 8(3):263–392.

_____. 1955. *Theory of Culture Change: The Methodology of Multilinear Evolution.* Urbana: University of Illinois Press.

Steward, Julian H., and Louis G. Faron. 1959. *Native Peoples of South America.* New York: McGraw-Hill.

Steward, Julian H., R. A. Manners, E. R. Wolf, S. E. Padilla, S. W. Mintz, and R. L. Scheele. 1956. *The People of Puerto Rico: A Study in Social Anthropology.* Urbana: University of Illinois Press.

Swartz, Marc J., ed. 1968. *Local Level Politics.* Chicago: Aldine.

Swartz, Marc J., Victor W. Turner, and Arthur Tuden, eds. 1966. *Political Anthropology.* Chicago: Aldine.

Taussig, Michael T. 1980. *The Devil and Commodity Fetishism in South America.* Chapel Hill: University of North Carolina Press.

_____. 1987. *Shamanism, Colonialism, and the Wild Man: A Study in Terror and Healing.* Chicago: University of Chicago Press.

Taylor, Christopher C. 1999. "A Gendered Genocide: Tutsi Women and Hutu Extremists in the 1994 Rwanda Genocide." *Political and Legal Anthropology Review* 22(1):42–54.

Tedlock, Barbara. 1992. *The Beautiful and the Dangerous: Encounters with the Zuni Indians.* New York: Viking.

Terray, E. 1971. *Marxism and "Primitive" Societies.* New York: Monthly Review Press.

Thapar, Romila. 1984. *From Lineage to State.* Bombay: Oxford University Press.

Thompson, J. E. 1933. *Mexico before Cortes: An Account of the Daily Life, Religion, and Ritual of the Aztecs and Kindred Peoples.* New York: Scribner's.

Titiev, Mischa. 1944. "Old Orabi: A Study of the Hopi Indians of Third Mesa." *Papers of the Peabody Museum of American Archaeology and Ethnology* 22(1).

Titus, Charles H. 1931. "A Nomenclature for Political Science." *American Political Science Review* 25(1):45–60.

Todorov, Tzvetan. 1990. *Genres in Discourse* (translated by Catherine Porter). Cambridge, England: Cambridge University Press.

Trevor-Roper, Hugh. 1965. *The Rise of Christian Europe.* London: Thames and Hudson.

Trigger, Bruce G. 1969. *The Huron: Farmers of the North.* New York: Holt, Rinehart & Winston.

Turnbull, Colin M. 1962. *The Forest People: A Study of the Pygmies of the Congo.* Garden City, N.Y.: Doubleday & Company.

Turner, Victor W. 1957. *Schism and Continuity*. Manchester, England: Manchester University Press.

Tyler, Stephen A. 1969. *Cognitive Anthropology*. New York: Holt, Rinehart and Winston.

_____. 1987. *The Unspeakable*. Madison: University of Wisconsin Press.

Tylor, Edward. 1889. "On a Method of Investigating the Development of Institutions: Applied to Laws of Marriage and Descent." *Journal of the Royal Anthropological Institute* 18:245–269.

Ulmen, Gary. 1978. *The Science of Society: Toward an Understanding of the Life and Work of Karl Wittfogel*. Den Haag, The Netherlands: Mouton Publishers.

Vansina, Jan. 1962. "A Comparison of African Kingdoms." *Africa* 32(4):324–335.

Veblen, Thorstein. 1953 [1899]. *The Theory of the Leisure Class*. New York: New American Library/Mentor.

Vincent, Joan. 1968. *African Elite: The Big Men of a Small Town*. New York: Columbia University Press.

_____. 1990. *Anthropology and Politics: Visions, Traditions, and Trends*. Tucson: University of Arizona Press.

Von Fürer-Haimendorf, Christopher. 1969. *The Konyak Nagas: An Indian Frontier Tribe*. New York: Holt, Rinehart and Winston.

Wallerstein, Immanuel. 1974. *The Modern World System: Capitalist Agriculture and the Origins of the European World Economy in the Sixteenth Century*. New York: The Free Press.

Warren, Kay B. 2000. "Conclusions: Death Squads and Wider Complicities: Dilemmas for the Anthropology of Violence." In Jeffrey A. Sluka, ed., *Death Squad: The Anthropology of State Terror*, pp. 226–247. Philadelphia: University of Pennsylvania Press.

Weatherford, Jack. 1985. *Tribes on the Hill*. South Hadley, Mass.: Bergin and Garvey.

_____. 1993. "Tribal Politics in Washington." *Political and Legal Anthropology Review* 16(1):36–39.

Weber, Max. 1964 [1947]. *The Theory of Social and Economic Organization* (edited by Talcott Parsons and translated by A. M. Henderson and Talcott Parsons). New York: The Free Press.

Weiner, Annette B. 1988. *The Trobrianders of Papua New Guinea*. New York: Holt, Rinehart and Winston.

White, John E. W. 1963. *Everyday Life in Ancient Egypt*. London: Balsford.

White, Leslie. 1949. *The Science of Culture: A Study of Man and Civilization*. New York: Farrar, Straus and Giroux.

_____. 1959. *The Evolution of Culture: The Development of Civilization to the Fall of Rome*. New York: McGraw-Hill.

Wikan, Uni. 1996. The Nun's Story: Reflections on an Age-Old, Postmodern Dilemma. *American Anthropologist* 98:279–289.

Williams, Bruce. 1994. *Bambo Jordan: An Anthropological Narrative*. Prospect Heights, Ill.: Waveland Press.

Williams, Raymond. 1977. *Marxism and Literature*. Oxford: Oxford University Press.

Wilmsen, Edwin N. 1989. *Land Filled with Flies: A Political Economy of the Kalahari*. Chicago: University of Chicago Press.

Wilson, Monica. 1951. *Good Company*. London: Oxford University Press.

Wittfogel, Karl. 1957. *Oriental Despotism: A Comparative Study of Total Power*. New Haven: Yale University Press.

Wolf, Eric R. 1955. "The Mexican Bajio in the Eighteenth Century: An Analysis of Cultural Integration." In *Synoptic Studies of Mexican Culture*. Middle American Research Institute Publication 17. New Orleans: Tulane University.

_____. 1956. "San Jose: Subcultures of a Traditional Coffee Municipality." In Julian Steward et al., *The People of Puerto Rico: A Study in Social Anthropology*, Part 7, pp. 171–264. Urbana: University of Illinois Press.

_____. 1959. *Sons of the Shaking Earth*. Chicago: University of Chicago Press.

_____. 1964. *Anthropology*. Englewood Cliffs, N.J.: Prentice-Hall.

_____. 1982. *Europe and the Peoples without History*. Berkeley: University of California Press.

_____. 1990. "Facing Power—Old Insights, New Questions." *American Anthropologist* 92:586–596.

_____. 1999. *Envisioning Power: Ideologies of Dominance and Power*. Berkeley: University of California Press.

Wolf, Eric R., and Edward C. Hansen. 1972. *The Human Condition in Latin America*. New York: Oxford University Press.

Woost, Raymond D. 1977. "Nationalizing the Local Past in Sri Lanka: Histories of Nation and Development in a Sinhalese Village." *American Ethnologist* 20:502–521.

Worsley, Peter. 1955. "The Kinship of the Tallensi: A Reevaluation." *Journal of the Royal Anthropological Institute* 85:37–75.

Zorita, Alonso de. 1963 [1570s–1580s]. *Life and Labor in Ancient Mexico: The Brief and Summary Relations of the Lords of New Spain* (translated by Benjamin Keen). New Brunswick, N.J.: Rutgers University Press.

INDEX